EXECUTIONER: PIERREPOINT

'I operated on behalf of the state, what I am
convinced was the most humane and the most
dignified method of meting out death to a
delinquent – however justified or unjustified
the allotment of death may be – and on behalf
of humanity I trained other nations to adopt
the British system of execution . . . I do not
now believe that any one of the hundreds of
executions I carried out has in any way acted
as a deterrent against future murder. Capital
punishment, in my view, achieved nothing
except revenge.'

Executioner: Pierrepoint

Albert Pierrepoint

CORONET BOOKS
Hodder and Stoughton

Copyright © Albert Pierrepoint 1974

First published in Great Britain 1974 by
George G. Harrap and Company Limited

Coronet Edition 1977
Second Impression 1977
Third Impression 1977

Printed in Great Britain for
Hodder & Stoughton Paperbacks, a
division of Hodder & Stoughton Ltd.,
Mill Road, Dunton Green, Sevenoaks, Kent by
Hunt Barnard Printing Ltd., Aylesbury, Bucks.

ISBN 0 340 21307 8

To ANNE my wife
who in forty years never asked a question
I dedicate this book with grateful thanks
for her loyalty and discretion

Acknowledgment

My friend over many years, Mr S. Parr, C.B.E., Q.P.M., D.L. Chief Constable of Lancashire, has given me unstinted technical aid and advice during the preparation of this book, while naturally being in no way responsible for its form or content. I should like to make this sincere acknowledgment of his generous help.

A. P.

Contents

Preface

For the first fifty-six years of the present century the name of Pierrepoint has appeared on the short Home Office list of qualified executioners for Great Britain and Ireland (being also accepted by the Irish Republic when that territory became independent), and for most of that time a Pierrepoint has been nominated as the Official Executioner, or 'Number One' as we have called him in the craft. These Pierrepoints have been, in succession, my father, Henry Albert Pierrepoint; his brother, Thomas William Pierrepoint; and myself, Albert Pierrepoint. Only one other family, the Billingtons, has undertaken this 'hereditary' exercise of the post of executioner, and that only for a score of years reaching into the beginning of this century. I myself was the last 'Number One' Official Executioner in this country, because when I resigned the post in 1956 – for reasons which the Home Office has asked me not to reveal fully – the decision was taken to appoint two executioners with equal precedence; and the comparatively sparse series of executions which took place during the eight years after my resignation ended on the 23rd of August 1964, when the two executioners who succeeded me carried out simultaneous 'last' executions in different places.

I consider that history welcomes and even requires the documentary record of a family which has upheld a unique tradition of service to the State for over half a century by supplying an officer whose integrity as well as skill has been totally reliable. A prison governor told a Royal Commission on Capital Punishment: 'A man who wants to be an executioner must be in a class by himself.' Both my father and myself had a keen ambition to take this post from an extraordinarily early age. I believe I owe to posterity this account of my family and myself, our methods and innovations, and some of our experiences, for there will never be a similar family, or similar experiences, again. This conviction is strengthened by my own firm belief that I was chosen by a higher power for the task which I took up, that I was put on earth especially to do it, and that this same higher power, after protecting me through my career, influenced and governed me when I resigned my calling.

I operated, on behalf of the State, what I am convinced was the most humane and the most dignified method of meting out death to a delinquent – however justified or unjustified the allotment of death may be – and on behalf of humanity I trained other nations to adopt the British system of execution. It is a fact which is no source of pride to me at all – it is simple history – that I have carried out the execution of more judicial sentences of death (outside the field of politics) than any executioner in any British record or archive. That fact is the measure of my experience. The fruit of my experience has this bitter after-taste: that I do not now believe that any one of the hundreds of executions I carried out has in any way acted as a deterrent against future murder. Capital punishment, in my view, achieved nothing except revenge.

A.P.

My Father and my Uncle Tom

I was nine years old, and starting an important one-man expedition. The only thing that vexed me was that I was wearing short pants.

Travel, that was good, what I always wanted. And I felt like the man who went round the world in eighty days when I took this first independent train journey to Bradford in Yorkshire. I think the haul was six miles and had cost my father three ha'pence. But in order to halve the outlay he and I had previously trekked – Father shouldering my pack with handsome muscular ease like my gallant uncle relieving Lady Smith (women and children first?) in my version of the South African War – what seemed another half-dozen miles from our home in Huddersfield to an outlying station. He bought my ticket, slipped me a penny, took a bearing on the nearest pub, and saw me to the platform. The train came in and we waved goodbye like shoplifters, not wanting to be seen. He went off, and I knew where. I realise now that I loved him, but I could not say it then, never did, because he died when that sort of thing would still have embarrassed us. But I did know that he was 'easily led'. I think that was a phrase which my mother first put into my mind, for me to make some allowance for what could seem injustices to us as a family – and I hoped that when he left me at the midway station my father would not easily find leaders. But he had such personality, he was so sociable, he could talk so well, made you laugh. And beyond this he had a sign somewhere on him, like a freemason's gold badge on his albert, a mark of mystery that other people would somehow catch, to proclaim HARRY PIERREPOINT, the . . . somebody I did not know quite what. And they would fasten on him like jovial, curious, leeches and draw him out, and he would respond to the recognition and give, give, give; not only his rich personality but sometimes Mother's money for the rent and the week's keep. I did not seriously worry about it. My father was good enough for me, and I tossed the shadowy fear out of the wide-belted train sash-window, and fought the immediate shiver.

But fancy having to travel in short pants. I had a mission in life, and although I was not yet absolutely sure what it was I knew that it asked dignity from me, and there was no dignity in short pants.

I tried to hide my knees, and I day-dreamed of the time when I could wear long trousers and not be fussed over by people like the lady opposite me in the train. I stood up, pretending to look out of the window, but really in order to wriggle and shrink my belly. And my pants, which were not short at all by modern standards outside Bermuda, dropped so that the hems were within an inch of the tops of my stockings. I tried to act as if they were Norfolk knickerbockers. How do you act as if they are Norfolk knickerbockers? Stand with firm Sandringham dignity, elbow crooked for the fowling piece from your loader, as if you are just ready to shoot pheasants, like King George the Fifth. I half-squinted round to see if the woman was impressed. But the sentimental gaze under the huge feathered hat was fixed indulgently on my squint rather than respectfully on my legs. 'Eh, Blue-eyes!' she simpered. I blushed. I scowled, and that at least straightened my blue eyes.

The train huffed and puffed its way into Bradford. There were soldiers in lines on the platform, soldiers with flat hats cutting off their eyesight and – would you believe it – khaki Norfolk knickerbockers sharply creased over their puttees. We'd soon be fighting the Kaiser, my father had said. I felt in my pocket for the train ticket, got the reassuring touch of the copper I had been given for my tram fare, and

'Will you be all right, lad?' asked the soft woman.

'Yes, thank you,' I answered with dignity, as I thought then – perhaps conveying stolidity or even sullenness as I reflect now, after seeing many other young lads fight their private wars of independence.

I jumped eagerly down on to the platform and edged my portmanteau off the train. I swung it a little clumsily as I made my way to the tram stop. It was an old, battered, squared basket-box with straps and, as I carried it, it rubbed and nagged at my leg on that maddening inch of skin below my pants. I might have been wiser to have brought a big shopping

hold-all or made up a string-and-paper parcel, as my mother
had suggested. But one was womanish and the other insignifi-
cant. I was as proud of that portmanteau as if it had carried the
labels of hotels in faraway places like Marseilles or Monte
Carlo, Brindisi and Bombay. It proclaimed that I was a traveller. Young Albert Pierrepoint was travelling – home.

Home happened to mean away from my mother and father.
That was the way of this busy world, for my father was a
traveller, too. He had emigrated from my birthplace nearly
twenty miles to where we now lived in Huddersfield. But Albert
Pierrepoint was travelling home to the countryside where he
was born, Clayton village with its Clayton smells of cake and
horses, the Clayton general stores which was really my Auntie
Lizzie, and the Clayton carrier who was my beloved Uncle
Tom.

The tram car stopped at its terminus at Lidget Green, and I
strode up towards Clayton. The road curved and dipped, but
for every slope it eased me down it produced a far stiffer hill to
climb up. It was the end of July, the end of the day, and I was
hot. I had already walked a fair whack from home to catch the
train where the fare was lower. I leaned against the gates by the
dry-stone walls, with my basket-portmanteau thrown into
the long hedge-grass. There were small wild flowers down
there, pink and white and purple with strong hairs on their
stems – I never knew their names because I never asked. I
grabbed the case out of their clutches. I took off my soft, broad,
peaked cap and slammed it violently in the air against the flies
and midges who had scented my sweat. I trudged on up the last
brow and came to the triangle of the village green with its
horse-trough in the middle, and the stone house with the
crammed shop-window at Town End. 1752, said the stone over
the upper window of the room where I would sleep. I edged
round the shop into the square, flowery front garden. There
was an enticing smell of fresh-baking bread as I went into the
house.

'Our Albert!'

'Auntie Lizzie.'

We spoke our greetings as statements of fact, announcements,
but warm just the same. We did not kiss, not in Yorkshire.

'You've grown.'

'Where's my Uncle Tom?'

'He'll be in shortly. Take your coat off.'

'Can I see the horses?'

'They're in the stable, same as they always are.'

'Can I have a drink, Auntie Lizzie?'

'Which do you want first, the horses or a drink?'

'I'd like a drink first, please, Auntie Lizzie.'

'And what would you like to drink?'

I hesitated. I had been thinking of it for the last two weary miles I had walked. Dare I ask? After all, they did have it in the shop, it wasn't as if they had to buy it.

My auntie knew what I was thinking and cut the knot for me.

'Would you like some stone ginger beer?'

'Oh!' Surprise not very well acted. 'Yes, please, Auntie Lizzie.'

She was pouring it in an instant, like a magician. She was solid yet quick and her movements were not dainty. She held the bottle and glass strongly and crouched to pour it out somewhere near her knees with almost as much effort as if she were pulling a cork. She wore round glasses, which I never really remembered and was always surprised to notice again. She was square of shoulder and in her long skirts she seeemed broad, and got increasingly wider all the way down until the last moment, like the stern of a Spanish galleon.

'And you'd better have a piece of spice cake while tea-time.'

I tipped the strong ginger beer into my mouth in a greedy cascade, and I could feel the muscles of my throat contracting and expanding as if my gullet had a separate life, and all the white dust of the last hour's tramp was washed away. I snatched the slice of spice cake and crammed the first great half-moon into my mouth as I ran out through the buzzing garden while my Aunt Lizzie was laughing. She had brought up two daughters and seen them married, and when I came it gave her real happiness to spoil a boy.

The grey gelding was out, but old Bess was in the stable, and in the other box a mule that I couldn't feel much warmth for, and Bess put her head inquisitively over the half door to see the cause of the scuffling. I pulled her hard bristly nose down against my sweaty cheek. She wouldn't take that, so I just let her go, and looked at her, and the stables and all that I could see of Clayton, very very satisfied. The houses of hilly Bradford were stacked in pyramids to one side far beyond the farm in the golden sun, and down in the valley past the stables lay the Gasworks fields where my uncle kept his homely domestic livestock, chickens and goats. It was not a Royal Academy landscape, just the mix of industry and small farming on the millstone grit peaks of urban Yorkshire in the days before the housing developers captured too many heights and dug in troops for permanent occupation. I did not then know of any better sight and did not want any more.

Uncle Tom came home with the grey in the shafts and the chain-horse clopping behind the cart – he always needed the extra horse for a full load on the testing hills round Bradford.

'Our Albert.'

'Uncle Tom.'

I looked full and smiling at him. Middle forties, middle height, the same impression of great bodily strength which my father gave, the same clear eye, but my uncle had a greater air of depth and reserve, he was not so eloquent or volatile as my father. I helped him unharness and stable the work-horses, and we tended them all. Uncle Tom peeled off the richness of carter's clothes he was wearing – so many coats and waistcoats, all with so many pockets, in the all-weather outfits of those days compared with the undervest and jeans of today's route-riders. I sat and watched him wash in the kitchen. I was quietly happy just to know that I was filling a space around the hearth of my auntie and uncle. I think I knew already, in the bossy way in which kids snatch at slogans, that I was the son they never had.

We settled down to Auntie Lizzie's enormous tea. Though there were the savoury delicacies to tempt a boy, the basis of it all was her fresh home-baked bread and her spice cake. To me the spice cake had something of the special-occasion symbolism of Christmas pudding, and possibly cost as much. Although ordinarily we spread a lot of meat dripping on the bread, and perhaps used margarine under jam – I didn't really register that – yet I know that only 'best butter' and plenty of eggs went in with the flour, currants and flavouring to make the spice cake that was served by the slice and following slice with slabs and slabs of cheese. My belly was taut and I was drowsily drunk with Clayton fare. I consented, after this crowded day, to go to bed before my time, with the red of the sunset bouncing off the neighbour's barn on to my sloping ceiling.

Next day I was up and around, re-exploring, getting domiciled. Uncle Tom had a few morning callers whom he received not absolutely cordially. Among his sidelines he ran a small bookmaker's business. There was a village tradition, which because he had a quiet sense of humour he did not discourage, that he was bad-tempered when he had to pay out. He made no secret of that side of his life, and later he used to ask me to help him in the dogsbody job of being a bookie's runner – which at that time was a formally illegal occupation. But there was still about him then for me the mystery of some craft, some awesome calling that linked him with my father. Everyone else in the village seemed to know about it, but they delicately sidestepped any direct mention of it, and never on any account asked a straight question. Only from the lads on the farm next door did I get any enlargement of my understanding. Uncle Tom had to go away occasionally on a job. The youngsters on the farm clearly looked forward to these jobs, because Uncle Tom used to give them sixpence to feed the chickens and milk the goats in his absence. From the boyish frank regret in their remarks to my uncle around the stables that Sunday morning, I gathered that there had been a recent hitch in one of these arrangements, something called a reprieve.

'Aye,' said my Uncle Tom gloomily. 'There'll come a bloody day when they'll all get reprieved.'

Across the village green there sounded a fervent finale from the Clayton brass band as they blew a determined halt to their weekly practice in an upper room next to the Black Bull. All over the village men came out of cottage doors adjusting their mufflers, because when the band stopped it was opening time. Uncle Tom went for a modest pint at the working men's club on an opposite corner of the triangle, where the beer was cheaper. Before he went he cemented his welcome to me by giving me sixpence. That was six times my normal weekly pocket money and it was a royal gesture – the gift really was like the money the King gave away on Maundy Thursday, for I never started immediate scheming how I should spend it. My father occasionally gave me a shining sixpence too, but more typically after having had a drink rather than before it. I turned back to the horses and busied myself in the stables, tirelessly absorbed in my lifetime interest. It was physical work and animal communion, but it was also getting my appetite into training to absorb the mammoth Sunday dinner with its great squares of my Auntie Lizzie's Yorkshire pudding filling the dinnerplates before the meat course.

A slightly restless afternoon: checking my landmarks in the village; sitting on the low window-ledge of the house where I was born, No. 5 Green End by the Black Bull, and renewing acquaintance with the children of Clayton; dodging home for the occasional snack from my Auntie Lizzie without disturbing my Uncle Tom, who was snoring on the sofa under a crackling canopy marked *Thomson's Weekly News*. And that completed my familiarisation course. I was ready to enjoy a month of summer, lapping up the indulgence of my auntie, accompanying her every Thursday afternoon when she shut up shop and took off for her weekly tonic of music-hall at Bradford Palace (I knew all the songs, or soon picked them up, but couldn't see all the jokes); and for the rest of the time working with my uncle in his carrier's trade in and around Bradford, caring for the horses, driving the horse and cart on safe roads, taking the fullest part in sharing my uncle's daily occupation, but knowing that if ever he mentioned that he would not be working at it for the following day or two – it did not behove me to ask questions.

Even my Auntie Lizzie, who was always very open and carefree and – as I remember it now – hardly ever stopped talking, seemed to freeze when any mention of these trips was overheard. 'Where did you say you were going Tuesday, Tom?' she was asking as I came in from the Gasworks fields on that first Sunday evening. I was rather proud of having been trusted to feed the chickens, and was looking forward to being taught to milk the goats, as my uncle had promised if I did the first job right. I looked expectantly at my Uncle Tom, but he kept facing away from me, and seemed to be waiting, and my Auntie Lizzie for once said nothing, so I went out into the garden. But 'Lewes', I heard him say in a low voice. 'Herbert Brooker. Him as did that woman in the train at Three Bridges. Said he were drunk at the time. Daft beggar.' And he raised his voice into the cheerful note he kept for me and called: 'Eh, Albert! Them goats! Come on!'

So he taught me to milk the goats. And strong fingers and forearms you needed for it. I was tired after only a few pulls at first. But from the one early and very lucky stroke when I pulled the milk out in a pencil of a spurt that foamed in the bottom of the bucket, I knew that there was a skill in this, and that it was a craft that I would master the skill of. By the middle of the holiday I was as persistent as any weight-watcher as I daily examined the finger-grip of my increasingly capable hands, and I admired the sinews rising in my sunburnt arms,

and innocently mistook the ridges for muscles: but muscles
were forming, just the same. Before long, I could be trusted to
milk the goats, which gave me the extra thrill of regularly chal-
lenging the billy-goat. The father and stud of the flock was tied
to a stake by a long chain in the middle of the biggest Gasworks
field. He had wicked red eyes and a skull of a hardness which
I never tested but always feared, especially since every charge
ended with an upward-spiralling twist of his horns which was
done far faster than any pay-off in a Spanish bull-ring. I used
to go down to the goats and, in passing, bait Billy by making
faces and clanging my buckets together. He was always game
for a fight, and, I suppose now but never thought it then, might
have been jealous of me as a male who could get nearer his
nannies than he could, except when they were in the mood.
Whatever the chemistry of my impact, the mechanics of his
reaction were always the same: a fearful Charge of the Light
Brigade against young Albert. It was the rattling of the chain
through a ring that I remember most, so I suppose that was the
toughest ordeal. I stood my ground as long as possible, thinking
I could judge the length of his chain, but knowing in advance
that my Uncle Tom sometimes altered the position of the stake
without telling me. Billy came crashing towards me like an
express train. Generally he was halted in time by a tremendous
tug of the stake on his chain, an arrest which, outside the Gasworks fields, I have seen paralleled only in television cartoons.
He went up in the air and sprang sideways to safety as the halter
– tied, as I now know, by an expert – ran back on his shoulder-
muscles. Once or twice I misjudged the distance. The total
terror which I experienced as I realised that I was going to be
hit at what I thought was sixty miles an hour was only capped
by the bliss of relief after a spontaneous back somersault, my
pails clattering as I revolved. I always fancied myself as a foot-
baller, but, looking back, I think that a few more sessions with
Billy might have put me prosperously in the circus business.

When I came up to the house from adventures like these, and
recovered some of my cool by knocking back a great flagon
of goat's milk – which was warm, and stronger than I could
ever take now – I thought I occasionally saw a glint of amuse-
ment – or comradeship – in my uncle's eye. But our harmony
was most complete when I went with him to feed the pony. He
had a little pony there he almost used to make conversation
with. Certainly my Uncle Tom talked. He used to ask him how

old he was, and the pony would say, by tapping his foot; and I never really knew whether the pony was right because I always gave my uncle the benefit of any doubt about whether the pony had tapped or just stumbled. My uncle would play with that pony like a baby, and I took it all in.

Sometimes Uncle Tom, being his own master, would decide to spend a working day in the yard keeping up the maintenance of his carts and their gear. He made all his own lorries, except for the wheels, and the wheelwright was very handy, just in front of the working men's club by the green. He did all his own repairs, even his own signwriting. On the brown-painted wagons there was spelt out in flowing yellow letters: *T. W. Pierrepoint, Clayton, nr Bradford.*

After the first weekend of my stay at Clayton my Uncle Tom put on his bowler hat and went away for a day and a half. On the second weekend my uncle had an extra day off for August Bank Holiday, and the Great War broke out. They said there were crowds around Buckingham Palace in London, but there were none outside the Black Bull in Clayton, which was the most prominent public building there. We took the Kaiser quietly at first in Yorkshire. Without radio or television, we gathered our news mainly by word of mouth in those days, for most families never saw a daily paper but invested only in the good read of the Sunday scandal sheets – which peppered its long accounts of the week's murders and disgraces with what I now see, looking back at the old copies, was really a very full coverage of political and public affairs. Song writers worked fast at that time, and on Thursday at the Bradford Palace the programme included a 'patriotic extravaganza' with lots of encouraging lyrics, sung against a backcloth of Our Sailor King, or some other bearded admiral, looking keen on the bridge of a dreadnought.

To me the Bradford Palace was always palatial. The crimson velvet and great gold hanging tassels combined with the magic of the coloured lighting and the confident brassy band in the pit to bring me into a gaiety and a spaciousness which I could not find anywhere else. Fortunately the patriotism didn't over-lay the pathos and comedy at Bradford, and after the Union Jacks there was still George Formby. 'I was standing at the corner of the street,' he used to sing, and his son sang it to me for old times' sake many years afterwards. I liked, too, Ella Shields – top hat and tails and an armour-plated, starched white shirt front – singing *Burlington Bertie*:

> I'm Burlington Bertie, I rise at ten-thirty
> And saunter along like a toff.
> I walk down the Strand with my gloves on my hand
> Then I walk down again with them off.
> I'm Bert, Bert, I haven't a shirt
> But my people are well off, you know.
> Everyone knows me, from Smith to Lord Rosebery,
> I'm Burlington Bertie from Bow.

That used to fix London for me as a romantic place I must travel to one day. I could understand Ella Shields. She didn't play in full Cockney, like Marie Lloyd – who, I believe, didn't come so much to the north because she didn't go down all that well in Lancashire and Yorkshire. Ella Shields was really rather refined. And she had a good voice. We used to judge other people's voices, and use our own singing voices, much more seriously at that time.

At the end of the show at the Bradford Palace they put on the Bioscope, as the climax. Judging it now, this jerky grey-and-white, generally goose-stepping spectacle seems to hold nothing like the warmth of life that I had just seen, with rich and comic characters in opulent surroundings. But it *was* life, not an imitation of life, and for us it had great glamour – this particular week, perhaps, more for me than for my Auntie Lizzie. It was a cinema newsreel of a fight between Gunboat Smith and Georges Carpentier, and I suppose it was the last time we yelled against the French for four years. Not that I ever had anything but admiration for Carpentier. Perhaps that film, at the end of such a memorable week, notched in my character my permanent interest in good boxing.

The holiday ended and I went home to Huddersfield, and that night my father came in cheerful, said 'Give us a tune' to my eldest sister, who played the piano, and sang *Genevieve, sweet Genevieve* and followed it up with his favourite:

> Just a violet I plucked when only a boy,
> When I'm sad at heart
> This flower brings me joy,
> And while life doth remain
> In my memory I'll retain
> Just a violet I plucked from Mother's grave.

The war gave my mother work, for the munitions industry was important in Huddersfield and she got a job filling artillery shells. The family – five children, two sisters older than I and two brothers younger – needed the money, for my father was having a bad spell. He was a very versatile man. He could put his hand to anything and do it well, but he could be thrown off course by an idea or an enthusiasm or a windfall of money, or, most often, by friends who were anxious to help him spend his windfall, and he could disappear for days, not turning up at work or at home. It was my father who had started the carrier's business in Clayton – he was full of good ideas and would work them up conscientiously – but then he might have a few gills and go off with his pals and throw it all in. My Uncle Tom took over the carrier's and made a steady business of it.

So my father was having a bad spell in Huddersfield. We used to go to the Queen Street Mission there, not only for religious observation but because they also gave us free clogs for our bare feet. Our family was not rare, many of our friends and neighbours were in the same boat. There were some wealthy men concerned with the Queen Street Mission and they had a lot of respect for my father. Besides being very competent, he could talk well and as long as he kept his enthusiasm for a job he was very responsible. These missioners approached my father and said that if he would give up alcohol for six weeks they would buy him a horse and cart and set him up in business again. He signed the pledge, went teetotal for five weeks, met some friends and broke out again. So he never got his business.

I felt very sympathetic towards my mother, who was mild and patient. All other things apart, she was never very happy in Huddersfield. She was born in Manchester and she always wanted to go back to her people and the place where my father, on his travels, had married her. Not all her family were now in Lancashire. One brother, Johnny Buxton, had emigrated to Canada, but now there was a war on there was a chance that he would join the army over there and perhaps come across on a troopship, and we would see him. I felt that my mother wanted these homely contacts. I was still at school when I decided that she had been led such a dance by my father that I would never get married while she was alive, but always look after her. It was a childish resolve, but, as circumstances governed us, that is the way life turned out.

Soon after the failure of the horse-and-cart mission my

father got a good job in the Huddersfield gasworks and held it
for some time. My mother's patient loyalty to him was justified. My father would come in and sing his songs again at the
end of the evening. When he sang 'I'll take you home again,
Kathleen' I used to fancy that my mother was quietly wondering if he ever would.

> I'll take you home again, Kathleen
> Across the ocean wild and wide
> To where your heart has ever been
> Since first you were my bonny bride.
> The roses all have left your cheek,
> I've watched them fade away and die;
> Your voice is sad whene'er you speak
> And tears bedim your loving eyes.
> Oh! I will take you back Kathleen,
> To where your heart will feel no pain;
> And when the fields are fresh and green,
> I'll take you to your home again.

During the second full summer of the war I became aware
that my father was in the middle of some business negotiations
which seemed very important and very different from anything
he had engaged in before. Men came to see him and he used to
sit quite long in the evening, writing. I didn't understand what
was going on and I wasn't encouraged to. The drama of the
days was made more solemn by a message which came to my
mother. Her brother, my unseen uncle Johnny Buxton, had
come over from Canada to fight for England, home and beauty.
He was put straight into the battle of the Somme on the 1st of
July 1916. On the 4th of July the first great thunderstorms
broke out, churning the battlefield into mud and making the
deep-stacked barbed wire of the unsuspected German defences
almost impregnable. Within another day my Uncle Johnny was
killed in action.

Then, on Saturday morning, my father called me very
cheerily and said, 'Come on, our Albert! You and me are going
to see your Uncle Tom. Spruce yourself up, sharp's the word
and quick's the action!' I was very happy. My mother saw that
I put my best clothes on. There were boots and fresh stockings
with garters that worked – I hated stockings that fell down.
There was a blue serge suit – pants still short – and a wide cel-

luloid Eton collar with a made-up bow tie which fastened on the front stud.

We walked a long way to the train as usual. My father was in very good spirits. He had his arm around my shoulder and he talked and joked and entertained me better than anyone at the Palace.

In the train I read from a thrown-away newspaper a war correspondent's report of the battle of the Somme. I have checked it since so I know what I then read of the way my Uncle Johnny went to death. But they never mentioned the barbed wire:

> The advance of our men through a double barrage and against machine-gun and rifle fire was as fine a thing as was ever seen on a battlefield. As we stood, in the shadow of some trees, twenty yards from the road, detachments of our troops could be seen swinging across country in half-companies, companies and battalions. Long before they came close one heard the steady roar of their feet — tramp-*tramp*! tramp-*tramp*! And always as they passed they whistled softly in unison. Some whistled *Tipperary*, some *Come back, my Bonny, to me*, and some, best of all in the place and the surroundings, *La Marseillaise*.

Thinking of it from that time on, I always imagined that it was my Uncle Johnny who had whistled the *Marseillaise*.

> They were always whistling. Now and again a laugh broke out at some unheard joke, a completely careless laugh, as of a holidaymaker. And, knowing what it was that they were going into, for the fiftieth time one marvelled at the way in which British manhood has proved itself in this most terrible of all wars.

From Bradford station my father and I walked to the stand where the carriers gathered. It was like a cab-rank outside a row of warehouses, but it was for goods-wagons and horses, and the carriers used to stand there and wait to be hired. When my Uncle Tom saw us he said he would give up work for the day, so we all got on his lorry and rode up to Clayton. From time to time my father talked to my uncle — I guessed it was about the important business he had been engaged in — but my uncle didn't seem to want him to be too open in front of me, and in his stolid way he stonewalled me from getting much of an idea of the subject of their talk. We came to Clayton and got a great welcome from my Aunt Lizzie. I slipped out to the stables and spent most of the afternoon there, allowing for a small pass at Billy the goat. We had my auntie's usual stupefying tea and then it was time to go home again.

My father and I began to walk down to Lidget Green. He sang a bit, just snatches of songs. He rested his hand on my shoulder and told me funny incidents that had happened to him. Adventures, too, like the end to some visit to London for a purpose which he did not clearly say.

'There were thousands of people, Albert, outside this place, and they were looking for my mate Billington and me. Just for curiosity, you understand, not that they didn't like us. But we didn't want to be nailed.'

'No,' I said defensively, not properly understanding, but wanting to give my father full support.

'They were packed right up the avenue to the gates. All the traffic was stopped. We had a rough time getting through, with so many people trying to follow us. But we fooled them. We darted into the nearest hotel, ordered a drink, slipped out through a side door and away to the station, and then we spent all the day at the Crystal Palace in peace and quiet.'

'Ah!' I said with relief.

'But this was not the end of a perfect day. We made our way towards St. Pancras Station to be ready to catch the midnight train. We called in at a saloon bar on the Euston Road for a refresher. Now this was the time when the Hooligans were terrorising London. Me and Billington was leaning leisurely on the saloon counter chatting, when in walked about eight young fellows, not above nineteen years old.

'It was the Hooligans!'

I didn't know who the Hooligans were, but from the conviction in my father's voice I was aware that they were terrible.

'One of them walked behind Billington and put a clay pipe on the counter behind his elbow so that when he moved he would push it on the floor.

'Now they hadn't placed who we were, you've got to remember.

'I saw what was in the wind, so I told Billington to be careful. But he didn't understand quite what I meant, and he moved his arm. The pipe went crashing on to the floor and broke.'

I looked up spellbound at my father. There was a note of drama in his voice.

'This is what they were waiting for. One chap asked Billington what the devil he meant, breaking his pipe. Billington answered back, and the fellow started squaring up. Immediately all the gang rushed up, pulling knives out of their pockets.'

I gasped, exactly as my father intended me to. He could tell a good tale.

'But we had them beat! We both used all fours – fists and feet, you understand. We drove them out of that bar without a scratch. The only casualty was that the barman jumped over the counter to give us a hand, and he knocked a stack of clean glasses over with his feet.'

'Dad!' I said.

'There were two gentlemen on the other side of the saloon. They came round to us. "That's the best sport we have seen for a long time," they said, and they took us by the arm and walked us all the way to St. Pancras and on to the platform for our journey home.'

My eyes were shining as my father finished. But we were at the terminus and had to run to catch the tram before I could ask any questions. I went over this adventure in my mind all the way to the centre of Bradford.

We walked to the railway station, where my father called on the stationmaster and announced that he was going to take him for a drink. It was still light, a pearly midsummer evening. They went to a near-by public house, and I stayed outside.

I saw a striking poster outside a newspaper shop. There was a man's photograph on it, and it looked very familiar. I read the print on the placard. But I looked back at the photograph. And I knew two things, for sure.

It was a picture of my father, taken recently. And he was ill. It had never occurred to me before. I had always pictured him as I had first seen him – strong, confident, wonderfully winning with his devil-may-care approach. But looking at that picture, outside a newsagent's shop, with the full moustache suddenly appearing to cover a mouth expressing anxiety, and the pose of the picture not showing the branching broad chest I knew, I thought for the first time: 'He's not the same. He's going down. My father is ill.'

The second thing I knew was less of a real surprise. It was the headline quoted in the printed newspaper bill. It said:

MY TEN YEARS' EXPERIENCES
BY HENRY A. PIERREPOINT
RETIRED EXECUTIONER

My father came out of the pub with the stationmaster and he introduced me.

'This is my eldest son,' he said. 'And one day *he* will be the Official Executioner.'

I looked up at my father and my mind was suddenly very clear. My mission, my one-man expedition, I knew what it was. And I knew what it needed.

'Our Dad,' I said. 'Can I go into long trousers?'

He looked at me with all the pride in the world.

'Yes, our Albert,' he said, 'You can. I'll speak to your mother about it.'

He came towards me, and turned, and put his arm round my shoulder, and faced his friend with me as if we were posing for a photograph. Then, with his firm hand still holding me, we walked together into the station.

2

Spellbound in't Cloggers Arms

It was in this dramatic fashion that, at the age of eleven, I was presented out of the blue with a solution to the puzzle of my father's mysterious apartness. My simple intuition extended this discovery, correctly, to explain activities of my Uncle Tom which I had not previously understood. And the same revelation gave me a glimpse of a calling which I also might attain to and which I took to my heart with a thrill of pleasure – understandable enough, as I reflect now, for there are few lads so young who are given the prospect of a strange yet very practicable vocation which may well fall to their lot through a sort of hereditary succession. Weekend by weekend for several months – for newspaper series had long runs in those days – I read 'My Ten Years' Experiences by Henry A. Pierrepoint, Retired Executioner'. The whole of Clayton village read them too, though I am sure they did not learn as much from them as I did, for my father, a good talker and I think an eloquent storyteller, especially in the Black Bull or the working men's club, had not been as guarded about his career in public as he was at home.

But, of course, I shared his revelations with a far wider audience, the 504,941 families publicised weekly as making up the certified readership of the penny *Thomson's Weekly News* in the autumn of 1916. These included our neighbours and my schoolfriends in Huddersfield, and since my father's photograph was on display for weeks at a time outside every newsagent's shop I suppose the Pierrepoint name must have achieved some celebrity; but I do not remember my own school pals as either giving me any special respect or treating me with any particular contempt or cruelty. What Albert's Dad did or had done, they seemed to consider, was nothing to do with Albert. So I kept my dreams – for I did begin to have ambition from that time – comfortably to myself.

The newspaper blurb which heralded my father's series gave him, I thought, a sober and respectful introduction before he took the stage. It did not approach the extravagances of a music-hall chairman announcing the next act. I know that I thought this then, for I had experience of the music-hall, but it was an approval that has hardened since, for I myself have had a sheaf of remunerative offers of public appearances – round the English variety circuits, bookings on the American lecture chain, or the publicised appearance in the TV chat show – and I have always turned them down with one comment: '*I am not a showman.*' The newspaper introduction, I thought, kept a proper dignity.

'This week,' it announced, 'Mr. Henry Albert Pierrepoint, of Huddersfield, who for nearly ten years occupied the post of public executioner, begins his remarkable life story. Mr. Pierrepoint is one of the most interesting men in the country, and no one coming into contact with him for the first time would ever guess that they were making the acquaintance of a man who had hanged no fewer than a hundred and five persons, specially if one found him surrounded by a happy family of a wife and five young children. He took part in exactly ninety-nine executions, six of them being double hanging affairs, and he carried out the capital sentence in thirty-eight different prisons in England, Scotland, Ireland, Wales and also one in Jersey, in the Channel Isles. Many notorious people passed through his hands, and of these persons Mr. Pierrepoint will have some astonishing revelations to make.'

And there the slightly awestruck tone ended, as my father took over, confident, easy and very authentic. I could hear his voice behind the print – I can today – as I read every word. Breezily, he came straight to the point. 'The word "hangman" almost invariably invokes a shiver from over-sensitive persons. They imagine him a morose, bloodthirsty sort of villain who takes a fellow creature's life in cold blood, and they think of him as haunted by the spectres of his victims.

'Well, I have executed over a hundred persons. But I've never seen a ghost yet. And as for the "bloodthirsty" stigma – well, I have a charming wife and a family of young children, and I would refer you to them as to whether I am anything in the way of a brutal villain.'

I could hear my father laughing, and looking over to me, Our Albert, his eldest son, for confirmation on that point, and

I gave it with all my heart. I read on, and was astonished to discover that he had conceived his ambition to be an executioner at just about the same age as he had presented the idea to me.

'Let me tell you how I came to take up this work,' he rippled on. 'It was through reading about the appointment of Mr James Berry as executioner and the carrying out of his first job in London that I got the idea of going in for it myself. I was only a boy then, working as a half-timer in a worsted mill at Clayton (Bradford). "That's just the sort of job I should like myself," I thought when I read about Berry's appointment, and from that day forward I had my mind set on becoming an executioner.

'No, I hadn't any repugnance to the idea at all, though I saw it would be useless to say anything at home about it. Perhaps the notion of seeing so many different towns had something to do with my desire, for I was very fond of travel.'

I thought to myself, 'Travel! Different towns! Both my Dad and I want the same things. We are globetrotters, really.'

'Being then only twelve years of age,' my father went on to explain, 'it was obvious that I could do nothing for some years, and it might be thought that the fancy would pass away as a mere childlike freak of mind. Not it. No matter what occupation I went to – and I changed about a good deal in my early years – that intention to become executioner whenever I was old enough remained firmly fixed in my brain.

'My father kept horses, which were used for bringing stone from the quarries near by, and there were ten of us children altogether. At the time of which I write only six of us were living, of whom one brother (who fought in South Africa) died this year.*

'After a time I left the mill and was apprenticed to a butcher in Bradford. I did not care for this, and left in two-and-a-half years and went to Manchester when I was about twenty years of age. I was now grown a big, strapping young fellow, and still had that idea of being an executioner firmly fixed in my mind. But I told no one of it. Four years later, I was reading about a number of murder cases which were then engaging public attention, and the thought came into my mind that the time was now quite ripe for trying to get that long-desired post.

'So I wrote as follows to the Home Secretary, Mr. Ridley:

*My Uncle, in fact, served with the South African Mounted Police. [A.P.]

Dear Sir,

I beg to offer you my services as assistant to Mr. James Billington, or for the post of executioner at any time Mr. Billington resigns his position. My age is twenty-four, and I am strong in build and health.

I am, dear sir, your obedient servant,

HY. PIERREPOINT.'

My father then told a tale of misunderstanding and disappointment which I followed with eager sympathy. I was too young then to marvel that he had had the nerve to write to the Home Secretary, but it was typical of him that he should. He had a few homely mottoes which he often repeated, and which I have remembered on his behalf all my life. The one that applied here was: 'Whatever you want done for you, lad, go to the top of the tree.' He had a speedy acknowledgment from the Home Office and this was followed by a letter instructing him to go next day for an interview with the Governor of Manchester Gaol. He went to Strangeways and told the gatekeeper that he had an appointment with the Governor. But when he was asked the purpose of the interview he was overcome by an embarrassment which I could well understand myself but could hardly associate with my hail-fellow, jaunty father: the fact that he admitted to it, however, made me feel even closer to him.

'I did not dare to tell them that I had come to try to get the hangman's job,' said my father. 'So I said I was wanting a post in the prison service – which was true enough in a way.' But the prison officials promptly stripped him and weighed him, gave him a rigorous medical examination, then finally measured him and sent him packing because they said he was under the standard height and therefore ineligible for the appointment. The very thought of my father, whom I always remembered as the steel-strong man who had tossed me around with casual competence so often in play when I was smaller, being rejected from anything on physical grounds filled me with loyal indignation.

My father immediately wrote to Governor Cruikshank at Strangeways Prison saying that he had been turned away without his promised interview. A reply came explaining that the officials had assumed he wanted a job as a warder, and fixing another appointment. The Governor saw him and approved of him, and said my father would have to go for a fortnight's training as an executioner in London, at Newgate Prison.

It was now necessary for my father to break the news of his strange quest to my mother. He was speaking of a time some years before I was born, when their only family was my eldest sister. 'I told my secret to my wife,' he recounted. 'She had never known anything of my inner desires up to that moment.' I recognised my father's mixture of autocracy and diffidence, never wanting to divulge a plan until it was successfully completed – but, knowing the open manner in which we had always lived in our small house, with official letters and official interviews almost impossible to conceal, I appreciated the barrier of reserve that must have grown up between my parents until the mystery was explained. My mother at first refused to believe my father when he told her his ambition, she thought it was one of his elaborate jokes, and then, when she saw that he was in earnest, tried to persuade him not to go on with it. I saw then, and I have understood much more fully since, that this is an entirely natural reaction on the part of a woman. She cannot be expected to condone any association with the taking of life, however strong and legal the justification. But my father had his way with my mother, as I was to do later.

And so my father, who for the first half of his life never moved outside the shallow triangle of Bradford-Huddersfield-Manchester, began his travels.

'In the highest spirits I at last set off for my first visit to London. And when I got there I was at first afraid to ask anybody the way to Newgate in case they discovered my business. I summoned up courage to ask a policeman at last, and in due course reported myself at the Old Bailey.'

Newgate Prison, after a continuous existence of over seven hundred years, was no longer the common gaol for London and Middlesex, but housed only those awaiting trial at the Central Criminal Court, which was then held in the old courthouse of the Old Bailey, adjoining it. It was still a principal place of execution, and maintained the grim reputation of its heyday as the showplace of London, earned when Tyburn was discontinued in 1783 and public executions were mounted outside Newgate until the practice was ended in 1868. My father found it a dismal pile, and the gloom was intensified when he discovered that he was assigned to what was called the Hangman's Room, a depressing attic at the top of a narrow flight of winding stairs, overlooking the execution shed and pitted with the names and initials of a legion of previous executioners, carved into the woodwork. He slept badly, and threw himself eagerly into the diversion of work next morning, when an inspection of the scaffold and a lecture about his duties began his training.

On the second morning he was ordered to carry out a dummy execution from beginning to end. The operation included a small skirmish of psychological warfare designed to test his speed of reaction. I could hear my father's lively voice setting out the anecdote for a taproom audience as I read it in print:

'I was taken to the condemned cell, and there in a dark corner the "victim" was pointed out to me. I advanced to pinion him as I had been instructed, and my heart did some heavy thumping when I found that the "condemned man" was a stuffed dummy with a hideously grinning face and right hand up saluting me! I had never expected this. I thought it was one of the warders whom I should have to practise on, and no doubt the real nature of the "victim" was purposely concealed from me in order to test my nerves.

'But if they expected me to flinch they were disappointed. I had had a shock, but I had the sense not to show it. So I pinioned the dummy, carried it to the scaffold, and "hanged" it just as though it had been the real man.'

My father hanged that dummy, or a substitute sandbag, continuously for another ten days, recalculating the drops for a change of weight and increasing his speed of operation. After a testing oral examination and a final 'snap' dummy execution, he was sent home with the warning that the next phase would be a searching investigation of his private character. But immediately after his first application he had had detectives enquiring about his character and associates at the business house where he was working as a furniture salesman, and the prospect did not vex him. However, as far as his new career was concerned, nothing happened for six months. 'I was just beginning to lose hope once more,' he recounted candidly, 'when I got a letter from Governor Cruikshank asking if I would assist at the execution of a man condemned for the murder of his wife. Joyfully I accepted the engagement, only to have a fresh disappointment. The man was reprieved.'

As a boy, I remember that I sympathised heartily with my father in this dashing of his hopes. As a man, a young executioner of exactly my father's age, repeatedly faced with the same set of circumstances at a time when one is anxious to prove oneself in one's craft, I am glad that I can honestly say that I never once experienced any mental rebellion at the news of a reprieve. I considered myself as the arm of the law, and I was content to accept the decisions of the wisdom of the law. I have never felt the slightest personal satisfaction in the judicial ending of another man's life, and I am happy to note now that my father immediately conceded this principle, although he acknowledged his impatience with a wry frankness: 'I contented myself,' he said, 'with the thought that I had been prevented from helping to hang a possibly innocent man, and waited more or less patiently for the next engagement to come along.'

I am sure that this attitude of resignation was more difficult for my father than for me. I have had plenty of time to assess our characters over the years, and I think my father had a more fiery temperament than I had, and was more inclined to be swept into the drama of a situation, whether from his own point of view or as the final instrument of justice. But I am convinced that a sense of detachment ought to be essential in an executioner. Regrettably, I cannot say that it has always existed, for I have known of assistant executioners, perhaps temporarily promoted because the 'Number One' was engaged elsewhere, who have demonstrated a suspect delight in their performance, and have done so not only within the craft but publicly afterwards. One man, after his first responsible operation, with the body correctly motionless on the rope, sprang into the air with his hands on his head and crowed 'I'm an executioner! I'm an executioner!' That was possibly an excusable pride in the craft, or the release of tension after an undoubted ordeal. But others have expressed themselves publicly as joyful avengers of the wrong done by a criminal. Vengeance is not and cannot be any aspect of an executioner's participation.

I will not deny that on occasions I have been emotionally involved in the fate of a condemned person, because of what I have previously read or heard about the crime, or the circumstances of the trial, or popular agitation for or against the prisoner which has erupted afterwards. It is the responsibility of the newspapers and of television that I, along with many millions of the public, have become involved in this way, and it has been a fatal flaw in this type of involvement – particularly when capital punishment was a reality – that its inspiration was entirely selective. It depended on published details of the virtue or age or sex of the victim or of the murderer which coalesced to fan a public mood. But other victims, or other murderers, whose circumstances have not hit the front pages, have been totally ignored.

As the executioner, it has fallen to me to make the last confrontation with all the condemned. It is I who have looked them last in the eyes, whether there has been popular agitation for their reprieve, or for the reverse on the boiling-oil principle that 'hanging's too good for them', or whether they have been entirely abandoned by public opinion so that any grounds for severity or mitigation of treatment have just not been canvassed. And it is at that moment, with their eyes on mine, and all the official witnesses huddled in a corner behind them, that I have known that any previous emotional involvement I may have had with them is to be regretted. There is only a final relationship which matters: in Christianity this is my brother or sister to whom something dreadful must be done, and I have tried always to be gentle with them, and to give them what dignity I could in their death.

I have always believed that I received a call to become an executioner, just as I was guided when I gave up the vocation. But I don't pretend that there was any mature shape to my thoughts when, in 1916, as a boy of eleven, I first read my father's reminiscences. In my imagination, and it was all imagination, Death was adventure – certainly when you met it individually, less glamorous, perhaps, when you lined up for it by the thousand, like my Uncle Johnny, for whom my mother never wept but often sighed. So Death was adventure, and Execution was romance. I had all the confirmation I needed on that point from my father's account of his first execution.

This was one of the last to take place in the old Newgate Prison, which was scheduled for demolition, so that the present Central Criminal Court could be constructed on the Old Bailey site. The condemned man was Marcel Faugeron, a young French anarchist who had killed a Clerkenwell jeweller during what was thought to have been a robbery to gain political funds. My father attended as assistant to James Billington, who had been the official executioner for some fourteen years but was then a dying man. Billington took his quarter in the attic known as the Hangman's Room, and my father – whether as a grim joke or a further test of his nerve – was assigned to a spare condemned cell utilised only for double executions and immediately next door to the convicted prisoner. Prowling around this cell after midnight, my father discovered that there was an inspection peephole in the wall which gave a clear view into Faugeron's cell. Since my father was very keen on his job, he took advantage of this observation point to make a further study of the physical build of the condemned man: Billington had already worked out the drop from the details of the man's height and weight and an estimate of the strength of his neck muscles, but my father understandably wanted to make his own observations and work out his private conclusion as to the length of drop which should be given.

Faugeron was walking up and down his cell, smoking cigarettes continuously. 'Then,' said my father, 'all at once the old church clock at the corner of Holborn boomed out its late hour. Faugeron held up one hand, and started counting on his fingers. It was two o'clock, but Faugeron continued to count until he had marked off the hour of eight on his fingers. Then he motioned to his warders and pointed his forefinger to the skies. He could not speak a word of English, and this was his way of saying that he was going to Heaven at eight o'clock in the morning. I could not help thinking about this, and when the clock struck the next hour I got off my bed to watch him. Still smoking, Faugeron counted out eight on his fingers and then raised his arm high. From time to time I continued my observations, and no matter what the hour was, he would go on counting it until eight and then theatrically point upwards.'

It is difficult not to agree with my father's description of this sight as 'theatrical' or with my own juvenile acceptance of it as Romance, for people much more cultured than I am would applaud that scene in the last act of a grand opera, if the condemned man was singing at the same time. The church clock was, of course, the famous chime of St. Sepulchre's Without Newgate, which had always begun the long tolling of its passing bell as the procession of victims in their wretched carts began to form up for the regular three-mile journey from Newgate to Tyburn in the old days. For a long time through my boyhood I kept in my mind's eye the picture of that dark young anarchist, unable to get a single word understood in that prison until, as he did, he made the responses for his last Mass on his last morning – counting and pointing, with the cigarette for ever in his mouth. That set piece was succeeded by a sort of strip-cartoon frame, with my father as hero, depicting the quick pay-off that proclaimed that he had been accepted as a master executioner. What had happened, my father recounted, was that two minutes after the execution he was in the break-fast room, 'just about to start a good meal'. Quite unexpectedly the prison medical officer came in. My father knew him as Dr. Scott, who had tested him during his oral examination after training, and who had just pronounced the condemned man dead. The doctor thrust out his hand. My father thought that for some reason he wanted to shake hands. He offered his own. But the doctor lunged forward and took his wrist. In a business-like way he noted the speed of the pulse. Then the doctor smiled. 'You will do,' he said, and dropped my father's wrist, turned about, and went out of the door. It was after that epi-sode that my father received an official letter from the Prison Commissioners stating that his name had been added to the Home Office list of executioners.

'During my first fifteen months as executioner,' he wrote laconically, 'I hanged fifteen persons, occasionally as assistant, but generally as "the" executioner. The second appointment I got after joining the prison service was as head executioner.'

By the time I went back to school in Huddersfield after the summer holidays I had read six or seven long instalments of my father's reminiscences, and I suppose many others who might have had something to do with me had done the same. I thought I might perhaps be treated differently as the son of a celebrity, and I did not look forward to this, for I was not a particularly cocky lad. But, as far as I could make out, no one took the slightest notice or made the faintest reference, neither boy nor master. I think it was different for my father at work, and, compared with my uncle for example, he was more a man to enjoy the revival of his fame. He then had a job in the Hud-dersfield gasworks. He wore an armband with a crown, and a big badge in his coat, to show he was exempt from army service, and, as he proudly reported and I proudly remembered, his employers had said 'We could do with some more men like you' – not because he had been an executioner but because he was a good worker and they were giving him this crown as conscription was coming in. But he was forty years old then and, as I now know, stricken with incurable disease.

And I myself was touched with the beginnings of an ambi-tion, or the realisation of a calling, based on my father's pride which had reflected on to me when he spoke about me to the stationmaster. It was not an idea that was constantly in my head, but it was rooted. Occasionally it prompted pictures in my mind, of the anarchist pointing dramatically upwards, of the executioner approaching sorrowfully, clothed in some dark and different costume. I never reconstructed any details of the actual death, never even had a picture of anything so sharply defined as a noose, so I do not think my imagination was working in a particularly bloodthirsty or abnormal manner.

Every morning I ran with my pals to Beaumont Street School to play football in the yard before the bell stopped. One day we came into class and my teacher, Mr. Hardcastle, set us an essay. 'What I should like to do when I leave school', I dutifully copied down at the top of the page. After that I was flummoxed. The only thing I was interested in, I thought, was horses, but I couldn't see myself getting a quick job driving a horse and cart. I gazed pretty blankly at the paper. The rest of the class seemed all set, heads bent down industriously as they got on with their compositions. I dipped my pen. 'When I leave school I should like to be the Official Executioner . . .' I found myself writing. I gazed at the words with a new interest, and somehow it didn't seem so impossible as getting a job with horses. So I expanded the idea with a few details of the duties I should have, taken from my father's story. Mr. Hardcastle, the schoolmaster, a short, spectacled man, was roaming round the classroom. He stopped behind me and read my essay over my shoulder. He smiled and continued to walk round the class. Towards the end of the period he came back and read some more. I had always thought he was a stern man, but he patted me gently on the back and walked away, still with a quiet smile on his face. I handed in the essay, and realised that I had actually committed an ambition to paper.

My father's reminiscences were still being serialised. I thought some of his stories were very moving. He told how he had been engaged to assist James Billington in the execution of Billington's old friend, Patrick M'Kenna who, as I read the details now, seems to have killed his wife in a state of mental confusion and was completely shattered by his own deed. The sentence was to be carried out at Manchester, and Billington himself was a distracted and over-wrought man, less apparently from the prospect of the duty he had to perform than from the fact that he himself was fading in an illness that was to kill him a fortnight later. Billington and my father went to view the prisoner through the inspection glass in his cell door. 'I never saw a more repentant man, tall in height, with his bushy prison beard, looking rejected and broken up.' They went back to their room, and Billington collapsed with his sickness. 'Ee, Harry,' he moaned, 'I wish I'd never ha' come.' In complete silence they went next morning to the condemned cell. 'The chaplain moved to the door and stood in readiness to lead the way and recite the burial service. As we pinioned M'Kenna he broke out in great sobs, crying "Oh, Lord, help me." It was only a few steps to the drop, but he walked slow and faltering. The strain was almost too much for him. Tears rolled down his cheeks all the time. The moment he stood on the chalk mark on the scaffold, he cried aloud "Lord, have mercy on my soul". Never in all my career as public executioner have I come across a more penitent culprit.' Billington soon afterwards died, and the people of Bolton, his home town and M'Kenna's, said it was because of the task he had had to do. But my father stoutly denied this.

Shrewsbury, Chelmsford, Usk, Londonderry, Cardiff, Norwich, Knutsford ... my father became a great railway traveller, even to prisons which have been pulled down now. He told a strange tale about an appointment at Ayr, in Scotland, a country which even then – the tendency became more marked later – indulged in comparatively few executions but used more consistently the policy of royal reprieves recommended by the Secretary of State for Scotland. Consequently, when there was a rare execution outside the populous cities, the local officials were both inexperienced and curious, and the local prison engineers sometimes built a scaffold that was awkward to operate.

My father began his account, like Captain Cook or some other explorer, with details of the course plotted and the route taken. These particulars always interested me because I saw a glamour, as I suspect my father still did, in the sheer spiritual lift of travel, even around Great Britain, where towns two hundred miles away were still genuinely 'faraway places'.

'I travelled through the north via Kilmarnock, then across country to Ayr, where I arrived late at night, and was met at the station, by arrangement, by the Town Clerk. After a little refreshment in the station, we took a cab that was in waiting and went straight to the gaol. I reported myself to the Governor and, noting that the hour was very late, I insisted on making my usual arrangements before supper. The Governor, the

Doctor, the Town Clerk and the Lord Provost were with me and eager to see everything, as they had not witnessed an execution before and were very interested in what was taking place. I went straight to the long execution-box which lay in the engineer's workshop, just as it had arrived, and which contained all the necessary tackle for me to carry out the job. Immediately I unscrewed the lid and took out the ropes, etc., I was surprised to see what great interest everyone had in examining the secrets of the box's contents. It put me in mind of children looking in a jack-in-the-box for the first time, and I had to smile, although I was as much interested in them as they were in me. Well, I explained to them all about the contents and what every article was for. Then I went to the scaffold, which was a new structure, built of very stout timber, elevated about twelve feet above the level of the ground with a rough flight of steps leading to the platform of the scaffold. I immediately told them that the scaffold was no good, the steps were far too difficult for a possibly half-fainting prisoner. But I saw that I would have to use it and I began to make my arrangements.

'All at once, in the stillness of the night as we stood about the scaffold – "Ring! Ring! Ring!" sounded heavily at the gate bell. It was then after ten o'clock at night, and the Governor could not understand it. He wanted me to wait, for fear that he would miss seeing anything while he went to enquire what the interruption was. And to everyone's surprise, it was a King's Messenger with a packet containing the reprieve of the condemned man.

'Of course this meant that my duties were at an end, and I packed up my ropes, etc. Then we had a consultation, all together, whether to inform the prisoner or wait until the following morning. It was decided to let him know at once. I was about to turn into my room, to consider what to do now that my services were no longer needed, when the Lord Provost invited me to go into the cell with them.

'Of course I accepted the offer. Five or six of us entered the cell believing we were taking the prisoner good news. But to our amazement, the prisoner received it badly. As soon as he heard that he was reprieved, he cried bitterly, with his hands over his face. He backed into a corner of his cell. We all stood close to him. He dropped his hands, and, looking me straight in the face, still crying, he pushed me gently on the breast, taking me for the Lord Provost. He said "I do not want a reprieve. Let me die".

'We left the cell, and adjourned for supper to a private room, where I can assure you I did justice to the meal, after my long travel and the excitement of my arrival at the gaol. After supper I decided to make the night journey home, via Kilmarnock. I was paid my fees and expenses in the usual way, then I left the prison for the station in a cab, in the company of the Town Clerk, who wished to see me off. I arrived home in good time the following morning.

'One would naturally think that a condemned man would be thankful for a reprieve. But I have known many cases where a reprieve has been granted against the wish of the prisoner. On the other hand, I have also hanged many who would willingly have gone through all the hardships and horrors of penal servitude to escape the scaffold.'

At home in Huddersfield such tales as these had never been told, although my father was often very jovial and spent his skill as a storyteller on other subjects, anecdotes of his experiences at work or memories of his boyhood in Clayton with my Uncle Tom. I understand now that there was a conscious bar against any mention of his career as an executioner. Although this may have been due to my mother's initial and continuing disapproval, both my parents honourably observed this ban, and this side of my father's life was never mentioned in the house: consequently we all read about it surreptitiously in *Thomson's Weekly News*. It is a policy of silence that I myself have always rigorously observed, but for different reasons. I have never discussed my work as executioner with my wife, not even years after any event, but this has been because, trusting my wife to the full and knowing that I have a support as deep from her, I have always respected the natural disinclination of any woman, as the giver of life, to be perturbed by details of the wilful ending of any life – and she has never asked me a single question. But it is also true that, unlike my father, I have never discussed my profession in detail with *any* friend or acquaintance, inside or outside my home, except for one ill-judged response to a newspaper which did not finally print my own words nor respect my deep feeling that I am not a showman. In this respect I have been, in character, more like my Uncle Tom, who was completely reserved on this subject even with me, until I officially joined his craft.

My mother had.had, in any case, more, I think, to tolerate than my wife Anne. My father – I can see it now – warm and likeable as he was, and so competent at anything that came to his hand, was a harum-scarum fellow, truly easily led and with an incomparable skill at finding someone to lead him. He might go off to Exeter to conduct an execution at a fee which at that time could represent a month's normal wages – but there was an equal chance that he might not come home afterwards until he and his friends had spent his fee. Only, it seems to me, when my Uncle Tom joined him on the Home Office list of executioners did he steady up his absences, but that was no great improvement on the situation, since, although it brought him home more quickly, it landed him sooner among a resident squad of friends who were only too pleased to beckon him out, and listen to the golden stories about his experiences which we could not hear at home. My mother was not a martyr, and not outrageously put upon. She was a typically patient and hard-working woman of her time, with perhaps more of the characteristic virtue of loyalty than some women cherish in these times. She was a fine mother, not reserved but very warm towards me, her eldest son. And although she was not demonstrative, and never joined in the song when my father would come bursting in like a comet in the late evening and call to my sister for a tune on the piano, I fancy that she felt some fulfilment and some relaxation in the family circle, even if she pursed her lips with a self-contained smile when my father would sing:

> Tell me, Mary, how to woo thee,
> Teach my bosom to reveal
> All its sorrows, sweet, unto thee,
> All the love my heart can feel.

I know that, as a Lancashire woman, my mother was 'never settled', as we say in the north, even although she was only a few miles across the Pennines into Yorkshire. And the time soon came when my father sang with literal accuracy 'I'll take you to your home again'.

Possibly bolstered by his receipts from the newspaper serialisation of his memoirs, he announced in the winter of 1916–17 that the family was to move to Manchester. He himself was to stay at work at Huddersfield – he had now left the gasworks and was employed at Hopkinson's Ironworks. But he was to come home every weekend. We were on our travels!

We were then living in 2 Emerald Street, our third home in Huddersfield in the six years we had been in the town. It was a house right against the railway, with an embankment dead in front of it and a railway arch to the side taking the main line to Yorkshire. I remember that during the war there were police-men on guard at the bridge twenty-four hours a day in case anyone tried to blow it up. My father arranged with the man next door, who had a lorry and horses, that he would remove our furniture to Failsworth, near Manchester, only a mile from my mother's birthplace at Newton Heath, at a cost of five pounds. The arrangement was that my mother and my two sisters and my youngest brother would go across by train, and – adventurous travel! – my younger brother Bill and myself were to ride on the cart on top of our furniture.

It was seven o'clock on a dark and blustery morning when the removal men knocked, and began to carry out the furni-ture. 'Brr! There must be a hanging this morning!' I said to my brother as we put our noses outside and shivered. It was a saying we used at school for this sort of dawn, and we had no family claim on it. The lorry was a low, flat four-wheeled wagon without sides, drawn by one horse in the shafts and with a chain horse tethered behind. By half-past-nine we began the long cold journey across the Yorkshire moors. The men soon had to put on the chain horse for the endless pull over the north side of the moors, and the horses were as relieved as we were when we stopped for food and an hour's rest at a halfway house on top of the Pennines. It was an old stone-built pub called the Floating Light, and my young brother and I snuggled luxuriously into the inset fireplace for a good warm. We set off again, and the misty night came down early. We had four oil lamps swinging at the corners of the load. We dropped into Oldham and followed the main road into Failsworth, with the men looking for Mill Street, where our next home lay. But I took no notice of the new house when we stopped, because I was concerned that one of the lamps had gone out, and as soon as I could scramble down I was trying to get it alight again. But I heard my mother calling 'Come on, Albert! Come and have your tea.' It was six o'clock, and I realised that I was starving.

We were soon settled in Failsworth, and my mother put me into the local school, Holy Trinity. I quickly made friends there, and hoped they would notice how promising I was at football. Perhaps they did, but they on their side could offer a far greater attraction. Some of them were already at work, and earning money. It was possible then for any schoolchild aged twelve-and-a-half to go to the cotton-spinning mills and work half-time – that is, do about six hours' work in the mill before midday dinner and then go to school in the afternoon. This prospect appealed to me, particularly as my mother did not find a job in Manchester to replace her munitions work in Huddersfield, and I began to make calculations on the calendar about my birthday. In the meantime, I speedily saw one great disadvantage of the new move. My father came home regularly at weekends, but unless I could be smuggled over for a quick return trip to Yorkshire on a Sunday, I had probably seen the last of my Uncle Tom and my Auntie Lizzie until the next summer holidays.

And this proved to be the case. Months passed before I rushed once more into that enticing smell of fresh bread, and saw my Uncle Tom standing with his spoon in a dish and champing at his 'pobs', as we in Yorkshire used to call this staple refreshment of bread-and-milk. It was the longest time I had ever spent without seeing the relatives who had been so close to me, and at the age of twelve, when a boy can be changing fast, the interval might have marked an alteration in our relationship. For I now knew that my uncle was an executioner, and complicating that knowledge was the fact that I was nursing my own ambition. But, staunchly, I never said a word about either fact, and if my uncle looked at me a little more knowingly I accepted it as the sort of understanding that exists between two men of the world. Perhaps I, too, looked a shade more knowing, for I had acquired a more adult awareness of the status of my uncle compared with my father. My uncle was the elder of the two, by some six years, and he was the steadier and perhaps in character the stronger. But it was my father who had the initiative and originality, he showed the spurts of flame, even if he also revealed their dying down. It was my father who had started the carrier's business in Clayton and Bradford, and once he had set it up he handed it over to my Uncle Tom. My father, also, had persuaded Tom to try for the Home Office list of executioners, as I knew from one of the very few oblique references which my father confidentially made to me about his craft. He had, in fact, trained his brother in the very stable at the back of the cottage to which, this time,

I had rather significantly *not* dashed as soon as I could gasp a Hallo. The instruction was so successful that, when Tom was sent to Pentonville for the statutory fortnight's training, the authorities sent him home within a week, with the comment from the prison engineer: 'You don't want any more. Your Harry's been teaching you!' And now, of course, Harry had resigned from the list and Tom was still on – as he was to remain for another thirty years.

Our relationship at Clayton had not changed. My stay there was a long summer month of paradise. My Uncle Tom ran his carrier's business, booked his bets, chopped hay with a peculiar cutter worked by a gas engine, ate his pobs, snored on Sunday, and quietly disappeared to hang a couple of people without a by-your-leave to me. My auntie, as talkative as ever, sewed up her mouth with such difficulty during his absence that I was sure that, when I was a year older, she would gossip to me with every confidence; meanwhile, she took me to the music-hall on Thursdays, and contrived a long solitary errand for me on one regular afternoon a week. I never knew until long afterwards that that was the time when she made her toilet, dragging the tin tub into the kitchen, barring the door of the general store, and putting a concise notice in the shop window: HAVING A BATH. I never even saw the notice between baths. As for myself, I fed the chickens, milked the goats, outwitted Billy, and even sold one or two of his offspring at the door as meat goats for Indians calling from Bradford. The price on the hoof was five shillings. On the more active side, I mucked out the horses, helped with my uncle's carrying, and finally mastered the gas engine driving the hay cutter.

I went back to Manchester, and the summer was suddenly cut off with heavy rains, and somewhere in France something called the Third Battle of Ypres developed into something called Passchendaele and wiped out some scores of thousands of Uncle Johnnys without much protest or impact on anyone notable except Winston Churchill. My own thoughts were on the date the 30th of September 1917. That was the day when I became twelve-and-a-half years old and I could legally go and work in the mill. And on that day I asked the master at my new school at Failsworth if I could have the form to complete which would allow me to start as a half-timer. He could not refuse me, although he seemed to want to, and after reaching for the form he asked me a number of questions and began to fill it in. In the interrogation I obviously must have revealed the truth that at Huddersfield the children did not have the chance to work as half-timers, because he loosed the remark, which I thought very unfair then and still do, that I had only come to Failsworth in order to start work. The fact was that I had never consciously heard of half-timing until I arrived, although my father had done it, and a fact of equal importance was that my mother needed the money. I could take home all of six shillings a week if I worked hard enough.

For this wage I had to work in the first week from six in the morning until a quarter past twelve. Getting up in the dark, and running to the Marlborough Mills with the other boys, I began to know the discipline of work – we ran, because if I was five minutes late I was thrown out of the mill, to the sick anger of myself, my mother, and, I suppose, the mill manager. After six-and-a-quarter hours' work I would come home, have some dinner, and go to school from two o'clock until half past four. On the alternate week I would go to school in the morning, and get to the mill by a quarter past one in order to work until half past five. My first job was as a learner tuber. This was a sort of initiation task that was only done by children, a continuous process of fitting the right-size tubes on to the right-size spindles, simple enough but non-stop. I took home my six shillings a week, and my mother gave me sixpence. That was the going rate for kids – a penny in the shilling.

On my thirteenth birthday I went full-time at the spinning mills and soon became a piecer, spending my working life, as I was to do for many years, moving and bending and dodging and joining as the slave of a rather ruthless pair of spinning mules which ran in and out all day, spinning the cotton. And that was the end of my education, or at least of any book-lore. But no teacher had really taken any notice of me from the age of twelve-and-a-half. I am very painfully aware that I had a restricted education. I continued to learn afterwards, from mixing and listening to people, and I think I have missed absolutely nothing ever since I was married. But I should have liked that completion when I was younger. I think education is the finest thing in the world. Any money I had I would spend on educating children, and never worry about leaving them money afterwards. I often think about this, the education I have missed.

My father came back from Huddersfield, and for a time was

unemployed. There had been an accident at work which had put him on the sick list for some time, and although this was not the end of his working career, it joined tentacles with the disease that was already mastering him, to pull him down. But he was never down-hearted and always had his eloquence. One day in Oldham Street, Manchester, he ran into the Reverend Somebody who had been one of his sponsors in the effort to make him go teetotal at the Queen Street Mission in Huddersfield. They had a long and optimistic chat together, and at the end of it the Reverend lent him ten pounds. I don't know that my father returned it. Soon afterwards he got a job in Mather & Platts, the engineers, and he got enough to keep us as best he could, with a little something over for the benefit of the landlord of the Cloggers Arms, the pub that stood at the end of our street.

I was making great efforts to get into the local league football team, and hoping desperately to be able to afford boots of my own. We lived no worse than many other people, but we didn't live very well. Soon after I went full-time the Great War ended, and for some reason work was not continuous any more even at the Marlborough Mills. At Christmas we had never had anything more than an orange and a few nuts as extras, there were no real solid presents: and now we didn't have nuts. No alcohol had ever at any time been consumed in our house, and, strangely enough, for my father was a man of free principles, he would never allow a pack of cards in the house, although occasionally he played outside himself – he had played with James Billington on the eve of Pat M'Kenna's execution to take Billington's mind off his condition.

Our only extravagance, even if we had to go deep in debt for it at the credit drapers, was that we had to have new suits for Whitsuntide. I think my father was as keen on that as my mother, and in my own mind I think I felt that every new outfit, always a little more adult, brought me nearer to my father, so that we might be able to go out for walks together, man to man, smoking perhaps – I never got as far as picturing myself having a gill of beer with him. A new outfit meant a new suit, new shoes, even new hat – and I was coming up to the point where a youth of my age would wear a bowler, or a pothat as we used to call it. The splash was connected with the traditional Whit Walks which are still held in Manchester and were much more strongly supported then: all the churches came out on different days with processions and banners. I had a strong connection with church life, because the only worthwhile football teams in my talent-band were connected with the churches, and you couldn't play for the church team unless at least you went to their Sunday school. I made a defection from Holy Trinity to Dob Lane, which was a unitarian church but a better football team. And at the Whit Walk they got me to carry the banner. I had managed to acquire a smart grey suit, and my first pot-hat, but the regular refined gimmick in those days was to wear elaborate sock-suspenders which were hoist round the leg and hooked and bracketed on to the sock with rather more to-do than women use to keep their stockings up today. I certainly could not afford suspenders, but I always hated to have my socks dragging round my ankles, so I made them fast below my knee with long lengths of string. But, earnestly carrying the banner through the city with both hands, I could not stoop down to make the necessary adjustments when both my string garters started trailing in the dust. And that had to be the day when my father decided to go into town and see Our Albert carrying the banner for the Unitarians. There was a smile of unspoken comment on his face when he told me what a grand impression I had made on him. 'Now let's have a tune,' he said to the rest of the family. He was flushed with the sun, looked more healthy than I had seen him for a long time, and he sang some of the Irish songs which he always liked, and which I do still:

> Believe me, if all those endearing young charms
> That I gaze on so fondly today
> Were to vanish tomorrow and melt in my arms
> Like fairy gifts fading away,
> Thou wouldst still be the same, as this moment thou art,
> Let thy loveliness fade as it will,
> And around the dear ruin each wish of my heart
> Would entwine itself verdantly still.

The time of fading was approaching. I had passed the age of seventeen and felt that I was coming much closer to my father. One early summer evening I was standing at the corner of the street with the rest of the lads, passing round the dimps, or cigarette ends, and hiding them in our hands between puffs, chatting, and chatting up any birds who might come along. We were straight opposite the Cloggers Arms and I suppose my

father could see me from the window. He came out of the pub.
'Come here, Albert,' he called, 'I want you.' I went towards
him with the usual vague feeling of guilt which a boy works up
on these occasions. 'Albert,' he said, 'I've seen you smoking,
and don't hide that cigarette any more. You're old enough to
smoke now, and smoke in the house. I've just won some Wood-
bines in there, so you can take them.' He passed me two packets
of five Woodbine cigarettes – which he never smoked anyway,
being a pipe man – and I lit up and began puffing away,
inhaling very flashily and chain-smoking when I had finished
one. But before I had ended my exhibition I was deathly sick,
and I never smoked cigarettes again. I tried a pipe, and that
had a worse effect. I was forty years old before I began to
smoke a pipe regularly, and I have given that up since.

That summer of 1922 passed, and my father finished working. In his condition he was too weak to go on. The family was
as hard up as usual. My father decided to re-write his reminiscences and sell them to another newspaper. He came to an
arrangement about this with *Reynolds News*. He got no advance payment, and he did not even have the money to buy the
paper to write on. I had a shilling, and I was saving it towards a
pair of football boots. But I lent him the shilling to buy two big
blue exercise books with, and in return he promised me a pair
of football boots to be bought when his money came through.
He began writing again, with a fluency that was now perfected
by practice, as with an after-dinner tale: more than once I had
been stopped by a neighbour in our street, and told in those
rather argumentative tones which they use for ecstasy in Lancashire: 'Eee, lad, I've just been listening to your father in't
Cloggers Arms, and he's had us all spellbound!'

The newspaper sent down the chief crime reporter, who
printed a profile of my father written, I thought, with a little
more southern rhapsody than the description which Thomsons
of Dundee had used six years before: 'Eyes clear as crystal . . .
His nerves are like unto finely tempered steel . . . He can inter-
sperse into narratives pregnant with haunting terror some little
human or humorous touch which stamps him as a born storyteller.' It was a bit too fanciful for me (though, as I still
remember, his eyes *were* clear as crystal), but I think my
mother liked the bit about her house: 'With pride he showed
me round his little home, every corner spotlessly clean. There
was a piano, a stack of sentimental and religious music, and a

delightful air of restfulness about the little house at the end of the street.'

The series ran in *Reynolds* for three months. On the week after it ended, in the issue of the 17th of December 1922, the newspaper printed my father's obituary. He had given me my football boots, and died. We buried him, with much love, at Holy Trinity. It was our parish, and his creed, despite a brotherly diversion to the Methodists at the Queen Street Mission. I grieved increasingly for my father. He went when I was at the age when I was beginning to come within his range in understanding, as well as affection. It was only a poor link with him that I could use his football boots, and only an inadequate sign of respect that I left Dob Lane Unitarians and crossed over to play football for Culcheth, where the church still upheld the Trinity.

3

My Inheritance

I was never a scholar, but there is one story from history which I have always vividly remembered ever since my schoolmaster told it to me. The Black Prince, son of the King of England, was being blooded in his first battle before he could be elevated to knighthood. In individual combat with a group of Frenchmen he was being hard pressed. The knights in the King's retinue saw his danger and looked to the King for permission to go and help him. 'No,' said the King, 'let the lad win his spurs.' That was the way I intended to reach my own recognition, and that was the way I did it. I saw my calling as hereditary, but I sought no family favours, and received none.

The death of my father marked the end of my boyhood. I was seventeen when my father told me I was old enough to smoke, slipping cigarettes into my hand with a result that he perhaps foresaw. I was still seventeen when I found myself old enough to be the head of the household – not the only bread-winner, for all but the youngest of the children were now doing work of a kind – but I was conscious that I was the eldest lad, and without any dramatics I set out to make of myself some sort of prop to my mother. She and I had a very warm relationship, undemonstrative though we were, and she both depended on me and deferred to me. She was always a wonderful manager, but I felt that she had come to rely on the reassurance of a man about the house. And so, very simply and perhaps without always knowing it, I became a man, and did in fact stay with her through two more bereavements until the end, over twenty years later.

But I still nursed my one ambition, and that was no longer childish. I kept it absolutely secret, but through all the years I thought always more about it. And I now had an inexhaustible source of inspiration which kept my ambition burning at full heat. My father's only positive legacy to me was the control of his files of papers – letters of appointment, communications from Sheriffs and Prison Commissioners, his diary of executions and his hand-written memoirs, set out in the blue notebooks I bought for him with my last shilling: I still possess them. My father bequeathed me one other thing, which I suppose it is now unfashionable for sons to confess. It was the memory of his voice, with a certain note of pride in it, saying 'This is my eldest son, and one day he will be the Official Executioner.' And when I heard that again in my mind, I still felt the touch of his firm hand on my shoulder. The documents and the memory were quite enough to fix for me the course I intended to follow, with the self-sufficiency which I suppose I also inherited from him, and, if I am to be honest, perhaps more dogged tenacity than he sometimes showed. People are individuals. Their characters and their ambitions are unique to them. This is what I was. This was my ambition.

So I read my father's papers openly – it was in any case impossible to be furtive over such an action in our small house – but I kept my thoughts to myself. My father's diary of executions was a thick, shiny black-bound pocket book with EXECUTION BOOK boldly inked across the edges of the pages, opposite the spine. It contained details of the date and prison for every execution he had carried out, with particulars of each condemned man – his name, age, height, weight and the muscular condition of his neck, 'thick-set', 'flabby', 'short' and the like – as noted by my father through the observation window of the condemned cell. The row of hand-ruled columns ended with one to record the length of drop which my father had calculated and given as a result of these physical details. (When I came to keep my own execution diary I added a note of who I had had as my assistant executioner, but I omitted any reference to the condition of the condemned man's neck, which I found a little distasteful to record.) My father's Execution Book, black like a Family Bible, also contained a record of the birth of all his children; and useful addresses of assistant executioners; with notes of expenses for various professional trips – fare to Belfast £1 11s. 3d., and a shilling for the cab; and also, my father's lifetime interest in horses and farm animals being inextinguishable, there was even a section on Horse Remedies and other veterinary medicine: for coughs and colds in cows, prepare a bran mash with half a pound of linseed and an ounce of saltpetre in the mash.

I learned from my father's diary that he had carried out as many as nineteen executions in one year, 1909, which was high by any standard in Great Britain before or since. But it was from his manuscript reminiscences that I drew the human details that had coloured his narratives and impressed all his listeners – except at home, where he had never discussed his craft. I read these stories again and again, since this was the nearest I could come at my young age to gaining actual experience of the calling. I had already determined never to discuss the subject even with my Uncle Tom until I had gained, by my own efforts, the professional status to enable me to meet him on this issue on level ground.

And so I gained a considerable familiarity with the attitudes and experiences that are peculiar to an executioner. My father's memories became mine. My mind held, as if the incidents had really happened to me, little pictures of the details of past tragedies, some pathetic, some graphic, some even grimly comic. I 'remembered', as if it had been part of my own life, the man at Leeds Gaol who had sworn to give as much trouble as possible all the way from the condemned cell to the scaffold, and who finally, as my father adjusted the rope round his neck, complained 'It's too tight!' I absorbed the detail of the man at Swansea who ignored the chaplain and smoked a cigarette all the way to the scaffold: my father let him continue smoking, and the butt was still between his lips when they took the body down an hour later. I saw in my mind the green lawn, closely cut, in the garden at Wandsworth Prison where all executed prisoners were buried, with a square stone let into the wall above their heads and only their initials marked on it with the date of execution. I re-lived the moment, illustrated like an engraving in a Victorian novel, of a sombre scene outside Wandsworth when a tall, graceful woman, clothed from head to foot in deep mourning, walked up to my father with an ashen face. 'In trembling tones she said to me "Is he dead? Is he dead?" I answered "Yes". Then in a moaning tone she said "My God, my God". Though there was a large crowd about, not one walked near me while I was speaking to that unfortunate woman.'

I saw through my father's eyes 'the bravest man I ever hanged', the soldier who had come home from the South African War and found his wife unfaithful. He carried his little daughter in his arms up the stairs of his North London home, and cut her throat, and then tore down the decorations which had been put up for his return, and took a Union Jack from them and placed it over the child's body. Then he went to the police and gave himself up. They asked why he had done it. 'So that she would not grow up like her mother,' he replied. He was sentenced to death at the Old Bailey. He acknowledged his action throughout, made no plea for mercy, and told the warders and officials in the condemned cell that he wanted to die and sought no reprieve. My father came to hang him on the appointed morning. 'Everyone,' he said, 'was standing at the cell door with bared heads until after the execution. I walked sharply into the cell. He stood up, ready, with his hand outstretched as if to shake hands, and a smile on his face as if he were glad that the time had come. I pinioned his arms and rolled down his shirt neck. He braced himself as if on parade, and seemed to be straining his muscles to walk as firm as he could, without a quiver. As I tightened the noose around his neck he did not flinch, and he smiled again as I placed the cap over his head. Then in a low voice he said "Lord have mercy on me". I drew the lever.'

This execution took place at Pentonville Prison and was, according to my father's records, only the second to take place there. My father actually officiated at the first execution to take place at this prison, after the closing of Newgate, where he had trained, and its demolition to make room for the new Central Criminal Court. This inauguration of Pentonville occurred on the 30th of September 1902, using what my father called 'the finest scaffold in the whole country, being fitted to hang three persons side by side. Before being installed at Pentonville it had been erected at Newgate, and previously it was in use at the old Horsemonger Lane Gaol. I have hanged a good many murderers on this scaffold, the one I was trained on'. I was interested to learn that it was this very first execution at Pentonville which marked the abolition of the practice of flying a black flag to show that a prisoner had been executed. By order of the Home Secretary a bell was tolled instead – but this solemnity, too, was later discontinued.

Later in my life I, too, came to use this historic scaffold at Pentonville. My father noted that it was fitted to hang three persons side by side, and this equipment still existed. In the old days of the Tyburn gallows, of course, prisoners were turned off a dozen at a time and allowed to strangle. Triple executions in public became common in the nineteenth century. English, but not Scottish, scaffolds continued to provide accommodation for three prisoners throughout my career. But, even though it has been my duty to hang 27 people in a day, when war criminals were being executed in Germany, I myself have never officiated at a simultaneous triple execution, and I should always decline to do so because of the confusion that would be involved. As far as I can ascertain, the last triple execution in England took place at Newgate on the 9th of June 1896. It was notable for a remarkable accident. The assistant executioner, Warbrick, was still strapping the third man's legs when Billington opened the drop. Billington could not see Warbrick, partly because the authorities had expected a fight on the scaffold between two of the condemned men and had posted four warders on the drop itself, two pairs of officers standing back to back on planks laid across the trapdoors on either side of the central prisoner. Warbrick heard the bolt being pulled out beneath him by Billington's lever and, as he fell through the drop, clutched at the legs of the man he had been pinioning. Though he dived head first through the doors, he kept his grip, and found himself swinging in the pit among the legs of three dead men.

My father notched another entry in the book of records of capital punishment by officiating at what was not only the first execution at Holloway Gaol – then quite recently adapted for exclusive use as a women's prison – but was also a double execution, which has been very rare in modern times when women were concerned. Newspapers printing my father's obituary said that he was privately opposed to capital punishment for women. I cannot confirm this, since he never discussed the matter with me. (My own views on the subject I shall record later, as they developed.) What I do know, from my father's writings, is that he had intense sympathy for the women prison officers who had to endure this cumulative three-weeks' ordeal of attending to the prisoners and finally seeing them die.

The women whom my father had to execute were often baby-farmers. This is almost an antiquated expression nowadays, but I suppose that, in its worst aspects, combining infanticide with cashing in on the shame and desperation of human weakness, to some minds it is little different from the darkest side of the abortion racket today. Baby-farmers were women who, exploiting the more censorious morality of Victorian and Edwardian times, 'helped' mothers of unwanted, generally illegitimate, children by taking them off their mothers' hands for a sum of money. The worst of the baby-farmers then murdered the children, and, if convicted and sentenced, they came eventually face to face with my father. The double execution at Holloway which he described was painful in much of its detail, with one of the women in an almost continuous faint having to be propped up by my father on the drop. But my father paid his sincere tribute to the prison wardresses, as their title then was: 'How bravely they went through the great ordeal! Every one was quite firm and calm, but after they left the death chamber one could detect stray tears trickling down their cheeks.'

Even baby-farming occurred in varying degrees of depravity. Some of those convicted seem to have been ruthless commercial murderers: in the rooms of the women executed at Holloway three hundred articles of discarded baby-clothing were found; the two crimes for which they were actually convicted brought them twenty-five pounds and thirty pounds for the 'sale' of the babies. In other cases distraught women seem to have been driven to the practice in desperation to gain money to live, as a brutal alternative to going on the streets. I fancy that my father had more sympathy for some of them, particularly for a woman he was called on, with my Uncle Tom, to execute at Cardiff. She had broken off a relationship with a man she had been living with and, in order to gain some money for support, 'adopted' a baby for the sum of £6, and, it seemed in sheer confusion, smothered it almost immediately in a train, haplessly leaving the body at the foot of her bed in her lodgings.

Her remorseful lover visited her in prison on the last day of her life, and the long night passed. 'It was a beautiful bright August morning,' my father said. 'The sun shone splendidly all around. I walked gently into the cell, my brother with me. There she knelt, saying her last prayers amid sobs, by the side of the prison chaplain, like one knelt at the penitent form in a church sanctuary. I touched her gently on the shoulder. She looked up, so pitiful, at me. I said "Be brave," and helped her gently to her feet. These words seemed to comfort her a little, and as quickly as possible we fastened her arms behind her back, and walked out into the corridor, the chaplain in his white surplice leading the way. It was only a few steps to the yard. As she stepped out into the open, what a glorious sight there was, no picture could be painted better. The sun shone brilliantly on her auburn hair, just for a moment, a prettier sight no one could wish to see. Thus ended the life of a bright woman who, but for her past misdeeds, might have been living a happy life today.'

This was the last execution of a woman in Great Britain for over fourteen years, and the last in my father's lifetime, for he died at the height of the public controversy over the sentence of death passed on Mrs. Edith Thompson. The year 1922, the year of his death, was marked by intense argument and discussion throughout the country on the practice of capital punishment. The kernel of the unrest was not that there was then a very strong abolitionist movement – this point of view had long existed but not noticeably grown. I can see now what was not so obvious then, that the basic reason for public disquiet was precisely the situation which has strongly influenced my own conclusions on capital punishment, upon which I shall enlarge at the appropriate time. It is not the fact that women could be hanged – this has carried no weight in my own final attitude although in my time I have executed around a score of women. It is the sheer *inconsistency* of decisions over whether to reprieve a prisoner or to refrain from interfering in the execution of legal judgments. One of the most glaring inconsistencies occurred in September 1922, when on the same day a reprieve on the ground of insanity was granted to the well-connected Ronald True, convicted for a commonplace sordid sexual murder, and simultaneously a reprieve was refused for the page-boy Henry Jacoby, convicted for what, at its worst showing, was a bungled and unpremeditated assault during the course of an 'inside' hotel robbery which led to the death of Lady White, a well-connected person. My father's last contribution to any newspaper condemned the inconsistency of these decisions. General public opinion did not see the issue in these terms, but, as always in emotional explosions like this, concentrated on sentimental reactions to the attractiveness or unattractiveness of the prisoners involved, and on personal estimates of their degrees of guilt and their suitable punishment.

Then, at the time of my father's death, the newspapers were filled with passionate discussion of the death sentence passed on Mrs. Thompson, whose ambiguous letters to her young lover Frederick Bywaters, interpreted on the one side as juvenile fantasies and on the other as direct incitement to kill her husband, had resulted in the conviction of both for the murder of her husband. My family had no direct involvement with the execution of Mrs. Thompson. My uncle hanged Bywaters at Pentonville at the same hour as Ellis, using two assistants, dispatched Mrs. Thompson at Holloway. But, although the alleged horror of the circumstances of Mrs. Thompson's death were used for thirty years more as propaganda for the abolitionists, I can say on the authority of an assistant at Mrs. Thompson's execution whom I afterwards personally consulted that the facts had no element of the sickening details that were almost immediately alleged – which were always indirectly reported, I have noted, and never with any basis of authority.

Ellis retired from the Home Office list of executioners fourteen months after he had hanged Mrs. Thompson, and shortly afterwards he attempted suicide. I must now touch on a delicate subject. It is my sincere wish, in writing this record, to give no pain at all to the families of any person, whether he or she was a convicted criminal or an executioner. For this reason I am deliberately not identifying most of the characters in this book, unless they occupy a place in criminological history – the Belsen criminals, for example, whom I hanged – or unless their names have been bandied about in subsequent propaganda, generally relating to the abolition of capital punishment, *when I know that propaganda to be false, whatever I think of the object.* And, even then, I decline to give details of how a particular named prisoner met his or her end. When I say that my calling is sacred I extend that cover to the victim. But I do intend, when it is necessary, to say that such-and-such a propaganda story is false, *because I know, because I was there.* I shall deny what I know to be lies, but not fill the gap with facts which I could swear to be correct, because my office as executioner held statutory obligations to the state and equally binding personal confessional relationships with the victims. For the most part, it does not matter, it is not ultimately relevant, whether a prisoner who, for example, met his death in a manner that convinced me that capital punishment is no deterrent, had the name Smith on his death certificate, or had the name Jones. The important fact is what actually happened, not the name of the prisoner, which I intend to withhold when I think there is any likelihood of causing pain to near relatives. But in cases like those of Derek Bentley or Ruth

Ellis, where names have been constantly repeated, sometimes with the permission of the family, to make some debating point, I must at least indicate where I know from my own experience that popular beliefs are absolutely wrong. The genuine criminological scientist will, in any case, be able to identify from his general background knowledge most of the personages I mention, and he can refer to me or my publishers in any case of doubt. The 'key' to such identities as I shall indicate will exist in a confidential record for the sake of historical accuracy.

It is a matter of historical fact that the executioner Ellis attempted suicide once and succeeded in a second attempt, years later: the fact has been falsely manipulated to indicate that his mind became unhinged because of alleged unnerving scenes at the execution of Mrs. Thompson. I shall not therefore mask his name, nor deny that there was friction between him and my father, Henry Albert Pierrepoint, and that it also existed to some extent between him and my uncle, Thomas William Pierrepoint.

The friction may be related to my father's retirement from the Home Office list of executioners. There is a mystery about his retirement which I have not been able to solve. All I am certain of is that it was not through any professional failure on my father's part. I have had the private assurance of prison authorities on this point, and I have indeed had the opportunity to read the reports on the conduct of individual executions conducted by my father, which prison governors submitted to the Home Office in their normal routine, making a note on the efficiency of the executioner. The Prison Commissioners have always been iron-hard in their insistence on two qualities in an executioner: first-class craftsmanship, and a completely correct and discreet attitude to the public for as long as the post was held. One human error, and a man was out for good. One resignation – on whatever ground, private circumstances or a professional difference of opinion – and a man was never invited back on to the list. This last rule held until my own resignation, over a professional conflict, and I am the only man on record who has been invited to reconsider his resignation and to come back on the list as the Number One Executioner.

I know that my father made no professional error, and I also know that he resigned from the list and, in accordance with the rules, was never asked to come back. He was succeeded by John

Ellis and my Uncle Tom, both acting as approved executioners but with Ellis claiming seniority – it was Ellis, for example, who executed Sir Roger Casement in 1916, and talked about it afterwards. I know that my father held a strong feeling against Ellis. I have heard him express it but not give the reason. 'If I ever meet Ellis,' I have heard him say, 'I'll kill him – it doesn't matter if it is in the church.' I report this without partiality to show the strength of the passion involved. I do know, from my later experience, that there has been a cut-and-thrust vindictiveness among certain executioners on the Home Office list – sheer dirty work aimed at getting the senior man disgraced – so that, apart from honourable exceptions, I have had to keep a careful watch on everyone working with me, knowing that, if I didn't, they would do me down. I never knew the force of the word Jealousy until I was an executioner. Some such consideration may have aggravated my father's sometimes fiery temperament and prompted him to resign. Or it may have been some official blunder which infuriated him: and, again from my own experience, I know that such unnecessary situations can occur, not on the part of the Prison Commissioners themselves, but occasionally in the offices of the Sheriffs, who traditionally have an independent and occasionally arbitrary role outside the control of central administration in the management of executions.

At the beginning of the year in which my father resigned there was one such blundering occurrence. The brief fact was that the authorities 'forgot' to pay my father and my uncle their fees for an execution at Kilmainham Gaol, Dublin, and after long and argumentative correspondence they never did pay. I suppose the explanation was that a file got lost in the Irish Office – Ireland was then a dominion of the British Crown – but that sort of smug civil service explanation is no comfort to an aggrieved man. It had been a badly-managed execution from the start, through lack of control of the situation by the officials responsible. As my father described it in the account he left to me, two priests were in attendance on the prisoner, a practice which was sometimes allowed in Ireland. 'The condemned man was very much broken up and his brain seemed to be in a whirl. When I had got him on the traps, at the last moment the two priests clung around him on the scaffold, holding a crucifix to his lips. I gave them every indulgence I could, until they became a pest to me, delaying me in my duty. At last

I told them to stand back. But they would not. So I had to push them off. The poor fellow in his anxiety was about to collapse. My brother held him up erect. It was a trying moment. I had to have my eyes all around me, taking in both the prisoner and the priests. Suddenly I saw my opportunity, and I took it like a flash and drew the lever. Afterwards I spoke my mind to the priests but they only looked at me with disdain. Later I reported them to the authorities.'

This was by no means my father's last execution. But neither he nor my uncle ever got paid for it. The fees involved were ten pounds for the executioner and two guineas for the assistant – an indication that the position of executioner can hardly be regarded as a lucrative career appointment. I myself worked on the same scale for my first ten years in the craft, in spite of thirty years of subsequent inflation. Whatever the ultimate reason was, my father asked to be removed from the Home Office list before the First World War, after nearly eleven years in the profession. My Uncle Tom continued for well over thirty years more. He finally retired at the age of seventy-five after completing a total of forty-two years' service as an executioner.

My relationship with my Uncle Tom grew even warmer after my father's death. He and my Auntie Lizzie treated me as their own son. I realised that I was the apple in the pie at Clayton, and I visited the village whenever I could. I always spent my summer holidays there, shorter though they were now that I was a working lad. Our mill always observed Oldham Wakes Week, then falling in the last week of August, and I remember that I had taken advantage of that holiday in 1924 to visit my Uncle Tom, now the undisputed Official Head Executioner. He was reading a newspaper at tea one evening when he suddenly exclaimed: 'Bloody hell, Ellis has tried to commit suicide!'

He thought for a moment, and then he added crudely: 'He should have done it bloody years ago. It was impossible to work with him.' I report this remark as a matter of record. I have found since from my own experience that many men on the Home Office list have not shown the temperament that one might expect of an executioner. Their personal reaction to the duty they have chosen is their own affair, and I would not hold it against them if only they had not usually combined it with a very self-assertive and exhibitionist manner *after* the execution – when they would go into pubs, leer confidentially across the bar with 'You know who I am, don't you!' and try to get some sort of brutal kudos out of their activities. This sensation-seeking sickened me. I have always prided myself that I have never once declared my identity, or sunned myself in any morbid reputation, in any public place or to any casual person, except that I have occasionally given my name to a policeman in a strange town when I was asking the way to a prison I had not previously visited.

An executioner can be excused an inner tenseness before he performs his duty. But if he lets it show, it also means that his attitude – perhaps of hysteria or panic – is communicated at the last minute to the officers and, most important, to the prisoner. This in my mind is the infliction of unnecessary cruelty. I have had assistant executioners quartered with me in my prison room on the eve of an execution who could never eat, never relax, would always prowl the cell, and smoke all night. I would wake in the dark at any time and see the assistant sitting up in bed, staring at the door, and chain-smoking. Yet this was the man who played the tough guy, loosing his mouth off afterwards at the way he dealt with murderers and the even tougher treatment he recommended for the future. In my opinion there is no call at all for any executioner to be a tough guy, or to pretend to be.

On that August evening in 1924 my uncle passed the paper across to me, and I read that John Ellis, after seventeen months in retirement, had been found shot at Rochdale with his jaw fractured from a bullet which had entered the neck under the chin. He was charged with attempted suicide. Addressing the prisoner in the dock, the magistrate said: 'I am sorry to see you there. I have known you a long time. If your aim had been as true as the drops you had given it would have been a bad job for you. Your life has been given back to you. Turn it to good use in atonement.' Ellis, on promising not to repeat the offence and to give up drink, was discharged.

My uncle, who had recently executed Vaquier, the Byfleet murderer, put on his best pot-hat shortly afterwards and departed to attend to Patrick Mahon, whose rather ghoulish efforts to dispose of his victim's body had led to his conviction for murder in Sussex. I was left to 'mind the shop' with my Auntie Lizzie. By this time I was nineteen years old and I knew perfectly well where my uncle was going, although he still confided to me absolutely no detail of that side of his life, apart from his spontaneous indiscretion over Ellis. My auntie was less inhibited, and in any case far more talkative, and since I was now like her grown-up son she never held back when the opportunity for a little natter presented itself. 'You know where he's gone, don't you?' she asked. I myself felt that I had a duty to be discreet, so I just nodded. 'He's doing that Mahon, at Wandsworth,' she went on. 'He's been busy this year. There's his diary over in the corner. Why don't you have a look at it?' True enough, there on a flat cupboard in the corner of the room was a thick shiny black notebook very like my father's Execution Book. I glanced through it and noted that my uncle was just coming up to his two hundredth execution. It interested me because I knew that Ellis's figure printed in the newspapers was two hundred and three.

When my uncle had asked me to mind the shop, it was not the Clayton General Stores he was concerned with, but his bookmaker's business. Because I had been seen out with him at the carrier's trade for years past in the summer months, most of his clients knew me well enough. Those who did not know me had only to be assured that Our Albert was Tom's nephew to be rid of the suspicion that I was either a welsher or a police informer; for street bookmaking was still illegal in those days. So, the day after my uncle went to Wandsworth, I walked down to Lidget Green, took the tram into Bradford, and went to the carriers' stand opposite the rows of mills and warehouses where the operatives worked who provided my uncle with part of his daily bread. I passed from one warehouse corner to another, from one bookie's runner to another, and at each call I collected a soft leather bag with a drawstring at the top to tighten it. I put the purses into my pocket, clinking with coins and rustling with the betting slips which recorded horse, race, stake and psuedonym. People then signed their bets with colourful fancy-names like Lucky At Last or Rule Britannia rather than reveal their identity as accomplice in the 'crime' of street gambling to the police, who might at any moment swoop down on the vagabond bookie – on this occasion, me.

I collected the bets and went on to the station to meet my uncle, coming back on the train from London. He was as unperturbed and as uncommunicative as ever. I learned much later that there had been a very rare mishap at this execution, but no detail of it was breathed to me until I was in the craft. As we stood waiting for the tram which would take us towards home, an old man plucked my sleeve, pointed to my uncle, and asked me confidentially, 'Is that *the* Mr. Pierrepoint?' I answered that it was. It was a renewed realisation, the first since the death of my father, that an executioner can command public prestige. The incident played its part in bolstering my ambition.

The more I studied my father's writings – and the word 'studied' is not too strong: I immersed myself in every account he had written, pondering his statements from every point of view – the more I realised that there were two important and different aspects of an executioner's life which had somehow got to be reconciled. On the mechanical side he had to master the technique of his craft. On the human side he had to *stay* human, which meant that he could not cut himself off from awareness of the condemned man as a human being about to die, about to send his own family into mourning. That humanity was part of his office, one of the reasons why he held the job of executioner, because it gave him the *flexibility* which made him far more valuable to the State than any mere machine designed to break a man's neck. Judicial hanging is not a simple job. As developed in Great Britain it demanded precise individual preparation and calculation, and such a practised familiarity with the equipment that an executioner's deftness and speed could ride the punches of any unexpected incident, yet not smother, for example, a last-minute confession of guilt – a statement which the authorities were always very glad to have. How an executioner reconciled within himself the two characteristics demanded of him – mechanical precision and human awareness – was his own affair. Human awareness involves memories, dreams and fears. I was later to find – from the number of assistant executioners who shot off the list with monotonous rapidity after two or three experiences – that it was the memories, dreams and fears that broke men up. But at that time, having every confidence in my own balance of mind, my youthful priority was to get the technique right and the speed unsurpassable. My father could despatch a man in the time it took the prison clock to strike eight – leading him from his cell on the first stroke and having him suspended, dead on the rope, by the last stroke. That seemed a very worthy intermediate ambition for me.

I knew that this striking performance was a fact, from a rare and historic press cutting which I possessed. It concerned the case of Abel Atherton, and I should like to present my father's account of his execution as well as the newspaper's. Together they set out the two aspects of an executioner's responsibilities which I have mentioned – the complete technical control and the human contact. But they are also, taken together, invaluable informative documents in the history of penology because they represent the last contemporary corroborative accounts of an execution in Great Britain.

My father began with a description of the crime for which Atherton was convicted – the murder at Chopwell, near Durham, of Mrs. Patrick: 'Abel Atherton, a miner, was charged with her murder, by shooting her in the doorway of her house. Atherton had been lodging for some time with Mrs. Patrick, and he had been paying too much attention to her daughter, who was only fifteen years old. Atherton was thirty years of age. Because of this, there were quarrels on several occasions, and Mrs. Patrick had to make him find fresh lodgings. But he was still a frequent visitor to her house. Another quarrel ensued. Atherton threatened Mrs. Patrick, then went to his lodging and got his gun. His new landlady tried to stop him, but he threatened her. He told her he was going to use it for sport, and went away, looking very fierce. He went to Mrs. Patrick's. When she saw the gun she said "You're not going to use that here." She struggled with Atherton and the gun went off, the shot going into the street. A second shot was fired, and Mrs. Patrick fell dead in the doorway. Atherton denied the charge of murder throughout, and said it was an accident, but his version was not accepted. He stood his trial at the Durham Assizes and was sentenced to death.

'The execution was fixed for Wednesday the 8th of December 1909. I was engaged by the Sheriff in the usual way. It was a cold wintry day when I arrived at Durham on the afternoon before the execution. I called in at an hotel opposite the prison from where the landlord used to send our meals across to the prison. While I was talking to the landlord at the counter, who should come in but Atherton's father and sister-in-law in deep mourning dress. Atherton's father was talking about his son and saying he was innocent. He pulled out some last letters they had just received from him while paying their last visit. I took a seat until they had gone, and pretended to interest myself in some curios that hung on the wall. It was now time for us to go to the prison, and as I was walking across the road I saw

Atherton's father and sister-in-law standing watching to see if I went into the prison. I knew they had guessed from my speech who I was when they came into the hotel.

'I made my usual arrangements after my arrival. Then I went to Atherton's cell. I found him fairly cheerful, but a sad downcast look upon him. He was only of short stature, 5 feet 1¼ inches high, but of strong build. Next morning all was in readiness in good time. Atherton was placed in a cell on the ground floor. Then, when all the officers arrived to witness the last dread act, I entered the condemned cell. Atherton was looking a little terrified. I pinioned his arms and prepared his neck. Then I gently tapped him on the shoulder, and said, "Keep your pluck up, my lad." This put life in him. I said I would get it over as quickly as possible. I brought him into the corridor. The procession started. Atherton was walking fairly well. On the approach to the scaffold I led him on to the drop. Instantly I fixed the rope around his neck. I was about to place the white cap over his head when he said in a feeble voice, "Yer hanging an innocent man."

'Whether or not, I could not flinch from my duty. I pulled the lever, which gave Atherton a drop of 7 feet 3 inches, and launched him into the hereafter.'

That is the executioner's account of his part in the drama. Putting it into perspective, there follows the narrative of an impartial observer, a Durham newspaper reporter. This account is itself of some importance, for it is one of the last detailed descriptions of an English execution as observed and published with absolute legality by a privileged professional writer. Its detail is very striking, and I do not dispute its accuracy.

The reporter wrote:

After the visit from his father Atherton seemed reconciled, and retired to rest at about ten o'clock on Tuesday night. He slept pretty well, and at half-past five was aroused, washed, and dressed in his own clothing. The Chaplain arrived at the Gaol before seven o'clock, and administered the Communion to Atherton in the condemned cell. Atherton partook of a light breakfast, after which the Chaplain again joined him, and remained with the condemned man until a few minutes to eight, then he left to robe to take part in the final act.

Wednesday morning broke clear and frosty. At ten minutes to eight Mr. A. A. Wilson, Acting Under Sheriff, entered the Prison, and was followed by the three Press representatives. Dr. Gilbert was the last of the officials to enter. Principal Warder Hunt took charge of the Press men, and at about four minutes to eight conducted them to a position immediately in front of the execution shed. Warders were already in position, at a signal from Engineer Stanton, to throw back the doors of the execution shed, and officers were stationed to signal to Warder Elliott, who had ascended to the prison bell, ready to toll the passing knell. Although all was perfectly quiet within the walls, imagination readily supplied the grim details which were being enacted within the Prison. The Acting Under Sheriff had demanded the body of Atherton for execution, two warders had been despatched to conduct him from the cell to the doctor's room, and there Pierrepoint and his assistant quickly fastened the culprit's hands behind his back, and bared the neck. The colliery buzzers had commenced to sound, and the first stroke of eight on the clock over the Assize Courts had sounded, when the voice of the Chaplain was heard reciting the opening sentence of the burial service: 'I am the resurrection and the life, saith the Lord.' A second later the procession came in view, in the following order: Chief Warder Barlow; the Chaplain, the Rev. D. Jacob; the pinioned culprit, with Assistant Warder Hutton and Assistant Warder Duke on either side; the executioner and his assistant; Principal Warder Lenthrall, and Schoolmaster-Warder Dawson; the Acting Under Sheriff; Capt. Temple, the Governor; the medical officer, Dr. Gilbert; Assistant Warder Jones bringing up the rear. The culprit, who seemed remarkably calm and composed, and walked with a firm step, fixed the Press representatives with a look which betokened that he had something to communicate. However, the procession hurried on, and Atherton saw the preparations which had been made for the carrying out of the dread sentence. From the beam there was the rope reaching well nigh to the floor. On the drop there was the ankle strap lying ready for use, and across the drop there were two stout boards with foot-pieces, ready for the attendant warders to render Atherton assistance if required. At the door the Chaplain stepped aside, and the remainder of the procession passed inside. The moment the threshold had been passed, Atherton's cap had been removed from his head, and the executioners urged him forward to the mark in the drop. The assistant instantly dropped on to his knees and fastened the ankle strap, and while Pierrepoint was adjusting the noose, Atherton in a husky voice cried out, 'Yer hanging an innocent man.' Pierrepoint whipped the white cap from his pocket, drew it over the condemned man's head, stepped aside and pulled the lever, and Atherton shot from view before – incredible as it may seem – the clock had ceased striking. Atherton was given a drop of 7 feet 3 inches, and death was absolutely instantaneous. As the Press representatives stepped forward and looked into the pit the body was hanging perfectly still. The execution house was then closed till nine o'clock, when the executioners withdrew the body from the pit, released it from the rope, and removed the other paraphernalia of their dread office. In the meantime the official notices were posted at the Prison gates, certifying that judgment of death had been duly executed on Atherton.

The inquest was held at nine thirty in the Governor's office at the Prison, by Mr. Coroner J. Graham, assisted by a jury of which Mr. J. Hall was the foreman. Prior to the enquiry the jury viewed the body of the law's victim which was lying on the floor of the execution house enclosed in a plain black deal coffin. Atherton's lips were very blue, and there was a swelling of the neck. Otherwise his features were placid, and gave no appearance of a violent death . . .

There are three special points of interest raised by these unique parallel accounts. The first is technical: the matter of the white cap, or hood.

The white cap – it was never black, as it has often been imaginatively described – has been used in British executions from the later days of batch-strangulation in public, long before the introduction of the long drop designed to sever the cervical vertebrae and cause instantaneous death. Its original purpose was to mask the contortions of slow strangulation, which were considered too horrible even for the ghoulish British public to witness, although the logic that public executions were a public deterrent against crime might strictly have been followed by exposing the ultimate horror in order to achieve the maximum deterrence. Later, the cap was still retained, partly for the sake of the official witnesses, since the varying drop did not always take a man's head below the scaffold floor, and partly as some mercy to the prisoner – and some aid to the executioner – so that the condemned man could not judge the exact moment at which the lever was to be pulled. (Some prisoners try to jump at the last moment. Even when hooded, there are occasions when their guess is right. The result can be clumsy, although, in my experience, it has not impeded instantaneous death. But the action can be disturbing to witnesses, as well as to the executioner.)

What is quite extraordinary in these parallel accounts – and it is borne out by other meticulous descriptions of executions which my father set down* – is that my father placed the noose round the neck first, and pulled down the cap over it. This is the reverse order to the practice carried out by every other British executioner I have had any familiarity with, including, naturally, my Uncle Tom and the laymen who trained me. The routine drill has always been for the cap – which is really a fairly capacious white cotton bag – to be swiftly slipped over the head, and the noose to be immediately adjusted over it. There is the practical advantage in this order of procedure that, with the rope holding the cap, no sudden up-draught caused by the drop can lift the cap from the face. I have no explanation of my father's preference for the other order of procedure, and I would indeed question my father's accounts of it, repeated though they are, if it were not for this report by an independent witness.

The second point of interest is the presence of Press representatives at an execution. When public executions were ended by the Capital Punishment Amendment Act of 1868, the responsibility for any execution was remitted to the High Sheriff of the County or his Scottish equivalent (in Scottish towns the City Chamberlain), and not to any central administrative body. The Sheriff could (and did) still invite private witnesses, including his bloodthirsty friends, to a 'private' execution held within the prison, maintaining the picnic spirit of the Newgate impresario whose invitations ran: 'We hang at eight and breakfast at nine.' But the general public no longer had a sight of the slaughter, and the ticket touts lost valuable casual income from selling places on near-by balconies or on the special grandstands which used to be erected for derby events.

Initially the new practice was to allow a relative of the con-

*See for example, 'the bravest man I ever hanged', page 52–3.

demned prisoner to see the execution, but this was abandoned. The Sheriffs continued to invite representatives of the Press. Their accounts, eagerly read, may have provided a continuance of the 'deterrent' factor formerly thought to be part of a public execution. The Press still had the status of the 'Third Estate', the responsible representatives of the people only yielding in importance to the House of Commons, and for many years the reporter-witnesses signed the Official Declaration that an execution had been completed, along with the prison governor and the chaplain and the separate corroboration of the doctor. It was in fact because newspapers were represented at executions, and reporters wrote their accounts without excessive reverence for the authorities, that the whole technique of hanging was improved. In the 1870s and 1880s the principle of the long drop, intended to break the neck instantaneously, was being painfully worked out, and unfortunately the only people to experiment on were the condemned prisoners. When an execution was bungled – often because the pet theory of the local prison doctor was being tried out – the newspapers had no hesitation in reporting it, as in the sensational decapitation of a prisoner by the executioner Berry at Norwich Castle in 1885. And it was the influence of newspaper reporting on public opinion and particularly parliamentary opinion which spurred the Home Office into much more serious research into instantaneous killing and the preparation of a standard table of drops, which was recommended in 1888.*

However, from the year 1888, the presence of newspaper representatives at executions was strongly discouraged, lest they should report the truth too accurately. It was part of the fast-growing general move towards official secrecy which has marked our once-public activities. Sheriffs, however, still had their theoretical autocracy, and some continued to use their power. A news reporter was present at Liverpool Gaol in 1891 when Berry, as executioner, made another ugly job of a hanging. The reporter mildly mentioned to Berry that he must have made a miscalculation over the necessary length of drop for that particular operation. Berry heatedly replied that his own drop would have been a completely different length, but the

*The table was a simplified extension of the formula:
$$\frac{1260 \text{ foot-pounds}}{\text{weight of the prisoner in pounds}} = \text{length of the recommended drop in feet.}$$
It was revised in 1913 to include another factor.

prison doctor, who was still theorising on lines outside the
Home Office circular, had insisted that an entirely unsubstan-
tiated drop should be given – and this was the result. (Berry
was, of course, absolutely wrong to give in to the prison doctor.
A master executioner is alone responsible for every detail of his
craft. He has to come to his own decision on the length of the
drop based on the Home Office table, varied by his own experience, and adjusted to the weight of the prisoner, his height, his
age and an estimate of the muscular and tensile strength of his
neck – which can be varied by such circumstances as a recent
attempt at suicide through cutting the throat, not an uncommon
occurrence after crimes of sudden passion. I myself have
listened to *advice* from a prison governor or prison doctor and
I have taken it into account, but the final decision has been
mine because the final responsibility for how a man dies is mine.
On the one occasion when a prison doctor *insisted* that I should
use the drop he recommended and I disapproved, I told him
that I would do what he wanted as long as he assumed full
responsibility for the outcome. He agreed to this, which
[although he did not know it] called my bluff – for I had no
intention of altering the drop, only of telling the doctor I had
altered it: the prisoner's fate was still my only care and it was
morally unthinkable for me to hand over the responsibility to
another authority. However, the situation righted itself. The
doctor cogitated for a long time on what he had taken on his
shoulders, and came to my room at midnight to wake me up and
tell me that he would not insist on his theory being carried out,
and he passed the responsibility back to me. I accepted this,
but, understandably, I was more than usually interested in the
subsequent post-mortem finding. And I knew that the doctor,
who, after all, was a man of far more specialised education than
I was, would, either out of malice or pride or for impartial
enlightenment, be even more interested. I was relieved when
the post-mortem examination showed an anatomically perfect
instantaneous death – 'fracture dislocation of the two/three cervical vertebrae; spinal cord severed'.)

Newspaper reporters were increasingly barred from execu-
tions by successive High Sheriffs, responding to Central
Government prodding. But Durham held out for many years.
The report I have quoted was written in 1909 – and in my
opinion it is accurate, informative, unsensational and humane.
Durham was finally persuaded to abandon the practice in 1914.

But the ultimate authority still lay with the High Sheriff, and occasionally he used his absolute discretion. As late as 1924 questions were asked in the House of Commons about the presence of Press representatives at executions. The Home Secretary replied that the law gave a discretion on that matter to the Sheriffs, and the law could not be over-ridden.

The third point of interest raised by the corroborative accounts of the Atherton execution is the 'last statement' by the prisoner – in this case, 'Yer hanging an innocent man.'

The authorities have always been gratified when they could get a confession of guilt from a prisoner, and until the policy of blanket official secrecy was introduced they gladly published these confessions. Even later, they occasionally leaked them. It was convenient to reassure the public, as well as the prison officials and the executioner, who were far more personally involved, that injustice had not been done and the 'final solution' had not been effected in error. The executioner Berry, who was a nonconformist preacher, was allowed to press condemned men not only for a confession of guilt but also an assurance that they had repented their crime and returned to the ranks of the godly. This was a privilege which would seem to put him in an unfair position of pressurising superiority, especially since he had the reputation (which he accepted to enhance his prestige, but probably did not merit) of mentioning to prisoners whose alleged crimes he disliked or whose attitude displeased him that he could easily alter the drop to provide a painful rather than an instantaneous death. No executioner after Berry arrogated to himself this status as inquisitor, although, as human beings, we were all admittedly interested in any confession. For some time the prison governor used to put the question to the prisoner at the last moment: 'Have you any statement or request to make?' *The Times*, in its formal announcement of every execution, would print the last words – which were obviously supplied to them by official authority – or else the sentence 'The culprit made no statement of any kind'. Some of these last statements were affecting in the simplicity of their remorse, and were, in the opinion of many better qualified to judge than I am, as useful public deterrents as any sermon – but I myself, being aware of the overpoweringly passionate and unpremeditated nature of many murders, am reserved about endorsing anything as a deterrent. The printed confessions did at least sometimes close a chapter of human

weakness, and bury the participants with some sort of epitaph
expressing the futility of it all. A labouring man from Battersea
who had killed his landlady said: 'I should like this to be known.
I stabbed Miriam because I loved her dearly. It was through
jealousy. Of course I had been drinking, or else it might not
have happened. So now the people of Battersea know why two
lives have been thrown away.' That was a more dignified head-
stone inscription than many another obituary verse printed in
The Times that day.

Some prison governors did not care to ask for last statements,
and some prison chaplains became over-zealous. The whole
practice, if prolonged, could seriously affect the smooth speed
which we executioners were trying to establish in the oper-
ational procedure, purely on humanitarian grounds. The issue
came to a head with the execution of the so-called Moat Farm
Murderer at Chelmsford. The trial leading to the sentence had
been a controversial matter, because the body of the victim had
been found at Moat Farm, Clavering, Essex, three years after
her disappearance, and another year passed before the conviction of the accused, who protested that he had had no interest in
murdering her because the victim had been keeping him. However, sentence of death was passed. The condemned man had
taken his place on the scaffold and all the adjustments had been
made, when the prison chaplain, the Rev. J. W. Blakemore,
peremptorily waved away the executioner and said to the
prisoner: 'Samuel Herbert Dougal, are you guilty or not
guilty?' There was no response from the hooded, haltered man
on the drop. 'Samuel Herbert Dougal,' the chaplain repeated,
'are you guilty or not guilty?' Again the prisoner made no reply.
The question was put a third time: 'Samuel Herbert Dougal,
are you guilty or not guilty?' There was a ripple of the cloth of
the white hood. 'Guilty, sir,' the man croaked. The chaplain
signalled to the executioner, who immediately operated the
lever. *The Times* reported the incident in part, but omitted the
dramatic torture of the repetitions of the question. The full
details of the encounter did, however, become known, and questions were asked in Parliament. In the ensuing commotion some
Members made the point that even an innocent man, trussed
blindfold for execution, when faced with the intolerable tension
of the repeated questions might say anything to end this hope-
less situation. Others argued that a minister of religion should
be allowed to go to any length to save a man's soul by ensuring

that he died with a confession of his guilt. The Home Secretary did not uphold this point of view. He announced that instructions would be promulgated to prison chaplains to prevent any future recurrence of such an incident.

Neither my father nor my uncle nor myself have ever made any such a harangue to a condemned prisoner as Berry did, nor have we, as far as we decently could, permitted any interference in our timing from anyone else present at an execution. I myself, needing a clear deck for my own speed, and out of mercy to the prisoner, have positioned any chaplain who actually mounted the scaffold well away from the prisoner on the opposite side to the lever. But my father was involved in one incident where the prisoner, who had maintained his innocence to his priestly confessors, admitted his guilt to the executioner at the very last moment. This occurred in Ireland at Armagh, where my father was carrying the execution through without an assistant. 'I had an interview,' he recounted, 'with the two priests who were in attendance on the prisoner. He protested his innocence, everybody thought he was innocent, even I did myself. At a few minutes before eight I went to the cell door. It was left just a little open. I could see the priest inside with the prisoner. In the middle of the cell a cross was erected, with beautiful white flowers around it. I heard the prisoner say to the priest, "I am innocent." The time was then up. All officials were ready. I went into the cell to pinion him. Then the prisoner started at a brisk pace, through the corridor and out into the yard in the chilly morning. We reached the scaffold. In a second I had him on the mark. Just as I was stooping down to fasten his legs he shouted out, quite sharply, "Executioner!" Then, as I stood up face to face with him to fix the noose, he said again, "Executioner!" and then the word "Guilty". He had kept this acknowledgment to the last moment. I was staggered, never expecting to hear a confession, the prisoner having carried himself so firm and collected. My blood was up. I pulled the lever violently. I felt I could have pulled it from its bearings. Never in all my career was I so much deceived by a condemned culprit. I reported the confession and, a few days after I returned home, I received a splendid letter from the Under Sheriff of Monaghan stating how thankful everybody concerned was to me as the disclosure made to me had relieved a great deal of anxiety in their minds. The authorities had, in fact, taken not a few days but only a few minutes to make this relief of their anxiety public. Hundreds of people accompanied me to Armagh station, and when my train arrived at Belfast hundreds more were awaiting me, while newspaper placards were prominent all over the city: "Confession on the scaffold. —— hanged this morning." '

I print this account as my father gave it. It illustrates the importance with which the authorities have always credited a final confession, and it also reveals something of my father's temperament. I myself have always tried not to become so emotionally involved with the personality of the prisoner, or the details of the crime he is supposed to have committed, or the swaying arguments over his guilt or innocence. I have tried to regard him as a *person*, but a person over whose character or about whose innocence it is vain and even damaging for me to speculate or become unduly partisan – for in that mood I cannot help him, only hurt him. And so I see him as a person who has a fixed and stony path decreed before him from which I cannot divert him, and therefore all I can do is to help him tread it as gently as possible.

I have never voluntarily discussed with my friends any of the details of the hundreds of executions which I have carried out, and normally none of my friends will introduce the subject, because they know my nature too well. But there have been exceptions among journalist friends. I am not ashamed to have some genuine friends among journalists, among those who have respected me and not abused my confidence, although it is also true that other newspapermen have printed what never happened, quoted what was never said, and invented grotesque tales of my joking publicly about my craft like a third-rate showman, which I can never forgive. It has been the journalist friends who – having the courage of their profession – have occasionally asked me 'Do you think so-and-so was guilty?' or 'How do you feel now about such-and-such?' naming convicted prisoners executed by me who have later rocketed back into the news on the impact of campaigns claiming their innocence, even naming other people as the truly guilty. I think back on the appearance of these men on the scaffold – I can remember them, they are not nameless grey faces whom I try to banish and forget. I say to my questioner, 'Who am I to judge?' Some retort with the protest that this is double-talk, dodging the issue. But it is not so. I do not need extraordinary humility to state that I have not the education, nor the specialised legal training, nor access to the results of expert police investigation, nor the ability to judge between plea and counter-plea, good and bad points of law. Who am I to judge? I accept that even educated men are fallible, I accept the possibility that an innocent man has been hanged in error by my hands, and it is not a pleasant thought. But I know that there never was anything that could be done about it by me, or the prison governor, or the Commissioners, or by anybody except the deputy of the Queen herself, the Secretary of State for Home Affairs. Who am I to judge?

I may add that there is never at any execution the situation where an unwilling executioner is ordered to take an action which he dare not refuse. This would be the parallel to the defence offered by some Germans accused of war crimes, some indeed whom I myself have executed, such as the men convicted of killing Royal Air Force escaped prisoners of war: that they were given orders which it would have been contrary to their oath of loyalty to refuse. No executioner is appointed under sealed orders to perform any execution as directed by his superiors. He is first asked if he is available to do that particular duty involving a particular prisoner on a particular date. If he says he is not available, the matter ends as far as he is concerned. He is an officer of the State, but his rigid obedience extends only to the duties he voluntarily opts to do. I have known of no other country where this humane attitude has been the rule, and I instance this as a further and little-appreciated factor in my broad belief that the modern British system has been the best in the world.

The wonder has always been that the system could command such integrity when it was being run so obviously on the cheap. In every other country which I have had experience of, an executioner has belonged to a highly paid profession. In Great Britain, when I became a master executioner, I received, as I have said, the same fee that my father had first taken forty years before – ten pounds, with three guineas for the assistant, and the indignity was that only half the fee was paid down, and the other half retained for a fortnight and only passed over 'if his conduct and behaviour has been satisfactory'. For an assistant executioner to go home contented with only a guinea in his pocket to show after missing two days of his normal work demanded a high degree of devotion. I did get the fees raised

by fifty per cent as one of my first actions after acceptance as
head executioner, but I can hardly claim that by so doing I
transformed the craft into a financially rewarding profession.

I knew all these facts while I continued to foster my ambition through my early manhood. In the material sense our
family, if never on the rocks, was often pretty near them. The
times were the years of the post-war slump, massive unemploy-
ment, the shadow of the stigma of the dole, all worsening as we
were swept into the international maelstrom called the Depres-
sion. I had no trade, in the sense that I had not graduated in
any craft. My father had urged me to become an apprentice
joiner, but I did not stick at it because my mates were earning
far more at the mill than I drew as my tiny apprentice allowance. So I threw in my lot with my mates at the mill, and after
a few years' work the slump came. The mills would go on half-
time – working one week and playing the next. I began to
manipulate a system, dependent on friends in other mills, by
which I obtained a place in a mill whose week of idleness was
running alternately to that of my own mill. So I would work
my stint at the Marlborough Mill, be laid off for a week, take
up my job at the Hollinwood Spinning Mill and accept another
week's lay-off while I went back to the Marlborough. It didn't
always work, but this was the sort of trick we had to get up to in
order to live with any pride.

My social life was limited to knocking about with the lads. I
played football, which was still my main sporting interest,
though I think I have had a go at most sports, including boxing,
in my time, and not been particularly clever at any of them. To
play club football I had to belong to a church. The church ran
socials of which the brightest was the Saturday night dance.
The girls came to support us at our football matches on Saturday afternoons and to dance with us at the church hall on
Saturday nights. And, just as a penny bus-ride to another club's
pitch was about the limit of my travelling – except for my visits
to my Uncle Tom in Yorkshire – so also, a regular dance with a
regular partner was about the limit of my courting. I did not
fall in love because I couldn't afford to pursue it. And if anyone
says that that is making false explanations with thin logic, or a
denial of any capacity for Romeo-and-Juliet romance, or sheer
miserly Yorkshire caution, then I know that the protester was
never living in the North of England in 1926. My attitude was
not untrue to life. I know, because it was my life, and this is

how my mates and I lived it. You just didn't fall hopelessly for a girl when you'd no money and no decent clothes on your back, when work was very hard to get and a fatherless family was depending on it. You developed your own sense of responsibility. You didn't become too involved with a girl too early, because your own maturity told you that all too easily it could only lead to two people becoming very miserable.

Even my fixed will to become an executioner was not a 'way out' from this sort of life. It certainly would not bring me more money, and might very understandably spoil many human relationships already existing. But I think I can see now, more clearly than I understood then, two strong attractions about acquiring the post. I did appreciate them then, but perhaps did not properly estimate their force. The first attraction was the individual social status that might make me something more of a person than the scores of thousands of anonymous worker-ant millhands who toiled or idled alongside me in grey industrial Lancashire. I am sure that many of them had their ambitions, and some of them achieved their aim, to be an individual, in politics or the Buffaloes or football. I had another target.

The second attraction was the opportunity for travel that would come to me. Travel today seems to imply only long journeys – to South Africa or the Mediterranean or the Riviera – and I have made all these trips in my time. But people forget today how much of *our own country* was a romantic faraway dream when I was a young man. Many parts of it a chap like me could only afford to see if he was paid to take the journey. There was no run-of-the-mill car jaunt out to interesting countryside, because no one in my circle ever had a car in the 1920s. You could only get away by train, only do it frequently if your expenses were paid. There was still an enormous glamour in the idea of travel within the home country, and in travel by the railway. That and the prestige were the 'perks' of the job which my father appreciated most, and I could read it in his narratives time and time again. My father used a travelling rug – almost as old-fashioned as a Sherlock Holmes fore-and-aft cap in modern eyes. For many years the most typical image that I had as the memory of my father was the picture of him coming in from a journey through the front door and putting his plaid travelling rug down on a chair. My father, travelling to attend an execution in Swansea, contrived to go by rail from Manchester to Conway and the Menai Straits, then on south on 'a lovely journey which I really enjoyed', going anti-clockwise round almost the whole of the scenic Welsh coast on railway lines that no longer exist, and recording his deep pleasure at being able to make the journey in this way – for the purpose of undertaking an execution.

I think the most memorable expedition which combined for my father the prestige of his position with a sense of exploration was a rare professional visit to Jersey which he narrated with enormous gusto. He described his train journey – who now ever 'describes' a train journey? – to London and Weymouth, 'where, arriving late at night, I just managed to get a little refreshment through the kindness of a friendly police officer. Then I made my way along the quayside to the S.S. *Reindeer*. It was a cold dark night, I could scarcely see anything but the black waters of the sea dashing their weight against the quay.' He got aboard the steam packet, which sailed at 2 a.m., and after generous entertainment by the crew – I have no doubt that he entertained them in his turn – he landed at St. Helier in Jersey. 'Hundreds of people were waiting to see me arrive and many followed me to the prison, riding their bicycles by the side of the cab. After doing justice to a good breakfast I had an interview with the Governor, and found that it was thirty years since an execution had taken place in Jersey. On the last occasion the prisoner was led through the streets with a halter round his neck, right up to Gallows Hill where the execution was carried out in public. The law had only lately been altered to prescribe private executions.' My father was shown the newly erected scaffold, and expressed his concern at the ten-foot-high set of wooden steps which the prisoner had to climb at the last. 'I carefully tested the new scaffold, then I leisurely passed my time about the prison. I was visited by the Sheriff and several other gentlemen. In all my travels I never received so much attention. Next morning I made my final arrangements and went to the cell. All the officials arrived, and to my surprise they all entered the cell, to ask the prisoner if he had anything to say. Then one pulled out a packet and read the death sentence to him again. I was dumbfounded, never having experienced anything like it before. Then I was beckoned to pinion the prisoner, which I did very smartly, as I was on my last seconds. As quickly as possible I pressed on the procession . . . All those who witnessed the execution were amazed, remarking 'Why, he's dead!' Some who were there had without doubt witnessed the execution thirty years previously, and were taken with surprise by the way I carried out the execution with such celerity.

'After I had completed my duties and had had breakfast, I was taken to all the principal places in Jersey, through the fire station and the Courts of Justice and many other places. In the evening I was taken to a supper at an hotel where sixty guests sat down, and later toasted my health. I had a good time and was invited to spend a week's holiday in Jersey any time I wished to go. I shall never forget the kindness that was shown to me.

'I slept in the prison again that night and caught the early boat to Southampton. It was a rough journey across the Channel but I enjoyed it. It was the roughest sea I had ever seen – it was the same day that the *Berlin* went down in the storm off the Hook of Holland. I was the only one allowed on deck, and I was strapped to my seat there. At dinner all the plates were switched off the table by a big broadside lift of the sea. On my arrival at Southampton I journeyed home by train with the pleasantest memories I had ever experienced.'

This, surely, was Adventure, I told myself as I read and re-read my father's story, and pictured him strapped to the deck as the ship battled with the howling storm. I don't think I put an entirely unreal romanticisation on the facts. I realised that the basis of it all was a sombre duty which had to be very skilfully done. But the reality still lay demonstrated before me that along with this duty came experiences of drama, and the education that comes from travel, and the development and appreciation of a man so that he himself and all who met him recognised and even acclaimed him as a responsible character – sixty men turning towards him with glasses raised to drink his health. I could not see my own life being illuminated by such highlights as these while I remained solely a spinning operative on short-time at the Marlborough Mills. And it was in the reflection of such potential glamour combined with such responsibility that I changed my life, left my job, and, feeling that my age and my maturity were now acceptable, wrote direct to the Home Secretary in Whitehall requesting that the name of Albert Pierrepoint should be put on the approved list of executioners.

I said in my letter that I had a good idea of what the job entailed, from what I had gathered of my father's experiences, and that naturally I was prepared to take the training. I did not mention my Uncle Tom at all, out of some feeling of independence, though it would have been farcical to suppose that my unusual surname would not be recognised, and linked. But I had never mentioned my plans to my uncle and was certainly not going to use his reputation now.

I considered my application to be the most important letter I had ever written in my life, and no ordinary postbox was good enough to entrust it to. I took a tram into the middle of Manchester and went to the big General Post Office to put it into the special slot marked LONDON.

A few days later I received a long buff envelope marked OHMS. I tore it open to know my fate. I read that somebody was directed by somebody else to thank me for my letter of the somethingth and to advise me of his regret that there were no vacancies on the list of persons approved to act as executioners.

Disappointment would be a mild description of my reaction. I was angry, resentful, and in a way ashamed of being turned down, as if I had not fulfilled the promise my father had seen in me. My one great relief was that no one in my family knew about it – neither the surge of hope and ambition in my request to follow my father, nor the crushing defeat, as I interpreted it, of being rejected.

I had recently, as I said, taken a new job and had left the mill for good. I used my experience and love of horses to clinch a position at a wholesale grocer's. I was taken on as a horse-drayman, delivering to retail grocers' shops the orders which our travelling salesman had already taken from them. The postman who had the walk which took in my home knew me well, saw me driving in the street, and gave me the Government letter before he made the normal delivery. So I had managed to keep my rejection as secret as my application.

I settled down to make the best of things. I got on well with my job. I liked the life, it involved meeting people, being friendly, being helpful, and to a large extent working on my own responsibility. That was the sort of life I leaned towards. Hard work never worried me but being what they called a mill-hand did; I wanted people to use more than my hands, I had a brain and a personality that I didn't want stunted. Although I had joined the grocery firm to drive a horse-dray, horses were on the way out, and I was soon trained to drive a motor and was given my own lorry. Even that was good for my self-esteem. Not so many people could drive a motor in 1930. It gave me an extra skill in the labour market. Not that anyone would notice that from my wages. I earned £2 5s. a week regularly for years until I became a manager.

My family was changing. One of my sisters married and one of my brothers died. My mother carried on, placid and uncomplaining as ever, and I continued as the man about the house. I had not buried my ambition, but let it hibernate. Occasionally, when I read that my uncle had been engaged for a particular execution, it stirred.

Some twelve months after my rejection by the Home Office, I came home fairly late from work and saw a long buff OHMS envelope on the mantelpiece. It was addressed to me. I looked at my mother, and she turned her eyes away. I opened the cover and read a second letter from Whitehall. It said that with further reference to my letter of a year ago there now existed a vacancy on the list I had applied to join, and if I was still interested I should confirm with the Governor of H.M. Prison at Strangeways, Manchester that I would keep an appointment for an interview which had been provisionally fixed for me in a fortnight's time.

I said nothing, but sat down, staring at the letter. I had a feeling of exhilaration but also of exhaustion, as if I had just won a mile race. But the moment was overshadowed by the necessity to break the news to my mother, as my father had had to do some thirty years before.

I looked up at her and saw that there was no news to break. She had seen hundreds of these long official envelopes in her time.

She said: 'You're after your father's job, aren't you?'

I said, 'Yes.'

She said: 'I had enough of this with your father. I don't think you should take this up.' She was not bitter. She was speaking slowly, out of her experience and her concern for me. She had had most of the day to reflect on it, once she had put that too-well-known envelope on the mantelpiece.

I did not argue with her, but I did try to explain. I could see how she was thinking. She was not only influenced by the actual duty that I was seeking. Understandably that was distasteful to her. There was also the memory of how it had affected my father. Every time he had gone away on a job he had brought her deep anxiety.

'You'll have no luck at all as long as you live if you take that job,' my mother said. 'Your father never had any luck.'

But I knew I was a different person from my father. He led a different kind of life from me. I was a man now, and I could see that I was different. He would go off for an execution, and sometimes he would be away with his friends for a week and not come home until he was skint. But, even from when I was a lad, I had said to myself 'If I get the same chances as my father, I'll do different things with them. He was a good fellow, but he was too soon led. I mean to do my best with what comes to me, and I know I'll never lead the same life'.

I tried to explain this to my mother as gently as possible. I think she was convinced enough about my character but it was useless to try to overcome her repugnance to the actual post I was seeking. She recognised my resolve, and having done so, never made another protest. For as long as she lived she never directly mentioned the subject again. It was a curious revival of the atmosphere that had existed when my father was alive. On my side, I did not flaunt my attitude, or its consequences. I stayed up late that night until everyone was in bed, and wrote in private my letter of confirmation. I had some days during which to prepare for my interview in Manchester Gaol.

The appointment was for three o'clock in the afternoon of a Saturday in the winter of 1931. I had never been to a prison before. I walked cautiously around the streets leading off from the prison, prospecting it. There was a jingle in my mind that I couldn't banish, because the kiddies were singing a rough new song in the streets about a murderer. These songs, using current popular tunes, used to come up suddenly in the middle of the publicity of a big trial. I don't know who wrote them – perhaps the fast-working, music-hall lyric-writers knocked them off between Guinesses and gave them to their landladies' kids in Ackers Street. Usually the words, when clean enough to be repeated, were precisely on target. I remember that on this occasion they weren't too accurate. The tune was Eddie Cantor's *Making Whoopee,* and the words said:

> There was a man
> His name was Rouse.
> He had the key
> To every house.
> He was suspected

And then arrested
For making whoopee.

Rouse was in fact a man convicted of burning another man's body in his own car in order that he could officially disappear into the Death Register and continue under another identity to make his own form of whoopee – and my Uncle Tom was just about to deal with him. I didn't think the kiddies had got the message right on this one, but that was the song I heard as I drew a deep breath before stretching out my hand to take up the big iron knocker on the gate at Strangeways Gaol.

As I hesitated, the wicket gate opened. A man came out, some thirty to forty years old, stumbling over the raised lintel of the gate. He went off, weaving slightly on his course. He certainly looked as if he had had a gill or two. I wondered how a man in that condition could be coming *out* of prison.

Meanwhile the gate had closed and I was still outside. I banged the huge knocker. I heard for the first time in my life that fanfare to almost every action and movement that takes place in a prison, the jingle of a ring of keys for selection, and the rattle of the chosen key in the lock. The door swung open and I was looking into the worldly-wise but friendly face of a gate-keeper with whom I was to become very familiar later. He asked me what I wanted. I made no reply, but simply handed him the Governor's letter confirming my appointment for the interview.

He read it and smiled. He said to me, 'How many vacancies are there?'

'I don't know,' I said.

He smiled again, and shrugged. 'You're the tenth today.'

Ten applicants! That was a blow to me. I knew that there were only some four assistants retained on the list. The gate-keeper saw something of my misery, and invited me into the gate lodge to sit by the fire. One or two prison officers were there, chatting. I was dejectedly weighing up my chances. Suddenly I had a thought.

'The man who went out just before I came in,' I said. 'Was he one of the applicants?'

'Yes,' said the gatekeeper.

I felt much better. At least I had not had to have a few gills to give me the courage for the interview. I did not drink alcohol at all at that time. But I knew then that, even if I had had a drink, I should have had the nous not to show it.

A bell rang in the gate lodge. The Governor was asking for me to be sent up. I was escorted – doors being unlocked and relocked at every stage – to the Governor's office. I saw a man who conveyed authority and friendliness. I was nervous, but he charmed much of my anxiety away. He was like my old head teacher. 'Sit down there,' he said. 'I'd like to ask you a few questions.'

I sat where I was shown.

'Why do you want to be a public executioner?'

Not very eloquently, I stumbled out some of my reasons. I had always wanted from boyhood to follow my father. I thought he had wanted it too. It was a position of responsibility I thought I could fill. I knew from what my father had said that it was something to take pride in. In my mind I was remembering the striking words with which my father finished the life-story which he had left as my only inheritance: 'I was very ambitious for the duty. I loved my work on the scaffold. My only desire was to become an expert officer of the State'. I did not repeat any of this to the Governor, but I think that, because those thoughts were in my mind, I said enough to convince him that I had not made my application for any morbid or crooked reason.

He said, 'This is a real ambition?'

I said, 'Yes, sir.'

He said, 'Does your uncle know that you have applied?'

'No one knows,' I told him. 'And no one will know, until I have achieved my ambition.'

'Very good,' he said, as if he understood me well.

Then his manner changed. His tone became perhaps more critical. 'Don't you think you're too young for this job?' he asked.

'No, sir.'

'Why?'

'My father was Number One Executioner at twenty-four years of age,' I said.

'Never!' he exclaimed.

'I think, sir, if you will look up his record, you will find that is right,' I told him.

He hesitated for a few moments. Then he brought some forms out of his office desk and asked me to fill them in. I began to read them, wanting to get the next stage finished on the spot. But he stopped me, and explained that I had to get other signatures as some sort of reference, so, apart from filling in then a skeleton form with basic personal details, I should take the papers away. I realised that he had better ways to pass his time than to watch me fill in documents, and I rose to go.

'I think you will hear more about this,' he said, and rang for me to be escorted away.

I walked out in a dream, and managed to perform my own stumble over the lintel of the wicket gate. But at least I had not completely fallen at the first fence. Outside, the kids were still singing:

> Di dah di DAH DAH
> Di dah di DAH DAH
> For making whoopee.

Making whoopee! I found that I was humming the tune unconsciously to myself as I walked through the grimy streets of Manchester, with rain in the wind and a winter night pushing the fog down early so that all the corner shops were already lit up.

I got all my forms filled up, and I sent them in. 'I think you will hear more about this,' the Governor of Strangeways had said. But I didn't. Weeks passed, and the whole episode seemed to have sunk into history. Another spring came and I briefly saw my Uncle Tom. I was thankful that I had said nothing to him. On the week after I had visited him I got the letter. It was waiting for me when I came home from work.

OHMS. I was getting wise to the formulas now. I looked in a corner of the envelope to see who had sent it. The Prison Commissioners! My mother continued laying the table as if she had never recognised it, never checked it. I was instructed to report to the Governor of H.M. Prison, Pentonville for a medical examination and a week of instruction and training in the apparatus and method used for executions. A Monday morning. Report at nine. Your confirmation required.

I went to the head of the firm which employed me and said I had urgent private business in London, and could I either advance the date of my holiday or take unpaid leave? They gave me unpaid leave. Ours was the sort of fairly intimate family firm where nobody ever had 'urgent private business in London' without going into full and gossipy details about it. After all, the phrase does sound dramatic, and anyone acquainted with me knew very well that I had never been to London in my life. But I resisted the impulse to tell a colourful lie, principally because I hadn't the imagination to provide much colour. I stuck as close as an oyster to my guarded story, and probably got a temporary reputation for having an even more urgently dramatic private life than I could ever have invented. I did confide the truth of the matter to one pal. And he let me down. So that was the last time I discussed any future details of my career with anyone.

Report nine, Monday morning. That involved catching the midnight train from Manchester on Sunday. Going without a bed for a night meant nothing to a youngster, and I never considered any alternative – nor could I afford one. The train biffed me out into Euston Station at six o'clock in the morning and I passed for the first of so many times through that monumental portico, now pulled down, which really did give some dignity to the occasion – for me, always an occasion – of the northern traveller entering or leaving London. On this, my very first visit to the capital, it seemed like an arch of triumph.

I was just twenty-seven years old. I was not a rare bird for never having covered the two hundred miles to London. Nobody I knew at home had ever done it except my Uncle Tom, moving about on State business, and those whom the State had also shunted around when they were soldiers in the Great War. That is how 'provincial' we all were just a few years ago, before the motor car became the equivalent of a bicycle and during the genuine poverty of the long post-war slump. London – the very word spelt novelty and adventure. It did to me, as I stepped out of the portico of Euston Station into quite strong early morning sunlight – and wondered how the devil I should find my way through this endless town.

I walked in a straight line. Fortunately I had picked a principal road to start with, and it went on for miles. I walked and looked and marvelled. So this was Bloomsbury, that was Russell Square. Here we were in Holborn. And suddenly I saw trams coming straight out of the ground almost like colliery cages as they zoomed up into Kingsway from the Embankment. At the end of Kingsway I could go no farther. 'Aldwych,' said a crescent-shaped street. I had to go right or left and I went left. Australia House – and suddenly I saw a new road at right angles to my route so far, and it announced a name I knew very well: Strand. I ventured along it to the left for a little 'oranges

and lemons said the bells of St. Clements' but at the Law
Courts I saw that it petered out into Fleet Street so I crossed
over and came back. Just past Somerset House I looked around
and saw my first great cluster of theatres – the Gaiety, the
Lyceum, the Aldwych, the Strand. Strand Palace Hotel, very
refined. Savoy Hotel, unimaginably posh. The Tivoli! Suddenly I realised that I was in friendly country, well known both
to my Auntie Lizzie and me. My feet began to bounce a little,
with a controlled inner spring like a ballroom dancer who can
step left or right in the middle of his tango, but decides on this
step to go forward. I was sauntering!

> I'm Burlington Bertie, I rise at ten-thirty
> And saunter along like a toff.
> I walk down the Strand with my gloves on my hand
> Then I walk down again with them off.
> I'm Bert, Bert, I haven't a shirt
> But my people are well off, you know.
> Everyone knows me, from Smith to Lord Rosebery,
> I'm Burlington Bertie from Bow.

I looked around for possible acquaintances. It was still a long
time till ten-thirty, and I could hardly expect to see even the
shades of hard-drinking Smith, Lord Birkenhead, or the racing
Earl of Rosebery at this early time in the morning. But there
seemed plenty of friendly faces pouring out of Charing Cross
Station. With a very light heart to match my springy saunter,
I turned into the Strand Corner House and had a wash and
brush up within marble halls at what was the most palatial
public lavatory I had ever seen in my life. The linen-and-
fishknife-dressed restaurant tables looked for too imposing for
me to have breakfast at – so I slipped straight across the road
to the ordinary Joe Lyons' tea room on the opposite side of the
Strand. A cup of tea and a bun, and I was all ready to take on
Trafalgar Square.

I walked all round the Square, took in every statue from
Charles I to George Washington as well as Nelson in the
middle, and I set off down Whitehall. I saw the Horse Guards
and Downing Street, and I came to the Cenotaph. This meant
more to my generation than it does nowadays. I saw the men
raising their hats to the million dead as they passed it, even in
buses, and I took off my hat and looked across Whitehall at
the Cenotaph and beyond. I thought I saw a part of the profile

of a building whose picture I had seen, and I decided to go and investigate. I looked back at the building by which I had been standing, and great brass plates announced that it was the Home Office. I considered this a striking coincidence, and went to touch the plates for luck. I crossed the road and stood on the corner of a street coming into Whitehall by a pub called the Red Lion. I had recognised the profile aright. At the back of Cannon Row was Scotland Yard. I gazed with very intense, very shy fascination at this building. I have always remembered this moment because I made so many friends in Scotland Yard later – Bob Fabian, Flap Daws, Reg Spooner and a number of other famous detectives who, in their time, helped me in many a tight corner. So I used to drop into Scotland Yard to meet friends and have a natter whenever I went to London. But I never turned the corner of the Red Lion into Cannon Row without having a strong, warm memory of the wide-eyed Yorkshire lad who stood, not too sure of himself, staring at the famous building all those years ago.

I completed my morning tour with a swift identification of the Houses of Parliament and Westminster Abbey. As I came back into Whitehall I was reminded by Big Ben that the time was shortening and I still had to reach an unfamiliar destination, miles deep in London. Pentonville Prison. How did I get there? I hadn't the courage to ask. But I should never reach it unless I did. The idea of taking a taxi never occurred to me. I had never hailed a taxi in my life, Burlington Bertie had never taught me that, how much money did you need to command such a situation?

There was a very young policeman standing outside the Home Office as I re-passed it. I realised that I should have to swallow my embarrassment.

'Can you please tell me the way to Pentonville Prison?' I asked.

'The Ville!' he said, apparently surprised by such a request at such a time from the middle of Whitehall.

'Pentonville Prison,' I repeated.

'Yes. The Ville.' I acquired my first phrase of police and prison slang.

'Why?' asked the policeman. 'Who do you want to see?'

It seemed silly to tell him I was going to see the Governor. It was sure to make him suspicious. I wouldn't have believed it myself if I had been in his place. Perhaps he would have thought I was helping someone to escape. No, he couldn't think that. Fancy asking a policeman where to find the prison you're going to spring someone from.

I said: 'I'm not going to see anyone really.'

'No?' he said.

'I want a place, and it's somewhere agen Pentonville Prison.'

'The Ville,' he said.

'Yes.'

He looked at me with a sudden sympathy, as if he had just understood. Obviously it was my brother, probably the black sheep of the family, who had served a term (done his bird? had his porridge? – I cheerfully mixed up my gleanings from Edgar Wallace) in the Ville; he was being released today, and I was going to meet him at the gate and reclaim him into the family.

'Take a 77 bus from here,' said the policeman, all prompt and kindly, 'ask for King's Cross, ask again there, and you'll get a bus all the way to Pentonville Prison.'

'The Ville,' I said.

'Yes.'

'Thank you very much.'

I lifted the knocker on the prison gate at five to nine.

In a few minutes I had completed a short interview with the Governor, and was sent along to the doctor for a very stiff medical examination. There was another aspirant who was being given the training course at the same time, a Londoner much older than I, whom I shall call Sid Collins. We finished the medical tests and dressed. Then we were handed over to the foreman of works, the prison engineer who was to supervise our practical training. He was well acquainted both with my uncle and formerly with my father, and his attitude towards me seemed to me to convey something of the respect he held for them.

'Come along, Albert, lad,' he said.

I was already christened into the prison service. I was never called anything but Albert during all the time I served, except that when I began to work closely with my uncle he always referred to me as 'Our Albert'. So the prison officers used to take up with some affection, I think, this northern style. And soon they were calling my uncle only 'Uncle Tom'. He was well over sixty even at that time, and he stayed with them until he was seventy-five, so it wasn't incongruous. The High Sheriffs and Under Sheriffs never got so familiar. They always used our surname.

I followed the engineer through the prison. Keys jingling, key rattling, slam and lock again at every steel door. I was re-living everything that I had ever read in my father's writings. From the moment when I had lifted the prison knocker I was thinking 'This is what my father did'. Going through the gates, through the yard, along the corridors.

We were going to the execution chamber. In the star-shaped prison lay-out the execution 'shed' was not a separate building, but actually a three-storey set of cells halfway down one of the wings. The ground-floor cell was the pit, with the traps set in the ceiling. The first-floor cell of the set held the floor of the scaffold, and across its ceiling level – it had no solid ceiling – ran two parallel beams between which passed three chains. The cell above that carried the great beam from which the arrangement of chains was suspended. It was to one or more of these chains that the rope or ropes was attached. The engineer was leading the way around the outside of the prison block, and he finally unlocked a door and went inside. I followed. We were in the pit. I looked up. The trap doors were open, and I could see everything. I gasped with intense surprise.

I had so often imagined myself making a similar journey, and so far the facts had corresponded with the scene I had built up. I was trying to live my father's life the way I had read it. I had pictured myself going through the gates, the yard, the general sombre prison set-up, and until then was not taken aback. But the execution chamber stopped me in my tracks. It was spotlessly clean and trim, when I had expected something dark and neglected like a tomb, but that was a minor change. What made me gasp was to look up through the doors and see the noose.

In all my thoughts or day-dreams I had, as it were, gone through all the motions of an execution – always entirely alone except for the prisoner, curiously enough – but in my mind there was never even the suggestion of a noose. I never saw a noose. I was going through a complicated routine, alone, but there was never a noose at the end of the dream. I don't think I had ever thought about it in any waking analysis or rehearsal. Now, in real life, I looked up through the doors in the scaffold floor and saw the noose above me, and iron chains. I accepted it, and arranged it into the routine, but it was a completely new detail. I cannot explain this. I only record it.

The engineer led the way up from the pit to the platform of the scaffold. I gazed around. I examined the hole in the floor, the two hinged doors, some eight-feet-six by two-feet-six, held vertically in the rubber-backed spring clips which received them when they dropped. I followed the mechanism of the lever which withdrew the bolts holding the plates supporting the drops from either side, under the central crack where they met. I examined the blocks and tackle attached to the beam where the three chains hung above me – the central chain to be used for a single execution, the two outer ones for a double. I was intensely, technically interested as the engineer explained the equipment, the adjustment of the rope, the method of altering the drop, and the routine of the general movement and positioning of witnesses at an actual execution.

He unlocked a door leading not into the first-floor corridor of the prison block, but straight into a separate room. Another door in a side wall led to another compartment.

'These are the C.Cs.,' he said.

'I see.'

'Do you know the meaning of C.C.?'

'I suppose it is the condemned cell.'

'You're right, Albert.' The engineer began a sort of lecture and told me to take notes. He spoke rather like a Beefeater guiding a party of tourists round the Tower of London: very precise, no doubt very accurate, little jokes slipped in here and there, but it was all a bit lifeless, like a lesson he had learned by heart. He glanced occasionally at a paper to make sure he had left nothing out. I made notes, but I didn't get it all in my head at once, and when on the following days I went off-beam, the correction always came in the same words, an approved formula like that which sergeants learn when they have to teach rifle drill to squad after squad of recruits. I wondered how many times he had to give this training. If it was often, it must mean that assistant executioners were dropping off the list pretty frequently.

'Tomorrow,' the engineer concluded at the end of that first afternoon, 'tomorrow you meet Old Bill.'

Sid Collins, the other trainee, and I had been offered quarters in the prison and we both accepted them. After our tea we could go out until ten o'clock, and Sid showed me a bit of London. I saw some of the most notable buildings and streets, but mostly only in passing, because Sid was more of an expert on the pubs. He liked his pint, and I used to take a soft drink alongside him.

Next morning we met Old Bill. This was the dummy used for training executioners. I don't know how many times we dropped him that week. The first exercise, continually repeated, was to get the noose right. 'Draw it firm and tight with the free end of the rope emerging from the metal eye just under the left jawbone. There is no knot. That fancy cowboy coil of a "hangman's knot" is something we abandoned to the Americans a hundred years ago. In Britain the rope runs free through a pear-shaped metal eye woven into the rope's end, and the operative part of the noose is covered with soft wash-leather. Always adjust it to the left, because with the pull of the drop the noose gyrates a quarter-circle clockwise and the tug of the rope finishes under the chin – throws the neck back and breaks the spinal column, separating it at about the third vertebra of the neck. Adjust it on the right, and it gyrates to the back of the neck, throwing the head forward, not breaking the neck, eventually killing by suffocation. No good. Leave that to the Americans.

'Draw on the white cap, adjust the noose, whip out the safety pin, push the lever, drop. Cap, noose, pin, push, drop. Push the lever, never pull it. The lever is like a railway signalman's points lever. When the traps are closed the lever is sloping towards the drop. You've got to be quick, not take time to get to the other side and pull. There is a cotter pin on the lever near the floor, a safety catch, never to be drawn while there are more men than the prisoner on the drop. Pull down cap, adjust noose, dart to your left, crouching to withdraw safety pin, push lever, drop. Cap, noose, pin, lever, drop. Let's get some speed in it. Sid, you be assistant, Albert, you be executioner. Prisoner's arms already pinioned behind him. Sid quickly pinion legs from behind, and *race off that drop*. Albert facing prisoner, cap noose pin lever drop. Haul him up and do it again. Get those traps up. Let's have some speed. Albert, you be assistant. Pinion and scarper. Cap noose pin lever drop. *You've got to get it right.* There's no allowance for error. Haul him up and do it again . . .

'Now let's get on with how to calculate the drop. Basically it depends on the weight and age of the prisoner. The heavier the man, the shorter the drop. The weaker his neck, the shorter the drop. Get it right, we don't want any butchery. Now you've got your table, Home Office issue, table of drops, executioners, for the use of. Use it, but use your own judgment too. Remember it's only a guide, and you've got to vary it according to your experience. Pull the man's head off and it's no use saying "But that's what it had in the table." You're out! An executioner has to use his own judgment. That only comes by experience. You'll be an assistant at a hell of a lot of executions before they trust you as Number One. Watch the executioner. Ask him. Why this? Why that? Ask him anything, any time, but not at eight o'clock in the morning. Make everything you see a part of your own experience. Old Bill is a dummy. He'll stand up to any punishment. On the actual job you're dealing with human flesh. *You've got to get it right . . .*

'Decide on your drop. You've got the man's age, weight, height, and you've had a chance to study him in the C.C., size up his neck. How do you adjust for the drop? You've got the rope, some six foot long. Metal eye at each end, one enclosing the noose and the other to be shackled to the chain by a U-bolt. You've decided to give a drop of eight foot six. Eight foot six. That's the maximum, Home Office orders, you don't want him springing off the floor of the pit and saying "Look, I'm a bloody yo-yo!" What do you do if you get a feather-weight? Use your own judgment, but *it's got to be right . . .*

'Right. Now the rope's some six foot long. Measure from the mark on the wash-leather above the noose, the rest of the rope is reserved for his neck. Measure from the turn of the noose *here*. Six foot, and you want eight foot six. Another two foot six to find. You've got to take it out of the chain. The top end of the rope, with the metal eye woven into it, is fixed to the chain by a U-bolt and shackle. *You've* got to do that, don't think the engineer will take responsibility once you're on the job. Choose your rope from those provided, test it and fix it yourself. To the chain. A four-inch link chain. You can alter the height of that by pulling the cotter pin out of the plates through which the chain passes at the beams and getting the right height. You can see there are holes in the plate about an inch apart. When you've got experience you can learn to adjust it to the half-inch. Why not? You want a perfect job. It's got to be right . . .

'Take your tape-measure. It's thirty-three foot long, there's plenty of clearance. Sid, you get up and hold the top. Albert, measure off the drop. Sid, adjust the chain and plug in the pin . . .

'Now I've got a man aged twenty-four, height five foot six, weight a hundred and sixty pounds in his clothes. What drop would you give him? Look at your table. Six foot three, it says. You'd be wrong. It wouldn't kill him. Not that fast, it wouldn't, and you're here to deal out sudden death. Instantaneous death. Six foot eleven, more likely, with that age and that strength of muscle. Fix me a drop of six foot eleven. Take your time, the first time. Take your time all the time. You haven't got the Governor looking on while you're doing this. You do it first thing in the morning. Choose your rope the afternoon before. And that's the time you test that the drop works smoothly, to your complete satisfaction, when you've got the word that the prisoner is at exercise, or in the chapel, or wherever they've put it in his mind to go. You don't want to have him hear it, he's only next door. In the afternoon, fix a drop that's near enough. Let the rope hang all night with a sandbag on it, weighing slightly more than the prisoner. Work out your final drop in the evening, from all you've thought about it. Go to the execution chamber before breakfast. The rope is nicely stretched now. Take the sandbag off, get the doors up, lock with the lever, fix the safety catch. Adjust the drop to your last calculation, and *do it quietly*. A good executioner hardly speaks a word on the morning of the job. Right. Start from scratch. Get Old Bill back in the C.C. Age fifty-six, weight two hundred pounds, height six feet, there's a tricky one for you. I'll give you time to work out the drop and fix it. Then I want to see you do it right through. O.K.? In the corridor outside the C.C. in twenty minutes. Pinioning straps at the ready. Albert, you be Number One. Then we'll break for a cup of tea . . .

'Now a double execution. Very tricky. Need a second assistant preferably another for spare. I'll be Number One first time. Into C.C.1, pinion arms, second assistant to C.C.2 Pinion. Prisoner One starts walking through connecting door, which most times he's never suspected because there has been a wardrobe in front of it. Assistant Two sees through open communicating door Prisoner One walking to scaffold, gets his man moving through C.C.1 into chamber. Number One has capped Prisoner One, adjusts noose, Assistant One has pinioned legs, waits on drop for Prisoner Two escorted by Assistant Two. Pinion Prisoner Two and assistant off – at the double.

Cap, noose, pin, lever, drop, back to the old routine. Now let's see if you can do it . . . '

Double executions, prisoner with amputated leg, cap noose pin lever drop, so it went on, repetition on repetition and then a variation. The engineer said it all so beautifully and confidently that I got the impression that he had performed hundreds of executions in his time. I thought about it at night, and realised that he had never done one. 'Albert, facing prisoner, cap noose pin lever drop,' he could say to me, and he could do it himself like a flash on a dummy. But he had never chosen actually to face any prisoner on the drop, meet his eyes, whip the cap from jacket breast-pocket where it had looked like a handkerchief, draw down cap, adjust noose, drop down without a word to touch assistant's shoulder for urgent speed if leg pinioning not completed, in same movement stay crouching and go for cotter pin, push lever . . . drop. He had read all the books, but he hadn't broken his virginity any more than I had, and he didn't intend to.

Repetition, repetition, variation. 'You've got the Fat Boy from the circus, weight twenty-two stone, that's just over three hundred pounds, height only five foot nothing, neck probably as soft as suet, your experience likely tells you you could do it with a drop of three foot four. But drops less than five foot are strictly forbidden by the Home Office. What do you do? I'll answer that one. The first thing you do is consult the medical officer and discuss his report with the Governor. Consult and discuss, I said. *You* take the decision. Anyway, five foot is the minimum Home Office drop. This rope is six foot long. How you going to fix a five foot drop from a six foot rope? We've done it before, I'm only springing it on you. *Come on, Albert!* . . . '

Repetition and variation. But not all the variations. In actual experience there was always an unexpected detail, sometimes a new solution to an old problem. I worked out my own measures to deal with the situation of a condemned prisoner who had previously cut his throat. In the end, a man is always working on his own, but before a band of critical witnesses.

On most evenings I went out with Sid Collins, listening between his pints to his puzzlement and uncertainty, for he was not taking the training as confidently in his stride as I thought I was. One night I stayed in my quarters and wrote to my Uncle Tom. It was the first mention I had ever made to him that it was even in my mind to get on to the list, let alone that I had got as far as this. *H.M. Prison, Pentonville,* I headed my letter, and I told him that I was on my training course and I hoped I should pass. Love to my Auntie Lizzie, yours, Albert.

Training again. One sequence I had paid no thought to was a consequence of the fact that the executioner still had some responsibility for the prisoner after death. The rule still held at that time that the body had to hang for an hour. But the executioner still had to get him down. There was a separate rope running from a block and tackle on the beam. It was lowered and tied round Old Bill's trunk under the armpits. The dummy was hauled up high enough for the noose and cap to be removed. Then it was lowered to the floor of the pit for notional disposal in a coffin, in the provinces, or on a mortuary stretcher for the immediate post-mortem examination that was the rule in London. Although there was a strict drill for this, as for every other part of the procedure, I was to find in actual experience that this sequence, more than any other, was in rehearsal utterly remote from reality. In training, it made little impression. In actuality, it represented all. At this point I took on myself the ultimate responsibility which, because of the speed and busy precision required at the actual execution, I had not had the opportunity to shoulder before. A dummy is a dummy. A newly dead body is supple flesh, responsive to your handling and mutely asking your respect. Just as it is the total responsibility of the head executioner to dispatch a prisoner, so he, and not the assistant (who is confined to managing the tackle), receives and handles the body for its last deposition.

I have gone on record and been many times quoted with apparent irony as saying that my job was sacred to me. That sanctity must be most apparent at the hour of death. A condemned prisoner is entrusted to me, after decisions have been made which I cannot alter. He is a man, she is a woman, who, the Church says, still merits some mercy. The supreme mercy I can extend to them is to give them and sustain in them their dignity in dying and in death. The gentleness must remain. The tough operator has no standing in the action. I have had assistants who have never seen this, since they have never had to carry the burden but only a dummy, and their attitude has jarred sharply against mine, so that some of the sharpest rebukes I have ever uttered have been given in the deserted

Henry Pierrepoint demonstrating his invention of a strap for a one-armed man

Henry Pierrepoint (left) making his way to
Swansea Gaol with his assistant, John Ellis, on
8 May 1909

Thomas Pierrepoint (left) with his nephew
Albert Pierrepoint

Henry Pierrepoint in 1922

The author in 1948

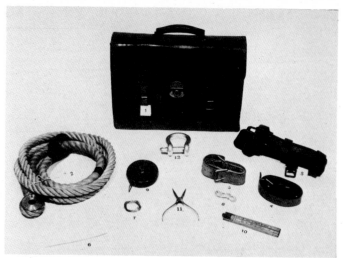

The tools of the trade, normally consigned in a box to the appropriate prison, can be enclosed in a demonstration carrying-case (1). They comprise (2) the rope, (3) wrist-strap, (4) leg-strap, (5) Henry Pierrepoint's innovation of a strap for a one-armed man, (6) the white cap, (7) copper wire, (8) packthread (twine), (9) tape measure, (10) two-foot rule, (11) pliers, (12) shackle.

Special wrist-strap of pliant calf-leather used by the author

The author deals with his correspondence

Albert and Anne Pierrepoint

The author

execution chamber when we have been alone with our responsibility.

Pentonville: repetition, repetition, variation, final test. On the last afternoon of our training we were examined by the Governor in the presence of the prison doctor, the engineer, and a senior prison officer. Sid Collins was nervous, but he did not infect my confidence. I went first. I was instructed to carry out a dummy execution from start to finish, the engineer acting as my assistant. The group of us stood outside the door of the condemned cell, the Governor with his watch in his hand. He looked at me and gave a slight nod of his head – the first of those many swift, almost imperceptible signals that I was to receive from Sheriff or Military Governor over the next twenty-five years. The chief officer unlocked the cell. I went in with the engineer, my wrist-pinion in my hand, and advanced on the dummy. The engineer carried it through the side door to the scaffold. Cap, noose, dismiss assistant, pin, lever, drop.

The group of witnesses said nothing. Then the Governor spoke. 'Outline to me the duties of an executioner, starting twenty-four hours before the execution,' he said. I replied confidently: be discreet and respectable at all times; avoid attracting public attention going to or from the prison; report at prison before four o'clock in the afternoon; be available for interview by Governor; receive physical details of prisoner from Governor; inspect, select and test apparatus provided by engineer; view prisoner without prisoner being aware; stretch rope; inform Governor of length of drop proposed; final adjustment of drop next morning . . .

The Governor interrupted me. 'That will do,' he said. 'You are free to go home now.' He gave no indication of whether or not I had passed the test. 'I'll take the other man now,' he told the principal officer.

I waited for Sid Collins. His examination seemed to take hours. He came out very uncertain of how he had done. We parted at the gates of Pentonville and he went home by tube. I took a bus, a direct bus, I knew the number now and had no inclination for sight-seeing, to the Euston Road and passed through the station portals to find a train for Manchester. I went to work as usual on the next Monday morning and found that my pal had talked, and the boss knew exactly what I had been doing. 'An executioner should understand that his conduct and general behaviour must be respectable and discreet at all times.' I never opened my mouth in public or private about any detail of my craft or any destination that had been allocated to me for the next quarter-century.

There was a letter from my Uncle Tom awaiting me at home. 'Thank you for your note,' he said. 'I am pleased you decided to apply to come on the list. Before this, I could not help you in any shape or form. I am sure you will be accepted to go on the list, and, when you are, I will try and see that we work together as much as possible.'

It was still some weeks before I received word from the Prison Commissioners that I had been placed on the list of persons competent for the office of executioner. I knew that one hurdle still remained for me to clear. I had to attend an execution, nominally as second assistant, but actually to do nothing, merely to observe the Number One and his assistant and to witness the execution. It was a final test of my nerve, and I knew that it had shaken many a man straight out of the craft so that he was never afterwards summoned.

I waited with some tension for this first call. It did not come. Every day I would go out on my delivery round, taking the loads of groceries to the corner shops of Cottonopolis in my Sunbeam lorry. I would come home, glance quickly at the mantelpiece for the long buff envelope, and it was never there. The summer holiday came, and I spent it as usual with my Uncle Tom. He was sympathetic about my suspense, but he recognised that I had not yet been blooded and he was as close as ever about the details of the craft.

The only comment he made on the subject was a pretty contemptuous reference to his predecessor Ellis, now some nine years retired from his position, who had been making an exhibition of himself in some side-show on the south coast, demonstrating to the public the method of legal execution. I came home and, about a fortnight later, read in the papers that Ellis had committed suicide. His former civilian profession had been as a barber, and this time he had chosen a more precise instrument than his revolver, and cut his throat. I did not know why he had done it, and did not draw any particular moral from the occurrence. A few weeks later I received my first offer of appointment as assistant executioner. Was I free to officiate at an execution at Armley Gaol, Leeds? I replied accepting the engagement. Shortly afterwards, a reprieve of the prisoner concerned was promulgated. Another invitation came. I accepted again, and again a reprieve was announced. This happened yet a third time, and I realised that the year was about to close without my having qualified as a fully accepted executioner, through failure to have witnessed an actual execution.

Just before Christmas, however, I was offered my first commission. It did not come in the long official cover, but in a small square envelope addressed in the flowing, very readable handwriting of my uncle. Uncle Tom had a job to do in Mountjoy Prison, Dublin, at the end of the year, and if I wanted to go and act as his assistant I was welcome. I wrote back immediately to say that I very much wanted to.

My uncle could freely offer me the job in Dublin because he worked independently for the Government of the Irish Free State. Ireland had no official executioner. It used to borrow Great Britain's Number One – Uncle Tom. But the deal was not done through Whitehall circles. Once they had got to know him, the Irish made a separate private contract with him, and they left the choice of his assistant to the executioner himself. My uncle cultivated this arrangement because it suited him well to be the only agent involved. I have mentioned the maelstrom of jealousy and in-fighting which has existed, in the experience of all my family, among assistants below the rank of master executioner, and the extremes of trickery which some of them have got up to in order to blast the reputation of the Number One. My Uncle Tom was determined that this should never happen on the Irish scene, and consequently, when he went to conduct an execution in the Irish Free State, he never took any person who was on the official Home Office list of men approved as qualified executioners. He did not want anyone in Dublin to know the names and addresses of these persons. He even preferred to take private friends, just for the expenses-paid trip and the couple of guineas at the end of it. He would 'train' them in a private session and, provided his estimate of their strength of nerve was correct, emerge safely on the other side. I don't doubt, however, that when he had the opportunity to take me – not only a relative who would never stab him in the back, but also a trained man – he felt a little relief. All I felt was gratitude.

I did not want to let my employers down. I knew that the minimum time I should take to go to Dublin was two working days, and to keep it down to that I should have to go without sleep for two nights. I worked hard until Christmas Eve, and when the deliveries had slackened almost completely after lunch, I said to my boss, Percy Sellers:

'I think I'd better have my cards, Percy.'

'What are you talking about?' he asked. 'I'm not sacking you.'

It was very difficult for me to mention the career that I was starting, which to me was so much more important than whole-sale grocery. But I managed at least to refer to it.

'Listen,' I said. 'You know what I went up to London for. It wasn't my idea that you should know, but you do. You know what I've applied for, and I ought to tell you that I've been accepted. I have been asked to go to Ireland next week. It will be two days, and occasionally there may be a few other two days. I owe it to you to put someone on the job who can be absolutely regular. I don't want to upset anybody in the busi-ness. But this is what I've chosen as my job, and I'm going to do it.'

He thought for a moment, and then went away to consult his wife's uncle, who ran this family firm. He came back and said, 'Albert, you can take those days off.' I said 'Thanks, but any time you don't want me to go, just tell me and I'll leave.' He said 'It all depends on how I find your books, don't it?' and he grinned. He was a very good fellow, Percy Sellers. He would throw pounds away if it was some way in which he could help a person, but if I was a ha'penny short in my account books I'd have to chase out where my addition was wrong, or else pay up. He had to have his books right. As long as I stayed with that firm, Frederick Harrison Limited, I gave Percy the chance to fire me every time I asked for time off. But he never took it, and I had to leave of my own accord in the end.

Christmas Day came. It was a Sunday. There were now only my sister Ivy and myself supporting my mother – who was now a little infirm, but never complaining – in our cosy little house at 2, East Street, Newton Heath. But we had a bit of a family party. I think the most heart-warming moment – especially for my sister Ivy, who was passionately attached to royalty – was when we were able to hear the voice of our King, George V, giving the first Sovereign's Christmas Message of all time on the wireless. 'Through one of the marvels of modern science,' he said, 'I am enabled this Christmas Day to speak to all my peoples throughout the Empire. I speak now from my home and from my heart to you all; to men and women so cut off by the snows, the desert, or the sea that only voices out of the air can reach them; to those cut off from fuller life by blindness, sickness, or infirmity, and to those who are celebrating this day with their children and their grandchildren — to all, to each, I wish a happy Christmas. God bless you.'

And 'God bless *you*,' we each of us replied.

On the Tuesday after Christmas I went on my rounds as usual, determined to put in a full day's work. I finished the day, and at six o'clock my Uncle Tom arrived on the direct bus from Bradford. We were settling down after tea when Uncle Tom said jocularly 'Well, our Albert, nobody has to worry about us in Ireland,' – and he pulled a huge revolver out of his capacious pocket. It was a wicked-looking black weapon firing bullets of much larger calibre than a rifle, and it was the first hint I got that being an executioner might be a dangerous job. My mother was terrified, both at the revolver and at the idea that it was necessary to carry it.

'It's all right, Mary,' coaxed my uncle. 'It isn't loaded.' And he pulled one of the wash-leather bags that he used for betting slips out of another pocket, and opened it to show that it was full of these ·455 cartridges. The fact was that my uncle never loaded his revolver. He kept the gun in one pocket and the bullets in another, and reckoned that just the feel of them was enough to give him security. It was only on his trips to Ireland that my uncle was armed. Executioners were not popular characters either in the North or in the Free State, and in the South the risk of a mobbing was much greater since the Free State was known never to use Irishmen but only to employ British executioners.

I myself soon became used to carrying a revolver in Ireland, and the police encouraged it. But for a long time, like my Uncle Tom, I never kept it loaded. Until one day, after an execution, when I had a long day to wait for the boat, and a policeman took me for a car trip into the country. As night came down we were in some rough terrain up in the hills, and the policeman said 'Don't worry, I'm armed,' and he pulled out his gun. 'Oh,' said I, making conversation like a schoolboy saying We're Quits, 'I've got one of those.' 'Can I have a look at it?' he asked. I unwrapped mine – it was a Browning, much smaller than my uncle's – and he examined it 'Why!' he exclaimed, 'the bloody thing's empty!' 'Oh, I've got a few rounds,' I assured him, and pulled out my own wash-leather bag. 'And a fat lot of good they'll be to you there,' he said, loading the revolver and adjusting the safety catch. Having a loaded revolver in my pocket didn't really make me feel any more comfortable at all, and I unloaded the thing as soon as I was off Irish territory, and locked it in a safe when I got home. But when I later had to go on professional business to Germany and other unsettled places – with the acting rank of lieutenant-colonel but no uniform more striking than my blue suit and brown trilby to back it up – I confess I did carry my loaded Browning in my trousers, with very special precautions about the safety catch.

On that night which began my initiation, with my mother suddenly more anxious for reasons she had never suspected before, my uncle packed his pockets in good time for the last tram – he never carried a travelling bag as it made him conspicuous arriving at the gaol – and together we travelled to the centre of Manchester. There were no special halters or personal tackle to take with us. Ireland bought its own hangman's ropes from the same traditional tentmaker's in the Old Kent Road which supplied execution equipment to the whole of the British Empire – but which made more profit from hiring out marquees for debutantes' dances and university balls. We should find everything we wanted when the engineer unlocked his box at Mountjoy Prison. But I did take one piece of personal equipment with me. This was a special strap invented by my father for pinioning a one-armed man. It was not so much a prudent precaution – though the happy-go-lucky Irish would never let you know in advance if the condemned man had one arm or one leg, and both sets of circumstances have their problems. I really took it with me out of a blind sense of keeping the continuity of my heritage. My father had been wearing that strap to demonstrate it when he had been photographed for *Thomson's Weekly News* sixteen years ago. That was the photograph on the newspaper placard at which I had been gazing when he introduced me to his friend the stationmaster. 'This is my eldest son. And one day *he* will be the Official Executioner.'

My father had been dead ten years. With patience and tenacity I had got to the beginning of the path he had trod, but I had never seen a dead man since. I had my ambition and my resolve, but I still did not *know* what depth or shallowness of courage I should show. The next few hours would tell much to me, as well as to others. I squared my shoulders and walked by the side of my uncle into the station forecourt. We bought our tickets. Uncle Tom sized up the midnight travellers and dossers with a shrewd glance, and led the way towards the Holyhead Boat Train.

4

The Blinds Flick Back

At some chill hour nearer midnight than dawn we left the train at Holyhead to transfer to the mailboat. Uncle Tom had a cabin reserved, and we hurried into its stuffy snugness, with the smell of hot engine oil soon yielding to my uncle's shag. Once the boat was under way he suggested a drink, seeking not oblivion but company – he only took an ale or two and I drank no regular alcohol at all. But he relaxed, and basked, and expanded his personality in the warmth of friendly recognition. I was seeing a new Uncle Tom. 'Eh, Tom! How are you?' Everybody seemed to know him, but avoided saying in what connection. There were friendly welcomes from the stewards, nods and smiles from farming types who, I supposed, were regular passengers, and knowledgeable beams – half worldly, half spiritual, wholly genuine – from a whole cohort of Catholic priests who had taken over the saloon in a very familiar way like ranchhands spending their rare and hard-earned time off in the nearest cattle-town bar. The only man who did not seem to know my uncle was a thick barrel of a man already propping up the bar. His ignorance did not affect his friendliness. He was a burly and talkative sea-lawyer from the Royal Navy going home in civvies to Ireland. As soon as I knew what he was I could see that he would have looked better in a Players Navy Cut hat and a fisherman's jersey with bell-bottoms rolled up to his knees. He was overpowering in his welcome as we joined him at the bar. He talked nonstop to Uncle Tom, asking as many questions as he supplied answers. And all the time my uncle sipped his ale, talked without giving any information . . . and smiled. I had never seen him smile so broadly and simply. It was as if, once he was on a journey to a job, he had no outside cares, but could give all his tolerant attention even to a busybody who was clearly already much farther gone than one over the eight.

I sipped my Bovril, and I watched it all, until the sailor went away to the heads, and never came back. The priests smiled to my uncle as if they were beckoning us with their blue-shaved faces, over to where they sat with their Guinnesses, hanging on to a rail or a bracket for support now and again, for the Irish Channel was choppy. We went to them. Uncle Tom accepted an ale, but I was in no need of Bovril. Someone was humming a tune. It was *The Rose of Tralee*. 'Give us a song, our Albert,' my uncle surprisingly said. It was like an echo of my father, saying 'Give us a tune'. I had a good voice, a light baritone, and I could take the top notes. I went straight into *The Rose of Tralee*, no fences barred. The priests looked delighted. My uncle beamed.

> She was lovely and fair as the rose of the summer,
> Yet 'twas not her beauty alone that won me.
> Oh no, 'twas the truth in her eyes ever dawning
> That made me love Mary, the Rose of Tralee.

The priests ordered another round of Guinness, which took time to serve, since at that time every bottle had to be uncorked. Uncle Tom indulged in another ale. I wanted nothing but another chance to sing. *Mother Machree*, hummed a priest, with benevolence aforethought. 'There's a spot in my heart no colleen can own,' I sang softly, like a pianist playing an introduction to get the chattering stilled. The company obediently hushed. 'There's a spot in my heart no colleen can own . . . ' I glanced at my uncle and saw that he was actually laughing – not hilariously, but crowing to himself like a child who has suddenly heard the angels. He sat there and looked straight at me, with that smile of fulfilment on his face, all the time I was singing, and the moment never went out of my memory.

> I love the dear silver that shines in your hair,
> And the brow that's so furrowed and wrinkled with care.
> I kiss the dear fingers so toilworn for me –
> Oh, God bless you and keep you, Mother Machree.

Respectable applause. One priest wiped away a tear. Another beat the bottom of his Guinness bottle on the table like an old-fashioned music-hall chairman. Offers of drink from various quarters, all discreetly refused. Other singers got into the act, but the self-elected chairman saw that I got my share of the action. And it brought me out. It nourished my self-esteem. It confirmed horizons of the sociability that I had always suspected was open to travellers. Dublin Diary Highlights: 'Our Albert' Pierrepoint, already a familiar figure in London circles and well-known in the Strand, was warmly welcomed by fellow globe-trotters aboard the Irish Mail last night when he sang his way into the hearts of all with a superb rendering of *Mother Machree.* Mr. Pierrepoint, with his Uncle Tom, is in Dublin to . . .

Four in the morning. 4 a.m.! I had never stayed at a party so late in my life. My Uncle Tom, his face a bouquet of smiles, seemed in no mood to go to bed. I myself had the lust of the recitalist in me. I joined in when anyone else was singing, and snatched my chance as soon as I got the wink from my dog-collared chairman.

> Oh Mary, this London's a wonderful sight . . .
> And they're all of them digging for gold in the street.
> At least, when I axed them that's what I was told,
> So I just took a hand in this digging for gold.
> But for all that I found there I might as well be
> Where the mountains of Mourne sweep down to the sea.

The applause had mounted from the respectable to the tumultuous. Admiring steward at elbow. Kingstown ahead on the port bow, sir, but you'd better learn to call it Dun Laoghaire. L-A-O- – never mind the spelling, it's still Dunleary. Train for Dublin leaves as soon as the main party are ashore, don't delay too long, for it doesn't wait for the drunks.

'So *there* you are!' said the friendly talkative seaman in civvies who had disappeared from the bar some hours before. 'I couldn't find you anywhere.'

'We've been here all the time,' said my Uncle Tom, gazing into the red-rimmed eyes of the sailor. 'Time to get our bags from the cabin. Nice to have met you. Happy New Year.'

Beyond the barrier, as we passed from the landing stage to the railway platform, there was a fair-sized crowd. They were all looking for somebody, as you would expect at a terminal. What I did not understand was that a proportion of them were looking for my Uncle Tom and myself.

There had been a great deal of feeling in Ireland about the case which had ended in the death sentence which we were about to execute. In addition there was the usual resentment that the Irish authorities had asked Englishmen to hang another of their citizens.

As we went through the barrier a policeman recognised my uncle and greeted him cordially. 'Everything all right, Tom?' he asked.

'If that had happened in London,' Uncle Tom growled at me from the side of his mouth, 'a uniformed man setting up a plain clothes man in public, there'd have been hell to pay.'

'Pierrepoint!' I heard a shout from a lean group of youngsters, not too sober. 'Where's Pierrepoint?'

My uncle guided me quickly away from the barrier to the rear of the train. We then began to walk up to the front. We had not gone far when two iron-hard hands descended on our shoulders, and we were swung round and propelled into a compartment which we had just passed.

'I was keeping these seats for you,' said the drunken sailor.

Sitting opposite us was a man reading a morning newspaper. Suddenly he jumped up and shouted: 'Pierrepoint is on this train!'

The sailor rose to his feet, not too smoothly. 'I know Pierrepoint very well,' he said. 'I will go along the train and have a look.' He lurched out of the door.

I was beginning to see the point of carrying a revolver, and I looked down with more satisfaction than previously at the bulge in my uncle's pocket. But he nudged me to be quiet.

Soon the sailor came back. 'Pierrepoint is not on this train,' he announced with possessive authority.

'Pity!' I said, and looked round into my uncle's face. But he had given up laughing for the morning.

We walked from the station to Mountjoy Prison. My uncle presented me to the Governor. 'You will be interested to know that this is my nephew,' he said. We had breakfast, and then were taken over by the engineer. He showed us the box of equipment. My uncle examined the ropes and selected one. Then he went to sleep, with his usual ease. In the afternoon we viewed the prisoner through the inspection panel, and tested the scaffold while the man was out of the condemned cell. My uncle adjusted the chains to fix an approximate drop and left a sandbag on the rope to stretch it overnight.

Once we were in the prison he had discussed details of the job with me, on and off. He had never mentioned it on the journey for fear of eavesdroppers. But there was no question of his building up the importance of the occasion, or any crucial aspect of my work. 'All I want you to do,' he said, 'is to get those straps on his legs quickly and step back off the drop as fast as you can.'

At nine o'clock we went to bed in a room in the prison officers' quarters. I slept right through until six, when I was awakened with the offer of a cup of tea. We had a good breakfast of ham and eggs, and I went with my uncle to the execution chamber to make the final adjustment to the drop which he had decided on the previous night. We brought up the trap doors, and by a few minutes before eight we were waiting outside the condemned cell.

My uncle stood, relaxed, sucking a sweet, with the armpinion in his hand. I never saw him otherwise at any execution, very calm, with a flat sweet in his mouth, the white cap folded in his breast pocket and the strap in his left hand.

At eight o'clock an official gave us the signal. I followed my uncle into the cell. I noticed that a priest was there, and saw little else. I followed my uncle the short distance on to the scaffold, strapped the legs, moved back, and had hardly time to get my balance, let alone look up, when there was a bang and then a space of complete silence. The traps were open, the rope was straight and motionless, the man was dead.

My uncle went into the pit by some side steps to open the prisoner's shirt for the doctor's stethoscope. The doctor confirmed death, and I suddenly realised that the chief prison officer was holding a glass of whisky out towards me. He had somehow produced a full bottle and some glasses, and was pouring drinks for all the witnesses.

'No thanks!' said my uncle quite evenly, but very firmly. I looked at him and saw that he was speaking for me as well as himself. 'No thanks,' I said, and the others stood savouring their drink for a few moments and then went away. The execution chamber was locked, and we followed the engineer to our quarters.

We had an hour to wait. I cannot say that I experienced any strong reaction. I was neither stunned nor relieved. My principal impression was of the astonishing speed of the operation.

My uncle and I went back to the execution chamber, and into the pit. A coffin was lying there. As the body hung on the rope, we removed the pinions. From tackle on the upper beam we fastened another rope in a loop under the arms. We hauled it up sufficiently so that the tension was released and the noose and the cap could be removed from the level of the scaffold. My uncle went below, and I eased down the rope so that he could receive the body and place it in the coffin. He came up, and we dismantled the equipment and put everything tidily back into the box. We left the chamber and told the engineer that we were ready to report to the Governor.

The Governor noted the few official details which we had to give him, and congratulated my uncle on his efficiency. As we took leave of him, he said:

'I hope you don't run into any trouble outside.'

It was then that we learned that there was a hostile crowd awaiting us at the prison gates. My Uncle Tom put another sweet in his mouth as we stood inside the wicket.

'Come on,' he said to me. The gate was opened.

The cul-de-sac outside Mountjoy Gaol was crammed with people. Many were holding banners. Some of them read: 'British hangman destroys Irishman. Abolish the system and abolish crime.' 'Pierrepoint the British Hangman hangs Irishman. Is this justice?'

My uncle calmly threaded his way through the crowd, never saying a word. I followed, not knowing what to expect, with my free fist clenched ready for the first sign that we were cornered. But my uncle looked so unconcerned, so obviously not on the defensive, that no one was prompted to challenge him, and we glided on through the turbulence of the streets into the calm of Phoenix Park.

'I think we'll go and have a tour of Guinness's brewery,' said my Uncle Tom. 'I have a friend who works there.' I was beginning to find that he had friends in most places. We called at the brewery and my uncle drank a sample or two. I had one glass myself, of some special new porter they were introducing, but I found that it did not agree with me. We retired to Phoenix Park – there was a long day to pass until the overnight mailboat. My uncle settled down, with the skill of a lifetime, to sleep. He gave one preliminary snore, which woke him up for the moment, and he opened his eyes and looked around at me long enough to say:

'You have done very well today, lad.'

I could not have asked for warmer praise. Unfortunately it did not come at my most receptive moment. The unaccustomed porter was playing havoc with my stomach, but I was determined not to let my uncle down. In the awful uncontrolled agony of nausea I waited until he was safely asleep, and then teetered away to get safely behind the nearest tree.

When my uncle awoke I was sitting decently beside him. He gave me another long look and said:

'Young fellow, I'm very glad you didn't take that drink in the execution chamber this morning when the chief came round with the whisky. You did very well on this job today, our Albert. But you'll always have to rely on yourself. That means you can't blow yourself up, or drink yourself up, to be anybody else. You've got to be yourself when you're doing this job. If you can't do it without whisky, don't do it at all.'

I thought then, and I think now, that it was very good advice. I have been alongside assistants since who have had to get themselves half-drugged with drink in order to pass the night before an execution. (Fortunately, nothing I have ever encountered has matched the scene in the past when a drunken executioner tried to hang the parson as well as the prisoner.) Nowhere except in Ireland have I known the bottle come out after an execution, but in Ireland it was the regular rule. However, even when I had become a moderate spirit-drinker I never accepted a tot when it was offered in the execution chamber. 'If you can't do the job without it, don't do it at all.' I stuck to that.

The winter night was blanketing the park, and, together, my Uncle Tom and I walked into Dublin. After a meal we walked the six miles down to Dun Laoghaire. We boarded the night boat to Holyhead and took the train to Manchester. We arrived at past five in the morning. The first tram did not run until six so we began to walk to my home in Newton Heath. Halfway home we heard a tram coming up the road, but my uncle did not consider it. 'Let's keep on,' he said, 'It's a nice night.' So we walked the last, probably our twentieth, mile of the day. It did not greatly bother us then, although my uncle was in his sixties. I put my key in the front door. My mother came into the kitchen with her tired face shining with relief. Uncle Tom broke bread into a bowl of milk, sucked up his pobs, and went straight down on to the couch, snoring in an instant. I washed and changed and went straight out to work, making my heavy Friday deliveries until late in the evening. I was conscientious. I prided myself on that.

I wrote to the Home Office saying that, although I had not

yet formally witnessed an execution in England, I had acted as assistant to my Uncle Tom in Ireland. I half expected a reply stating that it was no longer necessary for me to attend as second assistant under observation, and I could be engaged as working first assistant. But I was not given this exemption, and I can understand now that they preferred to have a representative of the Prison Commissioners personally noting my reaction to the infliction of sudden death rather than consult a prison governor in Dublin who – whether or not they were aware that he pushed out the whisky as a finale – had no official standing in the United Kingdom.

In a very short time the Governor of H.M. Prison, Winson Green, Birmingham, wrote to ask if I was free to take an engagement as assistant executioner for a prisoner whom he was holding, and I accepted. I soon checked that it was my Uncle Tom who was to act as Number One, and arranged to travel with him to Birmingham. When we met his appointed assistant at the prison, my uncle came to an arrangement with him that I should do the actual work. It made no difference to the assistant, who attended and took his fee in any case. But it did advance the close liaison between my uncle and myself as working partners.

At this stage in my life I had no particularly strong opinions on the efficacy of capital punishment as a deterrent. I suppose I conventionally accepted the line that it worked. But, much later, when I came to reflect on the problem in depth, my mind often went back to the details of this my first execution in England. For it seemed to show that a prisoner could be to all outward appearances unshaken by the prospect of his death. Put it down to his courage, his fatalism, lack of sensitivity, or, as some people far from the actual scene have often said, the brutal stupidity of the man about to die: the fact remained that this man met his death jauntily. And he was by no means unique. I came to experience much the same attitude in many other condemned men. The thought that kept occurring to me later was that the existence of the death sentence had not deterred them, and the immediate prospect of death had not consumed them with terror. Possibly the thought of the noose which hanged *them* deterred *others*, but the actual execution inspired respect for the man rather than revulsion. And if such an execution had been held in public, witnesses would have felt sympathy for the man's dignity rather than satisfied recognition of society's vengeance – which is not what the theory of capital punishment preaches.

I shall call the prisoner Gerald Hutchins. His offence was grave enough. He had been convicted of the killing of a mother of four young children. It was a love-affair murder, and the moment of passion had to be paid for. Sentence of death was pronounced. As a character, the prisoner aroused no disgust among the prison officers, who all called him Gerry, and it was through their friendly interest in him that I learned one of the details about the last day of his life which always impressed me.

My uncle and I arrived together at the prison, and we had just sat down in the lodge at the main gate when the noise of someone banging loudly on the knocker echoed towards us. The officer on the gate opened up, and let in a group of people. They were shown to a waiting-room on the opposite side of the gate lodge. When the officer came back to us he said, 'That is Gerry's sister with some of his relations.'

As their stay with him drew to an end, Gerry realised that it was up to him to put their minds at rest as best he could – it is surprising how often, in these circumstances, it is the dying man who has to comfort his mourners.

'Now I don't want you to worry about me,' he said. 'Don't crucify yourselves in the morning, waiting for me to go. And don't make too much of it afterwards. Don't send the house into mourning.

'At eight o'clock in the morning, I want you to get hold of the blind, and draw it down, but not let it stay down. Just let the blind flick back again, and say, "Poor old Gerry. He's gone." '

Gerry's family went away, and my uncle and I got on with our preparations for his execution. When the Governor visited him that evening Gerry spoke lightly to him: 'I should like eggs and bacon for my breakfast, sir, please. Not one egg and bacon, *eggs* and bacon, because I am going on a long journey, and I am going to be hungry.'

Next morning we were awoken at six by a prison officer bringing in hot cups of tea. It was a chilly dawn, and I was sipping my tea with the steam warming my face when I heard a great joyous voice singing. The sound came echoing through the stone prison in an unearthly fashion that makes me tingle now whenever I recall it. It would not be so remarkable today, when radios are commonplace in prison and there are even set hours for television. But *any* music in a gaol at that time was extraordinary, almost portentous, and when it came on that execution morning, very clear and resonant as it bounced along the walls of corridors and cells, it seemed to me uncanny. The voice was firm and free, and it was singing a song of the day:

> Sally's come back,
> Sally's come back,
> And she's living down our alley.
> Although she's been away
> For many a day,
> Sally
> Is just as sweet and pally . . .

'Sally's come back and brought the sunshine home . . . ' The song bounced on down the prison alleys. 'Who's that?' I said to the officer who had brought me my tea.

'That's Gerry,' he said.

Gerry sang on, for much of the morning that was left to him. There were only two hours to go. When my Uncle Tom and I went into the execution chamber to make the last arrangements and adjustments on the scaffold, only one wall separated us from the singer. He had a voice, and a spirit, to be appreciated. At a few minutes before eight we were waiting outside his cell. We could hear him joking with his guards. The Sheriff and the Governor arrived with their party, gave us the signal, and moved immediately into the execution chamber. We went into the cell, and Gerry turned round and laughed as we strapped his wrists.

We moved towards the scaffold. Before he set his foot on the drop, Gerry stopped and turned towards the group of officials who were to witness his death. 'Be good, everybody,' he said. 'And thank you for all your trouble.' Then he walked on to the drop.

And so he died. And one of the witnesses – I did not pause to consider who – was, I suppose, regarding me critically to assess my coolness and competence as a novice in executing the sentence of death. As we took Gerry down I was hoping that his sister was taking all the tragedy of this sad day with the resignation he had asked of her: the blind had been drawn; she had let the blind flick back. Poor old Gerry. He was gone.

In this fashion the 'firm' of Uncle Tom and Our Albert was

established. Not that we used any influence to get it going, for we could not. The Sheriff of the county chose the executioner, and the Governor of the prison appointed his assistant. My uncle had no rival as Head Official Executioner, but I had up to half a dozen aspirants on the list of the qualified executioners – a pack which was constant in number, but whose personnel varied from year to year as the assistants dropped off the list, deciding they could not continue. I think I impressed the authorities with my consistency and zeal, and I was picked to assist my uncle perhaps four or five times a year in the beginning, a higher average than any strict rationing of the executions would have given me. Indeed, very early in my career I was entrusted with full responsibility for an execution at Bristol, since my uncle was engaged elsewhere on the same day – but the prisoner was reprieved.

I think I gave something positive to the partnership of uncle and nephew, if only in a social sense at the start. It may seem strange to talk of executioners as social characters, but in the prison service, as in the corps of executioners, there were always old-timers and always new recruits. With the old hands, 'Uncle Tom and Our Albert' would slip immediately into familiar intimacy – which spells efficiency. With new staff, a little more effort was necessary, and making the effort came more naturally to me than to my uncle. He was close and taciturn until he had got to know people. I was always a good mixer, friendly by nature, the first to speak and therefore quick to get our duties going smoothly. Nowadays they call all this 'public relations' and set great credit on it, but it was just as necessary years ago when it had no name and was practised as part of the preliminaries in and around an execution chamber.

Even prison officers, perhaps attending an execution for the first time, possibly anticipating unusual trouble on the scaffold, have to be 'trained' – coached and coaxed – by the executioners. As an example, the prison officers who are the immediate escorts of the condemned man on the scaffold have got to be prepared for difficulties at the last moment, though it happens very rarely. If an executioner has not made plans for this contingency, even though it occurs only once in a hundred occasions, he is incompetent. These preparations include the briefing of the escorting officers. The two planks are always laid across the drop on either side of the noose for the officers to stand on – but how are they to hold the prisoner if it is necessary to restrain or support him? The 'natural' method is to hold his upper arm. But this is quite impractical since, when the man falls, they cannot detach their grip fast enough. The fall is broken, and they may lose their balance. Therefore we devised a hold effected by thrusting the hand of the escort, standing slightly to the rear, absolutely flat between the prisoner's upper arm and his ribs, and putting upward pressure high into the armpit, so that when the man fell the supporting forearm could be quickly lowered like a semaphore. Now this action requires not only careful explanation, but practical rehearsal. If we had a prison officer who was new to the duties of the escort, even if he had attended an execution in another capacity before, we could assume that he might be nervous – though neither we nor he might admit it. The manner in which we gave him emergency instruction like this was therefore important. If we made it sound too urgent or dramatic, it might only increase his tension. If I had already made a point of getting on good terms with him, he would accept the emergency drill in a workmanlike manner without building up any extra alarm. That, as I have said, was a better assurance of hundred-per-cent efficiency at the actual operation.

But, of course, whatever I gave to the 'firm' in geniality, my Uncle Tom gave a hundredfold in skill and experience. The executioner in Shaw's play *Saint Joan* speaks of his craft as 'a highly skilled mystery'. That is what I found it to be. And until I became the frequent companion of my uncle as he went about his work, I knew little of the finesse of it, in spite of my conscientious training. Before I was on the list my uncle had said nothing confidential to me. Once I was with him he told me everything, as patiently as a schoolmaster. In the little room in the prison where we were to pass the night he would explain to me his summing-up of the prisoner, the kind of man he was and the drop he was going to give him: why he was going to ignore the Home Office table and give perhaps a nine-inch longer drop because of his judgment based on what he had observed; what snags he anticipated, if any, and how he intended to deal with them. I would listen to him and absorb his experience, and know that he was really passing on to me my father's store of knowledge and the fruits of that experience, because it had been my father who had taught him. Uncle Tom would mention any information about the prisoner's condition passed to him by the medical officer, and explain how he was

taking it into consideration, what special measures he intended—
not only for the fairly obvious consequences of the wound from
a cut throat, but for other, more intricate, conditions.

There were even technical differences to be explained in the
manner of an execution in Scotland. Executions in Scotland
were rare. I think there was a gap in my time of a dozen years.
They were all getting reprieved, there was no one going down.
But I went up quite early in my career for an execution there,
and experienced the difficulty which always existed in Scotland
of making fine adjustments to the rope to ensure the drop we
had very accurately estimated. Outside Edinburgh and Glasgow, which had permanent apparatus, the Scottish authorities
used to send a mobile scaffold around from prison to prison.
When not in use it was folded up and stowed away in Duke
Street Prison, Glasgow. I remember I used it at Perth once,
and found it really rough. I had to walk the prisoner up a slope
to the scaffold because there was a runway that was hinged to
make the scaffold compact enough for mobility.

But it was the drop that was the trickiest part of the operation. In England, the chain holding the rope ran through a
slotted metal double plate, and the length of the chain could be
adjusted by pins put through the plates. In Scotland there was
no such means of adjustment. The metal eye at the upper end
of the rope fitted into a U-bolt connected to another U-bolt on
the crossbeam. The rope could be adjusted only by rather crude
shortening. We used to wrap the rope around a round piece of
wood and put in a double hitch knot so that it would not slip.
Sometimes the double knot made the rope too short, so we put
in a single knot. We had to allow for the drag on this knot, for
although the fairly thick rope could not be tightened by hand,
the sudden jerk of the actual drop would tighten it and lengthen
it – possibly only by an inch, but we were concerned with
accuracy and had to work against it. My uncle showed me how
to make the knot on the rope to allow for adjustment.

Technical difficulties were, of course, not confined to Scotland. With my Uncle Tom I carried out one execution at Exeter
Prison, the scene of the attempted execution of 'the man they
could not hang'. John Lee, accused on circumstantial evidence
of the murder of a woman at Babbacombe, and always protesting his innocence, was led out for execution there, and the trap
failed to drop – even though the executioner, after the first
stupor of surprise, stamped on it; then removed Lee from the

trap while he investigated (and it worked); then had Lee removed to his cell while he worked on the apparatus; then failed once more to hang his prisoner. Lee was dismissed from the scaffold and finally reprieved. There are many technical theories as to why this particular execution failed. I myself prefer to believe that it was an act of God. But at the execution which I attended – almost the last in the history of Exeter Prison – nothing out of routine occurred. Uncle Tom did not even bother to admit any feeling of relief.

Something which I think I also absorbed from my uncle was a sense of respect for the occasion. As I watched him working, I saw that he was a very dignified man. I don't mean that he was like an actor or the caricature of an undertaker. He was a man who did not try to snatch for himself any dramatic kudos out of the unique duty he was committed to. He was a man with recognition of his 'highly skilled mystery', a man who had that respect for humanity, for the humanity he had to handle, alive and dead, which I certainly developed with the courage of my own perceptions.

But Uncle Tom's gravity at the appropriate moment did not block his eye for the main chance when a variety of appointments was being offered. One of the hazards of a British executioner's life in this century has always been the chance of a reprieve – and a cancelled appointment meant a cancelled fee. My uncle, being a bookmaker, was skilled in assessing the odds on any man's death, so that he would often accept appointments on the same day in different parts of the country, making his own estimate of the form of the prisoners and their chances of survival through reprieve. (Since individual and independent County Sheriffs were appointing him as executioner, the fact that he had accepted two incompatible engagements never came to the eyes of higher authority.) He was never wrong, but at times he had the thrill of a photo-finish. Usually, when he had accepted two executions for the same day, he had read the trial reports so thoroughly that he was convinced one of the condemned men would appeal – which automatically shifted the date of his eventual execution if he failed.

But there was one particular occasion in my early association with him which gave me, at least, the cold shivers – and I think even Uncle Tom had to suck a few extra sweets under the tension. I had been offered an engagement as an assistant executioner in Manchester, and had accepted. Within a few days my uncle wrote to me saying that he had taken a job in Dublin and he had nominated me as his assistant – as he could, for Irish operations. The date of the execution in Dublin was the same as for that in Manchester. I wrote back saying that I had already accepted the other appointment. He replied, revealing that he was down to perform that execution, too. But, he said, he fancied that Manchester would not come to anything so I had better accept the Irish job. I was young, and I followed his judgment. Therefore, like him, I was engaged for both executions. The days passed, and no news came either of appeal or reprieve for the man in Manchester. In Ireland the prisoner had no hope. Both executions were fixed for a Tuesday, and we had to sail for Dublin on the Saturday night. The last week passed. I was very nervous indeed. The last night came. Still there was no news. On the Saturday morning I read in the newspaper that a reprieve had been granted for the man in Manchester, and shortly afterwards I received a telegram confirming this. At teatime Uncle Tom turned up at my house as cool as a cucumber, all ready to take the night boat to Dublin. He looked at me with his blue eyes, and he smiled so innocently. But I never again took such a risk. I was never a gambler, could never rely on luck. If I back a horse now it will drop down dead. I can't even win an argument.

I suppose it had been my uncle's shrewd knowledge of form that decided him to reject the engagement in Bristol, which was then offered to me, and to accept the appointment somewhere else in the country, at which he officiated when the Bristol reprieve was announced. After that early setback I had no invitation to act as head executioner for many years, and I became reconciled to working as junior partner in the accepted firm of The Pierrepoints: Uncle Tom and Our Albert.

I believe the name became familiar. I well remember being amused by the discomfiture of one country police sergeant. I went to pass the weekend with a friend in Yorkshire. On a very cold winter evening we went out for a couple of drinks – I was still on shandy in those days. We came back at about ten-thirty and settled cosily in front of a blazing fire. Suddenly there was a loud knock at the door, and I heard a woman's voice say 'Joe! Come at once. My father is hanging over the banister rail.'

'Come on, Albert,' said Joe, and together we ran to a house two doors away. There was a small crowd inside, but beyond I could see a man hanging from the stair rail. I asked for a sharp knife quickly, and told my friend to hold his shoulders higher in case he was breathing, and to avoid damage to his head when I cut him down. But when we had him down he was stone cold, and I could see that he had been dead for some time. I took a swift look at the rope. He had dropped only two feet and the knot had twisted to the back of the neck – he had died from strangulation.

The village police had been called, and in a short time a sergeant and constable arrived. They asked everybody to go home, as there was nothing else that could be done. My friend and I, who had been disposing the body, were the last to leave, and the sergeant pushed us gently in the back, saying, 'Come on, lads. This is not a fit sight for you to see.' We walked out without replying.

Some days later my friend was walking through his village when he saw the sergeant and asked him what the verdict on the old man had been. He was told 'Suicide'. 'You remember when you told us to go,' said Joe, 'and said it was not a fit sight for us to see? Do you know who was the man who was with me?' 'No.' 'It was Albert Pierrepoint.' 'Bloody hell, no! Not *the* Pierrepoint!'

As assistant to my uncle it became part of my duty to officiate at the execution of women. On the first occasion I questioned him closely as to whether there was any alteration to the routine. He put his hand on my shoulder and said, 'You've nothing to worry about, lad.' Clearly the drop could be calculated from the usual variables of weight and estimated muscular strength, and in practice we made no change at all in the procedure, save for shifting the position of the ankle strap for the sake of decency during the drop.

I am not inclined to dwell on details of the individual behaviour of the condemned during their last moments, though I think it is characteristic that it was a woman who made a strong protest against going to her death blindfold and masked in the hood: 'Must I have this?' she demanded as I adjusted the cap. But I willingly repeat that I told Sir Ernest Gowers in open enquiry, that a woman about to be hanged is very brave. The principal differences in the prison atmosphere during the execution of a woman were the appalling effect it often had on the woman prison officers, and the degree of commotion outside the gates. Soon after I began my duties Mrs. Van Der Elst, the wealthy propagandist against capital punishment, was beginning her emotional campaign, and she generally attracted more support when protesting against the hanging of a woman. She would stretch the pathos of the moment of execution to an almost unendurable pitch by playing hymns through amplifiers carried on cars outside the prison gates. *Abide With Me* and *Nearer, My God, to Thee* were two of her favourites. This affecting music stopped on the stroke of the hour. The crowd strained to hear the crash of the trapdoors. They never could hear it, but some abolitionist would obligingly thump the door panel of a car with a flat hand. Then the tension snapped into savage hysteria as the mob rushed the gates of the prison. It would be a crowd of this mood, though fortunately softened by a further ninety-minutes wait, that my Uncle Tom and I would have to encounter when we emerged from the wicket in the prison gate.

As the years crept towards Hitler's war I began to bring a new visitor to my auntie and uncle in Yorkshire. Two doors from the wholesale grocery store where I worked was a sweets-and-tobacco shop which I used. It was managed by a young lady from Bolton who had long been living in Newton Heath with her auntie. She was blonde, gentle, practical, and I liked her. Her name was Anne Fletcher. Eventually I took her home, and my mother got on famously with her. My sister Ivy, who was slightly older than I, became great friends with Anne, and together they joined the Nursing Reserve which had been formed as the threat of war grew. Ivy's real vocation had alway been nursing, but in those days it was difficult to get accepted, and the money nurses were given was no more than small change – you were supposed to be a lady, with no need of wages. So Ivy had very early become a tailoress, and a good one too. I was not sure that I approved the move when they both became volunteer nurses, for Anne worked long hours as it was, and the training cut down my chances of seeing her. I had bought my first car, a wire-wheeled Ford 8, almost new, which cost me a hundred pounds to put on the road – and I paid that by instalments: the first and last possession I ever got through hire purchase. We sometimes used it at the weekend to go over to Lidget Green, for my Uncle Tom and Auntie Lizzie had moved down the hill from Clayton. But the same welcome, and the same smell of fresh-baked bread, still greeted us. My auntie, who had always talked nineteen to the dozen, found a new confidante in Anne, and I could hear her rattling on when they went to bed – Anne sleepless in their room because the torrent could not be stopped, and myself sleepless because of the relentless snores of my Uncle Tom beside me.

At work, although I officially drove the delivery van, I became a jack of all trades, because I was interested in the business. I could do jobs with a practical skill like bacon-rolling, neatly cutting out the bone and tying up the side with string. Occasionally, particularly after I had the car, I filled in as a travelling salesman, going the rounds of the corner shops we supplied, taking the regular orders and attempting to coax a little more. I tried to model myself on my boss, Percy Sellers, who was a great commercial traveller. 'Now, have you forgotten anything?' he used to ask the shopkeeper. 'Aspro, Bacon, Beecham's Powders, Bile Beans, Blacking, Blacklead, Boot Polish, Butter . . . ' and all the way down the alphabet to Zam-buk Ointment and Zebra Metal Polish.

But I did not have much chance to develop my own style, for the proprietor of the business died. Mr. Sellers succeeded him as managing director, and he brought me in off the road to become manager. I got a small rise in salary, and it was the first I had had since I had joined the firm over seven years before. Anne had also done well. She had been made travelling supervisor of the chain of tobacco stores for which she worked. Things were going well. At the age of 34 I had faint dreams of domestic bliss. Then the war broke out, and Ann and Ivy went straight off to be nurses at £1 a week less their keep. My own job in food distribution was scheduled an essential service. I took my car off the road because there was no fuel to run it. And I continued my journeys to prisons around the country, in blacked-out trains with criss-cross tape gummed on the windows, and interminable delays, and with the young men who were to do the work and the dying standing endlessly in the corridors, in rough serge and hard boots, hearteningly cheerful, unconquerably patient.

Dunkirk came. My sister Ivy worked continuously for eighteen hours a day among the worst of the battle casualties. Winston Churchill came to power, and his first strategic duty was to counter the invasion of Britain, then being actively prepared across the Channel. I had an appointment in London, and heard him broadcast before I left my home to catch the train:

All goes to show that the war will be long and hard . . . Now it has come to us to stand alone and face the worst that the tyrant's enmity can do. We await undismayed the impending assault. Perhaps it will come tonight. Perhaps it will come next week. Perhaps it will never come . . . Should the invader come, there will be no lying down of the people in submission as we have seen in other countries. We shall defend every village, town and city. The vast mass of London itself, fought street by street, could easily devour an entire hostile army, and we would rather see London laid in ruins and ashes than that it should be tamely and abjectly enslaved.

This was the only nationwide speech ever made by Winston Churchill, as far as I know, which made a direct reference to British quislings or traitors, and the vengeance they could expect. I was particularly interested since, if ever their fate was to be settled by legal means, they would eventually come to me – as some did. But I fancy Mr. Churchill was speaking of a rougher justice. He was referring to the Home Guard – as he was to name the force a week later, although then it was still officially the Local Defence Volunteers, standing in support of the million and a half men under arms in the British Army: 'Behind these, as a means of destruction for parachutists, air-borne invaders, and any traitors that may be found in our midst – and I do not believe there are many, and they will get short shrift – we have more than a million Local Defence Volunteers.'

I travelled to London, newly aware that it might be fought street by street while I was in it, savouring the memory of Winston Churchill's voice and noting how his message had already strengthened the spirit of everyone on the train – the impact was as swift as that in those days. Within a week the Battle of Britain was at full force and I had to go to London again.

It was an assignment that was to have a great influence on my future. I was engaged to assist at an execution at Pentonville, but the chief executioner was not my uncle, who was engaged elsewhere. He was Sid Collins, with whom I had trained and who had previously acted only as an assistant. He and I were of the same seniority, having passed out from Pentonville together. But I had done more work than he had in the years between, and had, of course, been offered one head executionership at Bristol, though it had fallen through. Since my Uncle Tom was not available, I supposed that the London

Sheriff had selected Sid Collins from the list on the grounds that he was older in years than I, and he lived in London – which was convenient, since travelling by train had its uncertainties that summer.

I met Sid in the prison during the afternoon. We saw the Governor, later viewed the prisoner, and we went to the execution chamber at an agreed time. There was quite a crowd there. In London it had always been the practice of the Under Sheriff to inspect the scaffold on the eve of an execution so that he could be satisfied that the mechanism was working satisfactorily – a precaution which not all sheriffs took. In addition the prison Governor was present, with some senior officers in attendance, besides the engineer.

Suddenly I realised that Sid Collins was having a bad attack of nerves. I thought, possibly he had not expected the rather impressive audience, and they had given him stage-fright. But it was more serious than that. He had made no theoretical preparation for the execution, perhaps relying on having a chat with me quietly in the execution chamber. But in the circumstances this was now impossible.

'Eh, Albert!' he said to me out of the side of his mouth. 'What drop shall we give?'

'You should know,' I said. 'You're the boss.'

'I haven't a clue,' said Sid. He had a paper in his hand with the physical details of the prisoner which the engineer had given him. The Sheriff and the Governor, waiting in the chamber, sensed that something was amiss and looked keenly at us. I realised that something had to be done quickly for confidence to be restored.

I took the paper out of his hand and a pencil from my pocket. The truth was that I had already worked out in my mind an approximate drop from the details of the prisoner's height and weight which I had heard, and from my inspection of the condemned man. I put the paper up against the wall of the execution chamber, made a fast check that my memory of the weight was right, and wrote down a figure. I didn't bother to look at the Home Office table, because I was already using my own experience.

'That's the drop,' I said.

'I can't measure it!' whispered Sid in a breathy tone of desperation.

I took the tape-measure and began to mark it along the rope

with my fingers. Once I had started the routine he fell into the
old drill and helped me. We measured off the drop, adjusted
the chain, fixed and dropped the sandbag to stretch the rope
overnight, and the Sheriff and the prison officials went away
without a word.

'Thanks, Albert,' said Sid in utter relief.

'Why didn't you ask me before?' I said.

'I got flummoxed,' he replied.

In the evening I sat down and studied all the details, and
adjusted the drop to a finer degree. When the Governor asked
confirmation of the drop to be given, Sid told him.

We duly carried out the execution next morning, took the
body down, stowed the gear, and reported to the Governor. As
we went out of the prison Sid breathed a great sigh. 'I wouldn't
have got through, except for you,' he said, and he held his
hand out with some money in it.

'What's that?' I asked.

'It's half my fee. You got me out of that scrape.'

'I don't want it,' I said.

'You've got to take it. You should have the lot, really.' And
Sid went back to Fulham, never again to be called as head
executioner. He did officiate as assistant once or twice before
his death, which came quite soon. He was the only man I ever
acted as assistant to, apart from my uncle, and shortly after
this episode I received an important letter.

It came from the Prison Commissioners. It said that it might
be necessary to nominate an assistant executioner to act in
future as executioner. 'I have been asked by the Commissioners
to enquire whether in that event you would wish your name to
be considered.' I replied immediately in the affirmative.

I realised that I had been involved in a subtle trial of
strength. I know that the Under Sheriff, who had been intently
watching the action in the execution chamber, had drawn his
own conclusions, but he could appoint executioners only for
London. No doubt he was confidentially consulted by the
Prison Commissioners. It only confirmed to me the truth I had
always known since my father used to insist on it – the Prison
Commissioners allow no human error: one hesitation, let alone
a mistake, and an executioner is out.

It was with this realisation that I drove through a bomb-
devastated London to Pentonville Prison, and walked through
the gate to conduct my first operation as head executioner.

Probably I am a perfectionist, and I could be excused for any tension I felt along the lines of my old trainer's slogan 'It's got to be right!' I was also self-conscious. As on the occasion when I would not admit to the Whitehall policeman why I wanted to go to Pentonville, I was determined this time not to give away the fact that this was my first appearance as Number One. There was a sound reason for this: I had to inspire the maximum confidence in the other participants in the drama. And 'drama' is no idle word, just as its final catastrophe is no idle act. The swift but measured course of events which leads to the humane killing of a man demands rehearsed competence and unquavering confidence from all concerned. From my experience I must include in this company the condemned man. In his mind he has rehearsed this brief last act many times. I believe that frequently he is strongly moved to perform that exit with dignity, and stride rather than shuffle. In this determination I, as executioner, have always tried to support him.

On that entry into Pentonville I think I succeeded in at least arousing no anxiety among the prison officials. I was a familiar enough person to them, so that they did not need to enquire into my form, but accepted me at my face value – a man they approved of and whom the Sheriff had appointed. When I first came into the prison I asked who my assistant was to be, and I was told 'Wade'. That made me a little apprehensive. Steve Wade, a motor dealer from Doncaster, was comparatively new to the craft. Fortunately he did not fail in any respect, and later we were to form a quite regular team: but I still think it did him no harm on that occasion to conceal from him that this was the first time I had taken full responsibility.

I reported to the Governor. Then I met Steve Wade in the room which had been set apart for us in the prison. It had a bright fire crackling, and we sipped tea and talked. After some time the engineer, or foreman of works, came in and handed me a paper with the details of the prisoner's height and weight. He kept his eyes on me, and I knew it. He was not the man who had trained me, but I reckoned he had trained a few other assistants since my time – and that included Steve Wade. Steve was looking silently at me, too.

'What will the drop be?' asked the engineer in a casual tone of voice, but badly acted.

'I haven't seen him yet,' I said. 'Six foot three will be good enough for overnight.'

'Yes,' said the engineer. 'I guessed it would be very near that, myself.'

I thought, 'You can guess. There's no can for you to carry. I'm here to work it out.' But I said nothing.

'Shall we go?' said the engineer.

Steve and I followed him to the execution chamber. Rattle of keys. Grate. Slam. Rattle. The engineer opened the box of gear. Though I could see at a glance, like a sergeant-major at kit inspection, that everything was in order, he itemised every piece of the tackle in a civil-service sort of way. I fancy he had a shrewd idea that this was my first time in the lead.

I looked at the ropes. One new, one old, according to the regulations. Habitually I preferred the old. I examined it inch by inch, from the bend round the heavy circular steel eye at the top, where it was to be pinned into the U-bolt on the chains, feeling it all the way down to the pear-shaped metal eye enclosing the noose, and paying particular attention to the profile of the warps under the wash-leather covering of the noose, where the friction of the lower metal eye could be most destructive.

I cursorily examined the new rope, and picked the old. I tested the drop to see that the trapdoors opened smoothly as the lever withdrew the bolt. I had the traps closed again and bolted them with the lever. With Steve's assistance I measured off a drop of six feet three, and fastened the rope to the chain. I checked that the sandbag had been filled to a weight slightly more than that of the prisoner, and put it on the drop with four ropes fastening it to the noose. I pushed the lever again. The bag dropped, and I left it. 'Right,' I said to the engineer. 'When can we see him.'

The prisoner had been condemned for a crime that was then rare in London. It was a gangland killing resulting from a struggle for power in the underworld between two mobs in Soho. I knew nothing about the case, since most crime was very briefly reported in the thin war-time newspapers. I was interested that this execution was not to be the more common case of the first-time offender who had killed in passion. The prisoner was a professional criminal. It may seem strange to classify a man in this way, putting him apart from such 'professional criminals' as the multiple murderers Neville Heath, John Haigh, and John Christie whom I have dealt with. But this man was a gangster who had been convicted of killing one of his own kind, not even a criminal who had killed a police officer or a civilian during the course of a robbery. In the prison cages of Great Britain he was a rare bird.

I was taken to the corridor outside the condemned cell, and I looked through the judas-hole. This could not be an ordinary occasion for me, however successfully I acted as if it was just routine. For the first time I was looking at a man who was to die at my hands, studying him technically, but only to calculate how to be most merciful to him. I was interested in his physique, which affected my calculation of the drop I should give, and in his temperament and behaviour, which could give me an indication of how I could expect him to act next morning. Through the peep-hole I saw the prisoner close to the table in the centre of the cell.

He was talking to the prison officers who were his permanent escort. He was smiling. I noticed that he was handsome and, in spite of the prison drab he was wearing, he was somehow smart. I thought, 'He seems composed. He should give no trouble in the morning.' But this did not really make any difference to my preparations. Always I have made plans for the worst to happen, and briefed my assistant and the prison officers for the worst. Trouble was rare, and rarer still from an unsuspected source. But it did happen sometimes, and I was the calmer for being prepared.

Wade and I had tea in our room. Then I gave myself time to come to a final conclusion on the drop I should administer. I went over the next morning's routine with Steve, making him repeat it so that I was certain it came almost automatically to him. For the one thing I did not want on that scaffold next morning was the necessity to speak instructions to my assistant. This job had to go in perfect rhythm, with full understanding all round, as silently and as well timed as a team of commandos hi-jacking a German general from his own HQ. That is craftsmanship.

We went to bed early. In my mind I repeatedly went through every detail of the drill to be observed. Then I went to sleep, and I did not dream. I was roused by a warder at six thirty. Steve and I walked to the execution chamber and drew up the sandbag. We detached it from the noose and lowered it into the pit, disposing it in a corner. An empty stretcher was already in position, to one side on the floor of the pit. Steve detached the trapdoors from the rubber-clad springs which held them rigidly vertical, and stood on a stool to push them up flat. In the execution chamber above, I slid the bolt and plugged in the cotter pin and its guard at the base of the lever to act as a safety catch. Steve came up the side stairs by the wall, which was the communication between the pit and the chamber. With a ladder against the upper beam, and Steve holding the tape-measure, I re-adjusted the fall of the rope to the last half-inch, allowing for my last calculation and the overnight stretch of the rope. All this time we spoke hardly at all, and then only in whispers. We were next door to the condemned cell.

I made a final, official, measurement of the length of the drop and made a note of it. The noose was lying on the trap doors. I coiled the spare rope until the noose was at shoulder height. I held the coil where I wanted it, above the noose, and Steve put a light piece of twine around the coil and round the hanging rope. He passed the ends of the twine to me and I tied it, securing the loops to the rope. The rope then fell straight to the noose, but any sharp strain like the fall of a body would break the twine and let it pay out fast for the length of the drop.

I looked round the green-painted execution chamber to check that everything was in order. I picked up a stray thread of twine from where it had fallen on the traps. With a piece of chalk I re-lined the T-mark under the noose on the front drop where the prisoner's toes were to be aligned, the arches of the feet directly over the crack in the doors. I slightly shifted the cross-planks on either side of the T, and I made one final adjustment. I crossed to the lever and released a split pin that held the cotter pin fast, and I eased out the cotter pin for half its length, so that, while still resisting an untimely push, the end of it was flush with the side of the lever. In action, even the time it took to withdraw an extra half-inch was important to me.

'Right,' I said. 'Breakfast.' And we went away for bacon and eggs.

At five minutes to nine we were given the signal that the Sheriff had gone to the Governor's office. Wade and I walked across the prison yard with an officer who led us up to the corridor outside the condemned cell. I think the next minutes of waiting were the worst, not only then but on every occasion. It is impossible not to feel apprehension and even fear at the prospect of the responsibility of the moment, but with me the frailty passed as soon as there was action. At half a minute to nine a small group came down the corridor. There was the Sheriff, the Governor, the doctor and some senior prison officers. I suddenly had a strange realisation. I was the youngest man there, and the eyes of everyone were on me. The party paused at the next door to that of the condemned cell, the door of the execution chamber. A finger was raised and they passed in. The chief opened the door of the cell and I went forward with a strap in my hand.

The prisoner was standing, facing me, smiling. In his civilian clothes he looked as smart as I had already registered him. In my civilian clothes, amid all those uniforms, we might have been meeting for a chat in a club in Leicester Square – but who would have foreseen a robed priest in the room? I quickly strapped his wrists and said 'Follow me.'

The door in the side wall of the cell had been opened as I came in, and I walked through it into the execution chamber. He followed me, walking seven paces with the noose straight ahead of him, and the escorting officers mounting the cross-planks gently stopped him as he stood on the T. I had turned in time to face him. Eye to eye, that last look. Wade was stooping behind him, swiftly fastening the ankle strap. I pulled from my breast pocket the white cap, folded as carefully as a parachute, and drew it down over his head. 'Cheerio,' he said. I reached for the noose, pulled it down over the cap, tightened it to my right, pulled a rubber washer along the rope to hold it, and darted to my left, crouching towards the cotter pin at the base of the lever. I was in the position of a sprinter at the start of a race as I went over the cross-plank, pulled the pin with one hand, and pushed the lever with the other, instinctively looking back as I did so. There was a snap as the falling doors were bitten and held by the rubber clips, and the rope stood straight and still. The broken twine spooned down in a falling leaf, passed through a little eddy of dust, and floated into the pit.

I went to the side of the scaffold and walked down into the pit. I undid the prisoner's shirt for the stethoscope, and the doctor followed me. I came up again, and waited. The doctor came back to the scaffold. 'Everything is all right,' he said. It was a curious way for a doctor to pronounce death. I suppose his intention was to reassure the Governor, and possibly me.

We all left the execution chamber. Soon the Governor sent for me. 'I have seen your uncle work on many occasions,' he said. 'He is a very good man indeed. Never has he been any quicker than you have been this morning.'

At ten o'clock Wade and I returned to the execution cham-

ber. He went down into the pit and, kneeling on the scaffold
floor, I complied with a strange requirement. By regulation, I
had to measure from the heels of the hanging man to the level
of the scaffold from which he had dropped. This measurement
was longer than the drop I had given him. The extra length
was made up by the stretch of the man's body after death.
Since he was suspended from the jawbone, and the cervical
cord was broken, this stretch could only come from the flesh of
the neck. He had been hanging for an hour, and the stretch was
considerable.

This was the last ignominy in hanging, a relic from the time
when bodies were exposed on the gibbet. I had no heart for it, I
saw no reason for it, nor for the careful logging in registers of
the dimension of the distortion of the body. I was glad when,
years later, the Royal Commission's recommendation was accepted and the body was taken down immediately after death.

I put the tape-measure away, and went below. I stared at the
flesh I had stilled. I had further duties to perform, but no
longer as executioner. I had been nearest to this man in death,
and I prepared him for burial. As he hung, I stripped him.
Piece by piece I removed his clothes. It was not callous, but the
best rough dignity I could give him, as he swung to the touch,
still hooded in the noose. He yielded his garments without the
resistance of limbs. If it had been in a prison outside London, I
should have left him his shirt for a shroud, and put him in his
coffin. In London there was always a post-mortem, and he had
to be stripped entirely and placed on a mortuary stretcher. But
in common courtesy I tied his empty shirt around his hips.

Wade had fixed the tackle above. I passed a rope under the
armpits of my charge, and the body was hauled up a few feet.
Standing on the scaffold, with the body now drooping, I removed the noose and the cap, and took his head between my
hands, inclining it from side to side to assure myself that the
break had been clean. Then I went below, and Wade lowered
the rope. A dead man, being taken down from execution, is a
uniquely broken body whether he is a criminal or Christ, and I
received this flesh, leaning helplessly into my arms, with the
linen round the loins, gently with the reverence I thought due
to the shell of any man who has sinned and suffered.

5

Executioner at War

My sister Ivy was working at the emergency hospital at Winwick, near Warrington, in Lancashire when the lads came home from Dunkirk. For a considerable time she was on duty in the operating theatre for eighteen hours a day. She was, I know, a great healing influence in the wards. She collapsed and died of exhaustion. All she left was her autograph book. I have it now, with messages and home-made rhymes from men in the South Lancashires, the Green Howards, the Gordon Highlanders, the Royal Artillery, the Royal Air Force and the Royal Northumberland Fusiliers. There were many messages from Frenchmen and Belgians whom we had brought over wounded from the great German advance: '*Je souhaite que le courage des femmes d' Angleterre soit récompensé par une rapide victoire sur l'envahisseur,*' wrote a boy called Raymond: 'My wish is that the courage of the women of England will be rewarded by a speedy victory over the invader.' There was the lightheartedness of youth: a soldier wrote 'Always remember, Ivy, when you make a bed, make it properly – you may have to share it some day. Lawrence G., Royal Horse Artillery, 23.7.40.' To which my sister had later added a postcript: 'Some hopes you have, Lawrence. I.P., 26.7.40.' But another lad echoed the awareness of death which was not uncommon among the entries in this book:

> Every bullet finds its billet,
> Some bullets more than one.
> God, perhaps I killed a mother
> When I killed a mother's son.
> Jim Brady, Spr, RE 17.6.40 BEF Glasgow C3.

My mother went soon afterwards. She had always been very good to me and she had welcomed Anne when I brought her home. There was none of the jealousy that sometimes happens in these circumstances, indeed I think that Anne eased her loneliness. For, though she had come back from Yorkshire to live among her own people, they did not bother very much, friendly soul though she was, and often bereaved, as her fate was to make her. She was unassuming, she had never interfered with me in the craft I had chosen against all her inclinations. And just as she was quietly undemanding in life, she saw that she gave me no trouble in dying. She never said she was ill, and slipped away quite suddenly.

I stayed on in the house by myself. Anne was busy nursing. One evening, when she had missed me for several days, she came to the house and found me ill with influenza. I asked her to marry me. We had been courting for years, but I had always had the final hesitation before asking a woman to share my life, because of what that life entailed. I knew that she must have been aware for a very long time of what I did in the intervals when I told her 'I shan't be seeing you for a couple of days.' A northern mill town is as close as a village, and the name Pierrepoint is not a common one to hide under. But I never discussed with her the fact that I was an executioner, never named or described an execution, and did, in fact, go into marriage without mentioning the subject. My mother and I had behaved as though that side of my life did not exist. I do not know now how long I expected such an attitude of wilful blindness to continue without tainting the relationship of Anne and myself as full partners, and I owe it to Anne that it was smoothly resolved.

Anne left the general hospital and went to a children's nursery so that her working hours would correspond better with mine. I had been a careful man, almost a non-drinker, not extravagant in any way but not shirking family responsibilities – and I had saved just about a hundred pounds through my working life by the time I got married at thirty-eight. That was the sort of margin we had had to live on in Lancashire. I spent it all on the wedding. We were married at St. Wilfrid's Church, Newton Heath, on the 29th of August 1943 and we gave a party for two hundred guests at the Mowbray Conservative Club. There was a dance band and a stage show. Somebody did a sketch called *Randall In The Home Guard*, and somebody else sang *The Rose of Tralee*, which was intended to be a solo until I got my voice round it too. At the end they all sang *God Save The King,* and Anne and I went off to Blackpool.

When we came home to settle into my old house in Newton Heath there was a letter awaiting me offering an engagement at Wandsworth. I accepted. I left the letter around. Anne would not read it, and on the day before I left I said I would be away for a night and would take a clean shirt with me. I went to London, came back, kissed her, and said nothing. Anne said nothing either. A few weeks later I had a telegram from the Home Office summoning me to London. Only when I got to Whitehall was I told that two saboteurs were to be executed in Gibraltar, and that if I would accept the engagement I would be flown out that night. Security forbade that I should mention my journey, and I was forced to wire to Anne that I should be away for a few days. When I came back I told her where I had been, what I had done, and what my profession had been for a dozen years.

'You knew it all along, didn't you?' I asked.

'I knew, but I didn't ask,' she said.

'Thank you for not asking.'

'I wanted it to be you who told me.'

'I didn't want to tell you. I wanted to keep you out of it. I wanted to save you from all that goes with it.'

Then she told me for the first time about all the Nosy Parkers who had plagued and harried her since first we had started courting.

It was never going to be possible to 'save her from all that goes with it'. At that time I had no notion at all of the impact which public attention was going to exert on our lives: the understandable curiosity, the giggling, morbid quizzing, the anonymous letters which we each tried to intercept before the other could read them. I can only say that Anne has sailed through every storm as unaffected as a queen of the seas. She has still never asked a question. I have still never discussed my experiences with her. We have lived in mutual respect, as well as love.

For the wartime flight to Gibraltar we had first to travel by train to an aerodrome near Bristol, and from there we took off for Lisbon. It was at a time of heavy air raids, and dog-fighting in the Channel, and we flew on a big half-circle out to sea. When we came down at Lisbon I was astonished to see the airfield ringed with enemy aeroplanes, white Italian aircraft and

German machines carrying the swastika. As a neutral airport, Lisbon accepted all comers. But there was a severe airport discipline. By every aircraft there was an armed Portuguese soldier on guard, and his orders were not to leave that post on any account, presumably, among other considerations, to prevent sabotage of the aircraft by agents of enemy powers. The civilian officer commanding the aerodrome was a Briton who had married a Portuguese girl, and I was talking to him while I waited. 'You should have been here a couple of hours ago,' he said, 'you've missed a wonderful sight. You see that plane over there?' and he pointed to a German machine showing the swastika. 'The pilot was ready to leave, he went to his plane to take off, and just as he was going to climb into the aircraft he realised he had forgotten something. So he ordered the Portuguese soldier guarding the plane to go back to the central building and get it. The soldier said he was under orders not to leave his post, and refused to go. So the German spat in his face. So the Portuguese raised his rifle and shot him dead outside his plane.'

We took off from Lisbon. My pilot was Captain Gordon Bennett, who had recently flown Mrs. Winston Churchill out to Casablanca to join her husband after the conference with President Roosevelt. He invited me to the cockpit. 'We have to fly a certain distance from the Spanish coast,' he said, 'because although they are neutral they are on Hitler's side. If we go within their limits they will fire at us. I'll just show you.' And he brought the aircraft in over the sea towards the Spanish coast. Suddenly there were flashes bursting all around us. 'It's anti-aircraft fire!' I said. 'Ah,' he said, 'It's probably only warning rockets.' But he veered out to sea, just the same.

On the flight back through Lisbon our security had to be even tighter than on the outward journey. All aircraft departures from Lisbon were openly logged by the Germans, who had the communications apparatus to radio to air commanders in France the details of any aircraft which they decided would be best shot down. It was in this way that the actor Leslie Howard, travelling in a British civil aircraft, was killed shortly after my flight. It has been said that he was suspected by the Germans of being an intelligence agent. Lisbon was also the port of departure for a number of German spies who flew openly to England, generally with the identity papers of refugees, and indeed some of the spies who came to Britain in this way and were caught eventually had to face me. I think I dealt with every man sentenced to death under the Treachery Act, which was concerned with active spying within Great Britain, as well as the two men who were executed under the Treason Act – John Amery and William Joyce, 'Lord Haw Haw' – who were convicted for working for the enemy abroad, principally through radio broadcasts. The number of spies caught in the country during the war was quite small. The total was sixteen, four of them Britons, and all were hanged except a Portuguese, whose death sentence was commuted. When they were convicted by the civil courts they were not shot. I had a frustrating experience of the general belief that they *were* shot when I was travelling back from London after hanging two spies at Wandsworth in a double execution. I took a train from Euston with my assistant, Steve Wade, to return to the north, and two rather pompous gentlemen in the same carriage were commenting on the announcement in the afternoon newspaper that two spies had been executed at Wandsworth. 'Wandsworth!' said one. 'Impossible! They were shot in the Tower. They are always shot in the Tower. I was serving in the last war, and I know.' He seemed very positive. 'Am I not right?' he said to Steve Wade. 'I don't know, I wasn't in the last war,' said Steve, dodging the issue – but he had served, in fact. The man insisted on his argument at intervals throughout the journey. 'Wandsworth will be denied in the evening editions,' he said. 'They were shot at the Tower.' As we came to the end of the journey, Steve muttered to me 'Why don't you give him your card, Albert?' I should like to have done so, apart from the security considerations, but I have never had a visiting card made which gave any indication of my business, and never would. Berry, I believe, had printed cards which read: *James Berry, Executioner, Bradford, Yorkshire* and his notepaper was headed *The Executioner's Office*.

It was a German spy, parachuted into England at the height of the blitz, who gave me my toughest session on the scaffold during all my career as executioner. I shall call him Otto Schmidt. No details of his activities were published at the time of his conviction. But he had, in fact, been dropped from a Dornier near the village of London Colney in Hertfordshire. He holed up in a spinney for two days during which he used a light-weight trowel to dig a deep hole and bury his parachute, flying-suit, and swastika-marked helmet. The instant he took these off he became a spy. For underneath them he wore a British-made overcoat and a civilian suit, and had a loaded pistol, and six hundred pounds in English money along with a thousand American dollars. He had food in watertight packages, and a powerful portable radio set packed in two leather cases. He buried these, marking a nearby tree with his initials so that he could return to the spot, and on his second dusk after the drop ventured abroad to sniff the country.

He had been walking down the country lane for only a quarter of an hour when a lorry pulled up beside him and the driver asked him for directions – all the local signposts having been removed in wartime. The one thing Schmidt knew was his whereabouts, because he had had a long time to study his detailed maps. But he gave a surly answer, and that was his undoing. The lorry driver stopped a policeman who came cycling along the lane, checked his location, and mentioned that the surly so-and-so up the road had refused to help him. The policeman, Constable Alec Scott, thought it was odd to refuse help to a man in the twilight, and bicycled after Schmidt. His answers were unsatisfactory, and he was arrested after covering less than a mile of road in England. His four-day trial at the Central Criminal Court was held entirely in camera, for it was not intended that the Germans should know of his capture. He was sentenced to death.

I went to Wandsworth and made the usual preparations. My first sight of Schmidt was as he strode the prison exercise yard between two burly prison officers. His prison medical card gave me his height as six feet two inches and his weight as fifteen stone four pounds. In his grey prison suit, tied slackly with short tapes instead of buttons, I could see that he was a very strongly-built man. Above his bull neck his lips were shut in a grim line, and he was not trying to make any sort of conversation.

I was outside his cell on time next morning, and when the door swung open I got my first shock. Schmidt should have been sitting at the table with his back to me. It is usually arranged that the condemned man should be in this position, so that in three quick strides I can be behind him, tapping him on the shoulder and taking his arms to pinion his wrists behind his back as he stands up.

But Schmidt was standing at the far side of the table, glowering at the open door. I had to walk all round the table to reach him. His face was working angrily. His eyes were staring, very blue and dangerous. His big fists were clenched. Before I could reach him he heaved away the nearest prison officer and dived like a bullock at the stone wall. His head cracked against the masonry.

My first impression was quite irrelevant. It was the flurry of robes of the Catholic priest as he tried to get out of the way of the battle which followed. It may have been Schmidt's intention to stun himself so that he was hanged unconscious. I do not know. He stunned himself only for a moment. He lay like a log on the floor, then raised himself and shook his head. The two death-cell officers dived on top of him. He clawed and kicked them away. Two more officers rushed in from the corridor. There were five bodies thrashing on the floor, and one of the men in blue was an accomplished judo expert.

Somebody gasped 'Get your straps on him, Albert, for God's sake!' I was circling round the mêlée, waiting my chance to do this. I managed to engage one of his wrists. Then I brought the strap round the other. Officers were sitting on his legs and then they began to drag him to his feet. I turned to go through the cell into the execution chamber. It was not the sort of occasion when I would say sympathetically 'Follow me, lad. It will be all right.'

Suddenly there was a shout from behind me: 'Albert! Albert! Come back!' I turned and saw that Schmidt's arms were free and it was a free-for-all again. With his hands behind him he had strained on the pinioning strap around his wrists and split it from eye-hole to eye-hole. I would not have thought such strength was possible. I went back and got into the fray. Schmidt fought me, fought everybody. I managed to get a grip on the strap. Normally I had never put on the pinion very tight: I had found it was psychologically wrong to make the prisoner feel constricted, or angry because a buckle was nipping into his flesh, and that generally only the suggestion of restraint was enough, while for practical purposes the arms could not fly outwards anyway. This time I had no choice. I had to get the strap to fasten on an inside hole. I was strong, and I dug my knee into his back and pulled until the strap was secure in a second hole. Once more I started towards the scaffold.

The Sheriff and the Governor and their party had been watching this struggle from the execution chamber. Schmidt was now brought to the scaffold. A strap was quickly fastened round his ankles, the cap and noose were adjusted, and still he fought for life. Just as I was crossing to the lever, he jumped with bound feet. The drop opened, and he plunged down, and I saw with horror that the noose was slipping. It would have come right over his head had it not caught roughly at a point halfway up the hood – it had in fact been stopped on his upper lip by the projection of his nose – and the body jerked down, then became absolutely still apart from the swinging of the rope. I went down into the pit with the prison medical officer. He examined the body and said to me: 'A clean death. Instantaneous.' He sounded surprised, and I did not blame him. I was surprised myself, and very relieved. On my next visit to Wandsworth the Governor told me that the severance of the spinal cord had been perfect.

But the vexing thing to me was the fact that the noose had slipped. When it had been tightened round the neck a washer consisting of a plain round rubber ring had been moved up to it, and it was clear that this had not held the noose tight. In the arc of the man's upward jump he had gone higher than the hanging noose, there had been a droop in the slack of the rope, the washer had run down to the bottom of the loop under gravity, and the noose had consequently opened. This had been an eventuality which my Uncle Tom had anticipated many years previously, and he had in fact prepared an alternative stop. This was a rubber claw grip – a sort of thick ring with cut rubber spikes facing inwards from the circumference of the ring – which gripped the rope wherever it was placed and did not slip. Uncle Tom made a template of the shape he had thought out, and sent it to the Home Office with suggestions for its use. The design was accepted, models of the claw grip were made, and it became standard equipment on every hangman's rope.

My Uncle Tom was now walking about with a stick, but he would not retire, even though he was in his mid-seventies and had difficulty getting about. 'I'll do this job as long as I can walk,' he said. He could not help noticing, however, that more and more executions were being allotted to me rather than to him. He did not hold this against me, particularly as I had secured for him a higher fee for the executions that did come to him. My first action on being nominated a head executioner was to campaign for an increase in the payment. In a letter to the Home Office I said that I was being given the same fee as

my father had received forty years before. The most positive
outcome of this persuasion was that the fee for assistant executioners was raised from three guineas to five guineas an
execution. The man responsible for the payment of the executioner was the County Sheriff, whom the Home Office could
only advise, since the fee finally depended on his generosity.
On average through the country, however, the notional fee did
rise from ten to fifteen pounds – though this was never admitted
to the Royal Commission ten years later, where it was said in
evidence that an executioner 'had a right' to ten or eleven
pounds. It is a fee that I still have genuine shame in mentioning.

After one wartime execution at Wandsworth my assistant,
Steve Wade, said to me 'Albert, we have got to go and see the
post-mortem on this fellow.' 'Who says so?' I asked – it was a
common belief that executioners were compelled to go to the
post-mortems, but this was quite untrue, and I had never been.
'Dr. Keith Simpson says so,' Steve told me. 'He wants us to go
and see it.' I took a lot of convincing that Dr. Keith Simpson,
the famous pathologist who was then doing many London
post-mortems on behalf of the C.I.D., had really requested our
presence, but finally I agreed to go. My instinct was quite right,
for there was no requirement at all to go, and Steve Wade had
thought up the whole idea himself, but I did not discover this
until it was too late.

I was not willing to go at all. It would be accurate enough to
say that I was scared to death. Steve Wade led the way to the
mortuary, very confidently, went inside, and beckoned me in. I
had no taste for this butchery at all, and Steve advanced,
making smooth explanations as he went, towards the principal
tableau in the building. I saw a corpse on a slab, stark naked,
and a blonde girl sitting by the side of him taking notes on a
typewriter at the dictation of the man who was obviously Dr.
Simpson. I was more shocked at seeing the girl than the body
of the man. Steve introduced us, and we were welcomed, and
Dr. Simpson sawed round the top of the skull of the executed
man and took off his cranium. I was beginning to get interested
by this time, and when Dr. Simpson started cutting down, I
began to ask questions. I had always been taught that the
higher the severance of the vertebrae in the neck occurred, the
quicker and cleaner was the execution. The best separation, I
had learned, was between the second and third cervical vertebrae. I asked Dr. Simpson to explain this, and to point out the

vertebrae, which he very kindly did. I then asked a number of other questions, because I was discovering, to my great surprise, that anatomy was a fascinating subject – I have followed it up quite keenly since that first session. All went well at the time, but the blonde secretary wrote a book about her job long afterwards, and although she told a good story, she had not got the details or personalities right about this incident a dozen years previously. Her name was Molly Lefebure, and in her book *Evidence For The Crown* she wrote: 'We were doing a post-mortem on a murderer, a young Burmese who had kicked his wife to death. Suddenly the mortuary door opened and in came a young man in a blue suit, who stepped in briskly, gave us a cheerful smile, and said "Good morning, Dr. Simpson. If you don't mind I'd like to take a look at my handiwork." We stared at him with some astonishment, whereupon he introduced himself as Albert Pierrepoint, who had just taken over the job of Public Executioner from his uncle, Tom Pierrepoint. . . .'

It may seem over-fastidious to correct this story, but anything less brisk and cheerful than my entry into that mortuary would be hard to imagine, and I have never referred to a hanged man as 'my handiwork'. The important thing to me is that I have never in my career introduced myself to anyone as the executioner, and I should not like to have this fixed principle of mine cast in doubt by an inaccurate account.

As the war went on, and invasion forces built up inside Britain, the Americans became an increasing part of our population, and when a death sentence was imposed by an American court martial we were called upon to execute it. The American military prison was at Shepton Mallet, and they were allowed most of the American customs except the actual method of execution: no standard drop, no hangman's knot, but a variable drop on a modern noose suspended from a British gallows and designed to impart instantaneous death.

The timing of the execution was American-style. It was generally carried out at about one o'clock in the morning. Another custom which was strange to me was the practice of laying on a mighty feast before the execution. We were eating badly in this country at that time, but at an American execution you could be sure of the best running buffet and unlimited canned beer. The part of the routine which I found it hardest to acclimatise myself to was the, to me, sickening interval between my introduction to the prisoner and his death. Under British custom I was working to the sort of timing where the drop fell between eight and twenty seconds after I had entered the condemned cell. Under the American system, after I had pinioned the prisoner, he had to stand on the drop for perhaps six minutes while his charge sheet was read out, sentence spelt out, he was asked if he had anything to say . . . and after that I was instructed to get on with the job.

Even a few seconds can be a long time when a man is waiting to die. On my first execution in Shepton Mallet, long before the drop fell, the officer of the escorting party surrounding the scaffold was flat on the floor in collapse. Afterwards, at the continuation of the feast, a soldier said to me of the fainting officer: 'Just imagine a man like that leading you into battle!' I did not think his scorn was justified. A man can fight like a hero, and still be unable to face the death of a comrade in cold blood.

At the end of the war there came the treason trials, and spaced between the execution of the sentences passed at these tribunals I was called to Germany to hang the so-called Beasts of Belsen. The name today has a whiff of the absurd extravagance of a horror comic. Nobody thought so then. The staff of Belsen, who were identified at their trial as having previously served at other extermination camps, had in their charge, on the day they fled from the advancing British troops, forty thousand live detainees and the unburied corpses of thirteen thousand more who had died too recently for them to be buried. Once the British took over, another thirteen thousand were to die from the effects of starvation, beatings and disease. How many people had been liquidated there could never be stated as a firm total. The place had been for years a death-camp where the average life of an internee was twelve days. In 1945 people did feel emotional about that.

Unfortunately for my personal life, that emotion had a painful backlash on me. The announcement that I was to hang the convicted staff of Belsen was made from Field Marshal Montgomery's headquarters in Germany with far fuller publicity than had ever been officially given to executions at home. Because of what people felt about Belsen, and because they saw me as, in a way, their own stand-in avenger, not only for the wrongs of the SS but for all their grief at the deaths in this long war, I became a far too familiar public figure, and in private far too troubled. I had more reporters and photographers camped on my doorstep than a heavily suspected murderer before he is arrested. I was chased to my aircraft in the middle of the Northolt airfield by a pack of newspapermen who were to me about as unwelcome as a lynch mob. 'He should avoid attracting public attention . . . He should clearly understand that his conduct and general behaviour must be respectable and discreet . . . ' That was how I had been trained to be an executioner, and I could see it all going by the board.

I landed at Buckeburg at five o'clock on a December afternoon. I was met by a major and his driver in an old jeep. We had a forty-minute run through dark, devastated country to the story-book Pied Piper town of Hameln. In the back seat of the jeep I was freezing from the wind and drenched with the rain. Almost immediately after my arrival there was a conference with British Army officials, some of whom had been seconded from H.M. Prison Service. The discussions were lengthy, for I was to conduct the execution of thirteen persons in one day. Eleven were from Belsen, and two others had been sentenced to death by the War Crimes Commission. This was a revolutionary total in modern British criminological history, and the operation demanded careful planning. It was agreed that arrangements should be left entirely in my hands. I had thirty-two hours in which to complete my preparations.

I rose early on the morning of December 12th and looked out of the window at a cold, damp prospect. 'Brr! There must be a hanging today!' I remembered the old Yorkshire children's saying that I had used on the morning when we had moved house into Lancashire thirty years ago. I found my way to the prison and knocked on the gate. A German prison officer, very roughly dressed, asked me my business with impressive alacrity. I began to explain, but he could not understand English. I was rescued by a Regimental Sergeant Major in the Control Commission for Germany, as smart as paint in his freshly-pressed uniform. I took to R.S.M. O'Neil at once. He spoke fluent German, and in a few minutes he was escorting me around the prison. 'I've never seen an execution,' he told me cheerfully, 'but I'm going to see one now, because I am to be your assistant.' I was rather startled at being given a novice, but, as it turned out, I could not have hoped for a better man. Eventually he was to be my assistant at about two hundred executions of war criminals in Germany.

Inside Hameln Gaol on this day the Royal Engineers had just finished building the execution chamber, at the end of one of the wings. It lay on the right hand side of a long corridor adjoining the condemned cells, which were the smallest cells I have ever seen human beings confined in.

I got my first glimpse of the Belsen prisoners, all peering silently through the bars of their cell doors, as I walked down this corridor. The first one I saw was Josef Kramer, the former commandant. I recognised him at once.

As I went on down this dark corridor I could hear shovelling and scraping in the prison yard outside. It was a jarring and nerve-wracking noise in what would otherwise have been dead silence. I looked through a window and saw a gang of work-men busily digging thirteen graves for the following morning. There was no doubt that the condemned prisoners could also hear this sound. I complained about this to a prison official, but was told that nothing could be done to stop it. 'The graves have to be dug and the ground is frozen. It's full of pebbles and flints, and we must do the job today to be ready in time.'

I went on to test the gallows. We carried out a number of drops which convinced me that it was satisfactory. I walked back down the corridor, and the thirteen Belsen faces were still pressed close to the bars, watching me. Never in my experience have I seen a more pitiable crowd of condemned prisoners. I knew their crimes were monstrous, but I could not help feeling sorry for them. When I mentioned this to some young British soldiers who were present they said, 'If you had been in Belsen under this lot, you wouldn't be able to feel sorry for them.'

After lunch I faced a job I had never had to do before as an executioner. I had to supervise the weighing and measuring of the condemned thirteen, in order to work out my drops. In Britain this was normally done by prison officers before I arrived on the scene. At the far end of the corridor, with the faces always staring at us, we set up some scales and a height measure which we had taken from the prison hospital. Six German prison officers on the death watch stood by to assist us. 'Guards, close all inspection holes!' snapped R.S.M. O'Neil, and the officers slammed hinged, oblong doors over the small inspection grills. 'Guards, bring Josef Kramer,' ordered the R.S.M.

Kramer was in the farthest cell, and when the door was unlocked he came out stiffly and began to walk down the corri-

dor. His pace was slow, and I looked for a long time at the
original 'Beast of Belsen'. In cartoons he had often been de-
picted as half-man, half-gorilla. He was certainly an animal of
a man with a massive bone structure. His hair was closely
cropped. He had a square chin and a hard mouth. His small
dark eyes were set close together under very hairy eyebrows. He
had a broad nose with wide nostrils and his ears were set so
flat to his head that from a distance he appeared to have none.
It was clear that the months in prison had reduced his frame
considerably.

O'Neil asked him in German 'Are you Josef Kramer?' and
the man said 'Yes.' 'Age?' 'Thirty-nine.' This was immediately
translated to me. 'Religion?' I was busy making a note about
his physique, and I always regretted that I did not ask for a
translation of how he answered that question. 'Step on the
scales,' said R.S.M. O'Neil.

Kramer hesitated. Nobody said a word, but waited. He was
not prodded with a gun barrel, nor clubbed, nor whipped on to
the scales, nor casually shot down out of irritation. At his trial
a survivor from Belsen had given evidence that, on the day
before the British arrived, he and two others had casually shot
with Schmeisser guns out of the kitchen window at a group of
prisoners and killed twenty-two. Kramer stepped on to the
scales, had his height taken, and was sent back to his cell.

'Bring Fritz Klein,' ordered R.S.M. O'Neil. I was interested,
excusably I think, in his appearance, because in a long career
this was the first doctor I had ever met who had been convicted
of murder. Dr. Fritz Klein, who had graduated with Kramer
from Auschwitz, had made the daily morning inspection of the
naked prisoners shivering in the camp square, to decide who
should be sent to the brothels and who should be sent to the
gas-chamber that day and who should be allocated another
day's work. The naked victims chosen for the gas-chamber were
then loaded, three hundred at a time, into tipper-type lorries
which were driven to the gas-chamber chute. The trucks were
up-ended and the bodies sent sprawling down the chute into the
gas-chamber. Deliveries were continued until the day's quota of
three thousand human beings was fulfilled. Gassing and
cremation followed. Kramer, in his defence had said that there
could not have been a gas-chamber in the camp or he would
have known about it. Later he said that if there was a gas-
chamber he had taken no part in selecting the victims. Dr.

Klein, who had also killed prisoners by hypodermic injections but, the day before the British arrived, suddenly appeared with a Red Cross armlet saying that the sick 'must be very well treated', declared in his defence, 'I realise that I am responsible for killing thousands, but one cannot protest if one is in the Army.' This man, fifty-five years old, thin in appearance and matter-of-fact in his manner, now came walking briskly down the corridor and efficiently complied with the formalities.

At last we finished noting the details of the ten men, and R.S.M. O'Neil ordered 'Bring out Irma Grese'. She walked out of her cell and came towards us laughing. She seemed as bonny a girl as one could ever wish to meet. She answered O'Neil's questions, but when he asked her age she paused and smiled. I found that we were both smiling with her, as if we realised the conventional embarrassment of a woman revealing her age. Eventually she said, 'Twenty-one,' which we knew to be correct. This blonde girl of twenty-one, who habitually carried a riding whip to lash prisoners to death, had, it was stated by one of her fellow-guards in the camp, been responsible for at least thirty deaths a day. O'Neil asked her to step on to the scales. 'Schnell!' she said – 'Quick, get it over.'

Elisabeth Volkenrath was called. She, too, had made the selections for the gas-chambers. Apart from that, her general behaviour to the prisoners had made her, survivors said, the 'worst-hated woman in the camp'. I reflected that if she could top Irma Grese she must have been formidable. She was a good-looking woman. She did not flash the smile that Irma Grese had given, but she seemed steady, although nervous. She was followed by Juana Bormann, 'the woman with the dogs', who had habitually set her wolfhounds on prisoners to tear them to pieces. She limped down the corridor looking old and haggard. She was forty-two years old, only a little over five feet high, and she had the weight of a child, a hundred and one pounds. She was trembling as we put her on the scale. In German she said, 'I have my feelings.'

With the bundled records under my arm, I went back to my room and spent the next two hours working out the length of drop that would be required for each of the condemned persons. It was not a simple task, for I had to allow for the adjustment of the drop after each execution, and this controlled to some extent the order in which I took the prisoners. I was very anxious not to confuse any of the drops. It would have been

easy, in this unprecedented multiple execution, to have called
for the condemned in the wrong order. But, however it complicated the operation, I had come to the decision that I must take
the women first. The condemned cells were so close to the
scaffold that the prisoners could not but hear the repeated
sounds of the drop. I did not wish to subject the women for too
long to this. I determined to carry out the execution of the
women, singly, at the start, and follow with double executions
for the men.

I still had to go back to the execution chamber to make the
final tests. Back past the corridor with the staring eyes. We
went through a full rehearsal, and I knew that inevitably the
condemned must know what was going on.

It was a heavy day. As we went back to the mess R.S.M.
O'Neil said, 'Albert, I have read about executions, but I never
thought there was so much work to do.' 'Yes,' I agreed, 'it is
not as easy as you read.'

I was awakened by a batman at six o'clock next morning,
Friday the 13th of December 1945. I made my way to the
prison and met O'Neil and another officer. The mandatory
witnesses began to arrive, and finally the British officer in
charge of the execution came in. He was Brigadier Paton-
Walsh, whom I had known in pre-war days as Deputy Governor of Wandsworth. With him was Miss Wilson, Deputy
Governor of Manchester, who had to attend because women
were to be hanged. At a few minutes to the hour the Brigadier
asked, 'Are you ready, Pierrepoint?' I answered, 'Yes, sir.'
'Gentlemen, follow me,' he said, and the procession started.

We climbed the stairs to the cells where the condemned were
waiting. A German officer at the door leading to the corridor
flung open the door and we filed past the row of faces and into
the execution chamber. The officers stood at attention. Brigadier Paton-Walsh stood with his wrist-watch raised. He gave
me the signal, and a sigh of released breath was audible in the
chamber. I walked into the corridor. 'Irma Grese,' I called.

The German guards quickly closed all grills on twelve of the
inspection holes and opened one door. Irma Grese stepped out.
The cell was far too small for me to go inside, and I had to pinion
her in the corridor. 'Follow me,' I said in English, and O'Neil
repeated the order in German. She walked into the execution
chamber, gazed for a moment at the officials standing round it,
then walked on to the centre of the trap, where I had made a

chalk mark. She stood on this mark very firmly, and as I placed the white cap over her head she said in her languid voice, 'Schnell.' The drop crashed down, and the doctor followed me into the pit and pronounced her dead. After twenty minutes the body was taken down and placed in a coffin ready for burial.

Within another ten minutes I had prepared the rope for Elisabeth Volkenrath, and I went into the corridor and called her name. Half an hour later I had hanged Juana Bormann. We paused for a cup of tea, and I set about adjusting the scaffold for the double executions. I called, 'Josef Kramer, Fritz Klein.' Kramer came out of his cell first. Although he had lost two stones in weight since he was captured, he was still a powerful man, and I was thankful when I had strapped his thick wrists safely behind him. I marched him to the trap and put the white cap over his face. I came back to the corridor to pinion Klein, then brought him into the execution chamber. On the trap, Klein hardly measured up to Kramer's shoulder. I adjusted the ropes and flew to the lever. This first double execution took only twenty-five seconds. But there were inevitable delays between the operations. The bodies of the two men were taken off the rope, placed in coffins and taken away at once for burial in the ground outside the condemned cells. The morning progressed slowly, but the business was over by one o'clock. However, the winter dark was already on us when R.S.M. O'Neil came to me before the last double burial and said: 'There has been a mistake – we are a coffin short for one of the men.' We wrapped the body in hessian and put it in the grave. He was the thirteenth person to be hanged on Friday the thirteenth before thirteen official witnesses, and there was no coffin for him. But at Belsen they had been buried by bulldozers, and without hessian.

In the evening I went to a mess party. The boys suggested that I should be given a memento of my visit to Germany, perhaps an engraved clock. I said I should be returning to Germany very shortly and would be proud to accept it – I have the clock now: it is a treasured possession. In the morning I flew back to London and faced the mob of the Press once more. I was to go back to Germany many times, as the only British executioner ever called on, often under difficult conditions in that post-war wilderness peopled by desperate displaced persons. Major Thompson, of the Judge Advocate General's department of the War Office, said they were putting up my name for a commendation. I said that I refused to be considered, and this was accepted, though I was glad to know later that Regimental Sergeant Major O'Neil was recognised. The war, with all its grey treachery and inhumanity, was moving into the past, except for the final showpiece of Nuremberg. When a newspaperman asked Anne what was my most vivid memory of it she replied – with absolute accuracy – that it was the knowledge that I had shaken hands with Winston Churchill. But, for so many bereaved, the war would not be over for a long time. Not only mourning, but the thought of vengeance, could not be stilled. Every Christmas, for years after that act of finality in Hameln Gaol, I received a plain envelope with a five pound note in it. On the first occasion there was a scrap of paper enclosed, with the one word BELSEN. Later there was no message. Then the gift was stopped, presumably through death. Who sent it? What person, with what emotion? Did he find peace?

6

Declaration of Independence

Early in 1946 Anne and I took over a public house, which had the curious name of Help The Poor Struggler, at Hollinwood between Oldham and Manchester. My main reason for leaving my friends in the grocery trade was that I wanted to run my own business so that I should be under no obligation when I took time off. As far as this aim was concerned, and in every other circumstance, the move was entirely successful. I proved it to myself when I found that I could take a three o'clock plane from Dublin after conducting an execution there and be opening my bar without comment at half past five.

Keeping a public house was in many respects a difficult venture for a novice, but I received unstinted helpful advice from friends in the trade. What appealed to me about the business was that it was lively. I am a social character, I always enjoyed meeting people, and the pub became a cheerful local centre. Anne proved herself an excellent hostess, perhaps a rare one, for she did not drink. From the business point of view I was also under no illusions but that the Press did much to make the pub prosperous. However much I resented their over-personal interest in me, I could not deny that they gave the pub good publicity. If the interest of any casual customers was more morbid than social, they certainly got no change from me or from my stalwart regulars. I never mentioned my job as executioner in the bar – I was better known, in fact, for doing conjuring tricks. If the matter was raised meaningfully in conversation, I ignored it and changed the subject. I certainly made no jokes about it, as was sometimes said. If casual customers tried to pump the regulars, they got a dusty answer. I have often heard, from behind the bar, members of my 'home team' say to a stranger in a corner, 'We don't talk about that in here. The Guv'nor doesn't like it.' I was very touched to have their loyalty.

Because it was a Lancashire pub, and Albert Pierrepoint was the landlord, there was naturally plenty of singing – of what the Americans call the barber-shop style, mainly ballads and the old Irish numbers. I would give a song myself whenever I could. Everyone seemed to enjoy it except when it signalled closing time. At five minutes to time my great friend Jimmy Kemp used to call, 'Come on, Albert, it's your turn now.' And I would go up on the stage and sing *Danny Boy* or *Galway Bay*. Then the pennies would begin to fly towards me, or if my customers were short they would send a few beer trays clattering in my direction. It was good for a giggle and a well-tempered method of clearing the pub.

My Uncle Tom was, of course, in his element when he could slip over and see me. He had come off the list at last, being severely disabled by arthritis, but he was still very active and always anxious to help with suggestions for rather Heath Robinson mechanical contraptions which would, he thought, make the house, or sometimes the beer, run more smoothly. But I liked to see him in the singing-room with his gill in front of him, smiling with bliss as the melody rose around him. Though he was a quiet man, slow to melt into affability, he was soon completely at home with my mob, who included a number of off-duty policemen. It was the Manchester C.I.D. in fact who christened the pub almost with the full force of the corps. On the first day I opened they all turned up in a coach. I had to make a swift adjustment and open the club-room upstairs. I found myself short of pots, so a sergeant said, 'Give us some buckets, Albert!' I sent the beer up in great white pails and they all dipped their pint pots into it. The pub went dry in the first night, and I could only open next day with extra help from the brewers, for beer was fairly rigidly rationed then. My first full stock, I always remember, was exactly one barrel of mild beer, half a barrel of bitter, and six dozen mixed bottles of beer and stout. But through my first Christmas season I sold twenty-eight barrels of beer and four hundred dozen bottles.

Not only the Manchester police were my pals. I had become very friendly with a number of the chiefs in Scotland Yard. I was having a drink one day in the Fitzroy Tavern in Charlotte Street, Soho, which was kept by my friend Charlie Allchild, when he introduced me to a young C.I.D. officer in the Mets. This officer introduced me in turn to Bob Fabian – 'Fabian of the Yard' – and we found we got on together very well. Later, in another pub a house in Manchester called The Land of Cakes, some Manchester C.I.D. lads who had been giving evidence at the Assizes introduced me to a big man, a wonderful personality, who went on to become Chief of Scotland Yard's Flying Squad. He was Wilf Daws, always known in the Force as Flaps, because of his big ears. He introduced me to Reg Spooner and Bill Chapman, and so the circle grew. Whenever I was in London I used to call in at the Yard as naturally as going home. Every time I went in, I used to think of my very first morning in London, on the day when I had to report to Pentonville for my training, and I stood by the Red Lion and gazed with such awe at this historic building.

These Scotland Yard fellows were very correct and discreet. Never once did they put a single question to me about my craft. But they would help me in practical ways whenever they could, far more readily than the Home Office. On the afternoon before the execution of Derek Bentley, when the mood of some protesting members of the public was probably at its ugliest in modern times, I had called in at the Yard and was having a cup of tea with Wilf Daws. His chauffeur, a great man six foot four high who was naturally called Tiny, came in and said, 'There's a hell of a big crowd outside Wandsworth.' 'That's where I'm going in five minutes,' I said. He assured me, 'You'll never get in. Can't you get an escort from the Home Office?' 'They wouldn't even pay for a taxi,' I said. 'Tiny, get the car out,' said Wilf Daws. And I went through the crowd outside the prison in a police car, which was probably the only safe way to do it.

Bob Fabian is a very close friend of mine to this day. I particularly enjoyed his company when he used to show me the byways of London, and make the place live as I had never known it. He knew every street and alley in Soho, and would take me round, reminiscing about all the tough times he had had there as a young policeman. He was always a very well-known personality there – the barrow boys particularly always used to give him a 'Good morning, Guv!' I was wandering about these haunts one afternoon soon after the war, before keeping an appointment at the War Office concerning a professional visit to Germany. I was walking down Charlotte Street a little after two o'clock when I saw a crowd of people looking at someone lying on the pavement. I imagined somebody had been knocked down by a car, but time was pressing and I went on to see Charlie and Annie Allchild at the Fitzroy Tavern very close by, had a quick drink with them and then left for my appointment without paying further attention to the crowd just down the street.

I arrived at the War Office, got my instructions and papers for Germany, and went to the Rubens Hotel at Victoria, then a transit hotel for officers, where they had booked me in as Lieutenant-Colonel Pierrepoint, my honorary rank. At breakfast the following morning I read in the newspaper that an innocent bystander named Alec de Antiquis had tackled a gang who were making an armed robbery in Charlotte Street and had been shot dead. I realised that he had been the focus of the crowd I had seen the previous afternoon. That same morning I flew out to Germany, and came back to London a few days later. I always telephoned Mr Fabian when I arrived in the capital, and I was told that he was at the Fitzroy Tavern, which he was using as Murder Headquarters during the enquiries into the Antiquis murder. I joined him there. I was always as discreet about his work as he was about mine, but I did gather that at that time he hadn't a clue about who he was looking for. After a drink with the Allchilds I went back to Manchester.

A fortnight later I read in the Press that three men had been arrested for the murder of Alec de Antiquis, who was the father of six children. I thought to myself, 'Good old Bob! What a wonderful job you have done.' These men were brought to trial and two of them, Jenkins and Geraghty, were sentenced to death. The third man, Rolt, was sentenced to be detained during His Majesty's pleasure. Later in the year I hanged the two condemned men at Pentonville Prison.

This particular crime, with an earlier one related to it, was later cited by the Commissioner of Police for the Metropolis as an instance supporting the deterrent value of capital punishment. In a memorandum to the Royal Commission on Capital Punishment Sir Harold Scott, the Commissioner, said:

The following note refers to the gang concerned in the murders of Captain Binney in 1944 and Alec de Antiquis in 1947:

'On 8th December, 1944, a case of shopbreaking occurred at 23, Birchin Lane, City, E.C., when jewellery to the value of £2,563 was stolen. This crime was effected by several men using a stolen motor vehicle. They stopped outside the shop, broke the window with an axe, stole jewellery displayed in the window, entered the car and drove away. The offence was witnessed by Captain Binney, who, in an effort to prevent the thieves driving way, jumped in front of the car. The driver drove at Captain Binney who was caught underneath the car and dragged for a considerable distance (over London Bridge) to Bermondsey. Captain Binney was found suffering from multiple injuries from which he later died.

'Enquiries were made by Metropolitan Police Officers in conjunction with City of London Police Officers and, although several arrests were effected, sufficient evidence was obtained to convict only two of them, viz.: Ronald Hedley (the driver of the car) and Thomas James Jenkins. Hedley was convicted of murder and sentenced to Death; Jenkins was convicted of manslaughter and sentenced to eight years' Penal Servitude. Hedley appealed against Conviction and sentence of Death but his appeal was dismissed. The Death Sentence was later respited and commuted to Penal Servitude for Life.

'On 29th April, 1947, a case of Armed Robbery occurred at 73–75 Charlotte Street, W.1. which was effected by several men using a stolen motor vehicle. The men were disturbed and, in making good their escape, one of the men shot a man named Alec de Antiquis, who made an attempt to apprehend him. As a result of enquiries, three men were arrested and charged with the Murder of de Antiquis, viz.: Charles Henry Jenkins (brother of Thomas James Jenkins, mentioned above); Christopher James Geraghty, and Terence John Peter Rolt. On 28th July, 1947, the three prisoners were convicted of Murder. Jenkins and Geraghty were sentenced to Death, whilst Rolt, on account of his age, was ordered to be detained during His Majesty's Pleasure. Subsequent appeals were dismissed and on 19th September, 1947, Jenkins and Geraghty were hanged at H.M. Prison, Pentonville.

'All the persons concerned in these two cases were associates and resided in the Bermondsey district. They had formed themselves into a gang of criminals and, as events have proved, there was no limit to the steps they would take to avoid capture. After the result of the case against Hedley and Thomas James Jenkins became known to their associates, they (the associates) again came out into the open and became actively engaged in crime. Some of them were arrested and sentenced to varying terms of imprisonment but still they continued living their life of crime. Then came the carrying out of the Death Sentence on Charles Henry Jenkins and Christopher James Geraghty. Almost immediately, the gang disbanded. They have not been seen in their usual haunts since, and as far as is known, are not engaged in criminal pursuits.'

The witnesses for the Howard League for Penal Reform commented to the Royal Commission on this case as follows:

It was suggested that the execution of Geraghty and Jenkins for the murder of Mr. de Antiquis broke up a gang which had not been deterred from crime by sentences of imprisonment. It is a facile explanation and ignores the possibility that it was the removal of the leaders that smashed the gang, and that removal for ten years might have been equally effective.

And there, for the moment, I leave the controversy on this the most thorny of all the problems involving capital punishment, the deterrent effect on professional criminals who are determined to use violence when it is deemed necessary.

I have said that the murder of Alec de Antiquis occurred on the eve of one of my visits to Germany. I was allotted very heavy work during those years of retribution immediately following the war. On one occasion I had to hang twenty-seven people in under twenty-four hours. Twice I dealt with seventeen people in a day. The condemned men included doctors who were convicted of having given lethal injections to women prisoners, and twelve men convicted of the notorious shooting in cold blood of fifty prisoners of war from the Royal Air Force and other allied air forces who had escaped from a prison camp. I even hanged two executioners who had operated in the extermination camps. These multiple executions were exhausting mentally and physically – they were not morally repugnant to me – because of the great strain I worked under. I suppose, if my professional pride had been less insistent, a slacker approach would have passed. I was not working, as in Great Britain, under the keen eyes of half a dozen permanent officials who were resolved to maintain and improve an already meticulous standard. I myself kept to that pattern out of integrity to myself and humanity to the condemned. Often I did not know what their crimes had been, although I respected the judgment of the courts. The war had done so much, bred such brutality, eroded so much of the civilisation normally alive in simple people, and although these men and women had caused, God knows, appalling casualties themselves, they too were casualties – and they were sent to await me. They were not all the devilish villains of the concentration camps – I am convinced that many of these are alive and well and living in Germany. Some were displaced persons, rootless and propertyless, malleable adolescents who had been brutalised into some banditry that had ended in murder. It was a period of summary justice, martial law, and I do not claim that there was even time or opportunity to introduce any more merciful approach. All I could extend was my own final mercy of a quick death, and that involved the incongruous strain of measurements and calculations and adjustments ending with a crude list nailed to a brick wall and the tired order: 'Bring in so-and-so.'

The Press, who did not always know everything, had loudly announced that I was to execute the eleven 'supreme' war criminals, the German leaders who were hanged at Nuremberg. I knew perfectly well that, under the dominating influence of the United States at Nuremberg, dominating from considerations of both geography and prestige, this entry was a nonstarter. But I was as discreet about the executions I was not to undertake as about those that I was asked to carry out. A sergeant of the American Army conducted the Nuremberg executions, after the prime victim, Goering, had opened the cavity of a scar in his belly to extract a capsule of poison and escape him. There were indications of clumsiness, the newspapers alleged, arising from the unalterable five-foot drop and the, to me, old-fashioned four-coiled cowboy knot, which resulted in each bloodstained rope having to be cut above the halter to remove the body, since the noose was unusable for a second time. I did not go to Nuremberg, but instead hanged at Pentonville Neville Heath, who had certainly murdered two women and probably four in the pursuit of sexual sadism – a paltry score alongside the tally attributed to the men of Nuremberg.

It was an additional part of my duties to go to the British-occupied zone of Austria to carry out executions. This mission at least led to a reform in the method of execution previously carried out there, though it also set me on the run for some drunken Russian soldiers in the 'Third Man' setting of the demolition and rubble of post-war Vienna. I had been asked to put myself at the disposal of the British Control Commission for Austria. I flew to Vienna and was met by a Major who took me to an hotel and said he would pick me up next morning. I washed and had a meal, and then, feeling fairly tired after my flight, decided merely to stand at the door of my hotel and watch this strange world of occupied Vienna go by. It was a lovely evening, I was interested in the characteristic national costume of the Austrians and sympathetic with the appalling conditions in which they still had to live, when two Russian soldiers approached, very drunk. The taller of the two walked past me, which was lucky, since he was over six feet high. The shorter stopped and said something to me. I did not understand him, so I kept quiet. He then made a grab at the double-breasted gold watch chain which I was wearing, probably very foolishly considering the time and place, across my waistcoat. At one end of the chain was my watch. At the other end was a medal I had won for football when my local Manchester team took the local league championship twenty years before. And I think I was far more concerned about the medal than the watch.

I stepped smartly back. He missed the medal, grabbed the chain, but fortunately he did not wrench it from my clothes. I looked down at my torn button-hole and belted him hard on the chin. He yelled, and fumbled for his gun. His big companion luckily did not look round. And I ran like hell, not into the hotel, where I thought I might be cornered, but down the street and away into the ruins of a demolished building which was on the next corner site. I ran over the rubble and slid down the farther slope on my backside. All I wanted to do was to get a reasonably thick pile of bricks between me and the weapons of the Russians. I crouched in the hollow into which I had fallen, and heard the boots of my pursuers crunching. They faltered, there were voices, and then the steps seemed to go away. I waited until I thought all was quiet, and then worked my way back to the hotel. I scouted the vestibule, saw no signs of tension among the staff, and slipped quietly up to my room to brush myself down.

Next morning my escort called for me and we drove through most beautiful scenery to Graz. This entailed going through both the American and the Russian zones, and since I was not sure that the Russians might not be looking for a man in a blue suit and with a capitalistic gold watch chain who had socked one of their heroes, I kept my overcoat tightly buttoned. I was very glad when we finally came to the British zone and a young sentry took my papers, which correctly gave my birthplace as Clayton, Bradford, Yorkshire, and he gave them back to me with, 'Ee, lad, yer come from the same place as me – good old Bradford.' The major winced at the 'Ee, lad,' and the sentry noticed it. He saluted and said cheerfully to me, 'Carry on, Colonel.' But if I can read faces as well as I used to, his expression was saying, 'Yer crafty bugger!'

Next day after arriving at Graz we set out for Karlou Prison. The Governor there told me that he had eight men under sentence of death and that the execution was to be carried out the following morning. He could not sanction the crude Austrian method of judicial hanging, and he therefore wished me to carry out the task, demonstrating to the Austrian executioner and two assistants the routine which I followed. He had had new apparatus built in an execution shed, constructed by the Royal Engineers to a Home Office blueprint.

With the aid of an army Major who spoke German I spent two hours in getting over to the Austrian executioners what I wanted them to do on this occasion as my assistants. It was not a long time to convey, in another language, the routine to be followed for eight hangings. I could do little more than explain the principles of speed and humanity, instruct them in the pinioning which I was asking them to carry out, demonstrate the method of adjusting the cap and the noose and going straight over to the lever – 'Cap noose pin lever drop' – which I was certainly not going to ask them to do on this occasion, and beg them to watch me closely and learn as much as they could. I then went with them to the condemned cells to view the prisoners individually. I never saw a more dejected group of people in my life. They were unclean, very roughly clothed, spiritless and, to my eye, hungry.

The executions were over the next morning in under two hours. I put on four double drops at half-hour intervals. I flew home and, a few weeks later, received a letter from the Head of the Control Commission for Austria saying not only that they were most satisfied with the manner in which the executions had been carried out but that the Austrian executioners had announced that if the British method was not adopted permanently, they would go on strike. I had never heard of an executioners' strike, so I was glad to hear that the Commission had gladly acceded to their wishes. Before I went to Austria the execution procedure was that the prisoner mounted the steps of a platform about six feet from the ground, he was plunged through a trap door, and two assistant executioners seized hold of his legs and pulled as hard as they could to make the strangulation he was suffering as short as possible. It was a nauseating and degrading routine, and I was glad that my demonstration had done something to end it.

Almost immediately I was asked by the authorities in the Republic of Ireland if I would train an Irishman in the British method of execution, which had been entrusted to me and my family since the Free State had been formed. I answered that if they would get permission from the Prison Commissioners I would undertake it. They replied that the English Home Office had agreed that the training could take place at Strangeways Prison, Manchester, and the man under training would shortly arrive. Soon afterwards, I received a telephone message from the Manchester Police that a Mr. Johnstone had turned up to be trained as an executioner for Ireland. I later picked him up at the Manchester Police Headquarters and took him to the gaol for two nights' training. I did not think he had the character to be an executioner. He was old and short and timid. When I first took him into the execution chamber his face went as white as chalk. But I gave him the basic training and he went back to Ireland.

Two months later the Governor of Mountjoy Prison, Dublin, wrote to say that he had a man under sentence of death and he would be obliged if I would act as assistant to Mr. Johnstone, though taking the full executioner's fee. I duly crossed to Ireland and, on arriving at Mountjoy, reported to the Governor, who had known my family for many years and always gave us the greatest kindness. Johnstone was in his office, and I agreed that I should let him undertake the execution while I acted as assistant. We went across to the execution chamber, which was at the end of one of the wings, and started to prepare for the morrow. I stood back and waited for Johnstone to get things going with my assistance, but he had forgotten all his training and did not really have a clue. I stepped in and put things right, and finally we went back to our room and had a meal and a chat with the officer looking after us.

We had a sitting-room and a shared bedroom. Johnstone went to bed before me, and when I came in he seemed to be asleep. I went to bed and was soon fast asleep, but for a reason I could not fathom I suddenly woke up. I did not move, but opened my eyes, and there I saw Johnstone, out of bed, emptying all his pockets of wallet, letters and money and putting all his possessions under the pillow. I thought, 'Well, he can't really think I'm going to pinch the stuff,' and went to sleep again. Next morning I was awake before Johnstone, but did not get up. I deliberately did not even stir. He rolled over in the dawn light and said, 'Are you asleep?' but I did not answer. So he took all his possessions and put them back in his pocket. It occurred to me that it was his letters and papers that he was being most cautious about, and I concluded that they would bear his name, which was not Johnstone but something he was trying to keep secret. In retrospect, the Governor had seemed anxious not to emphasise his identity and, on the whole, judging by the violence of many Irishmen's condemnation of other people's violence, I did not blame an executioner in the Republic for wanting to keep his identity secret.

After shaving and washing we went back to the execution chamber for the last preliminaries, but again Johnstone had forgotten his part and I had to keep stepping in to help him. The Governor asked if all was satisfactory and I answered that it was as far as I was concerned. He asked Johnstone if he was all right and Johnstone said 'Yes'. But the Governor came once more to me and asked if I was satisfied. I said, 'Yes, sir, but I should not like to take any responsibility for this execution.' The Governor saw that I was not too happy, and he walked away to talk with one of the officers. He came back and said, 'Mr. Pierrepoint, I think you should take charge.' I said, 'That's up to you, sir.' The Governor looked across to see how Johnstone was reacting, and my own interpretation of his attitude was that he was very pleased. 'Very well, Mr. Pierrepoint,' said the Governor, 'you take over.' I agreed, and the execution was carried out to everybody's satisfaction. Immediately afterwards the Chief Officer came round with the usual bottle of whisky and, as usual, I declined. But I noticed that Johnstone was very glad to take a tot. When we left prison, Johnstone and I walked together down the main road and I asked him where he lived. He mentioned a small town about forty miles from Dublin and said he would catch a train to it. Outside the station we shook hands and he said he hoped he would see me again. Out of curiosity I let him go ahead, and followed to see what train he would catch. But he took a left fork and bypassed the station and went on into the town. My guess was that he lived in Dublin, and was keeping his address as secret as his name. And that was the last I saw of him, and the last he saw of the gallows. I was called to Dublin on a number of occasions afterwards and I never once saw Mr. Johnstone.

I could understand the unwillingness of anyone in Ireland to become the official executioner. One Sunday night I opened The Struggler, and as soon as the doors were unlocked there entered a man who spoke with a strong Irish accent and who was escorting a lady. They went inside the little snug, just near the front door, and when I went in he asked for a Guinness and a small port. As I served the drinks he asked, 'Is the Guv'nor in?' 'No,' I said, 'I'm very sorry, he's out, but he'll be in later.' The evening went on and the visitors continued to drink. The pub began to get crowded. After about an hour and a half the man came to me again and said, 'Hasn't the Guv'nor come back yet?' 'No,' I said, 'but he'll not be long.' Then things got really busy, and I could hardly disguise who I was since every customer called me Albert, and just before closing time the Irishman came to me and said, 'Guv'nor, I know you are the man I want to see, and I want to buy you the best drink in the house.' I said, 'Thanks very much, I'll have a glass of mild.' 'Go on,' he said. 'Have something good.' 'A glass of mild will do,' I said. 'Now before I go,' he said, 'will you come and have a word with me in the snug?' 'Yes,' I said, 'just let me get these chaps out first.' When I had shut the pub I went to the snug. 'I'm very pleased to meet you,' he said, and he told me his name. 'I am a member of the I.R.A. Now we've been trying to get you on many occasions in the past, but we could never find you. It's all over now, so it doesn't matter. Mind you, we only wanted to detain you. We had instructions to get hold of you and take you to one of our places, under arrest, but we wouldn't have hurt you in any shape or form. We should have treated you as though you were the King of England.' Coming from the I.R.A. I was not certain how to take this assurance. 'You could have anything you wanted, till this man . . . we were after . . . went free, was reprieved, or let free. As long as this man got away . . . But we could never find you. We waited at stations and airports and everywhere. Now it doesn't matter, so tell me for the laugh of it – which way did you travel?'

I thought very quickly. I told myself, 'You're due in Dublin again in three weeks' time.' 'Well, it was very simple,' I said. 'I used to fly to Belfast and then come down over the border to Dublin by train.' 'Did you, begod?' he said. 'We never dreamt of that.'

Needless to say, I never in the future travelled to Dublin by way of Belfast. But I had not done so in the past!

I suppose the most notorious execution in England as the early post-war years settled into peacetime was that of John George Haigh, who said himself that he dissolved the bodies of his numerous victims in a bath of acid after taking a draught of their blood. He was convicted because the police arrived just in time at his disposal-shed in the country to rescue from the sludge enough remnants of soft bone, denture and plastic jewellery to identify his last victim, the rich old widow Mrs. Durand-Deacon. When he was first arrested, Haigh said amiably to the senior officer present: 'Tell me frankly, what are the chances of anyone being released from Broadmoor? Oh, don't worry with all that "Anything you say may be written down" stuff. Tell me how you can prove murder if there is no body? Mrs. Durand-Deacon no longer exists. Every trace has gone. I have done the same with five other people – or is it eight?' And he blinked calmly from behind the gold-rimmed spectacles that had belonged to another of his victims, Dr. Archibald Henderson.

When the time came for me to carry out the execution of Haigh I took a special strap in with me to bind his wrists. It is a strap made of pliant pale calf-leather, no different in design from the straps I normally used, supplied by the Home Office in the box of execution apparatus, but it is personal to me. I have used it only about a dozen times. Whenever I used it I made a red ink entry in my private diary. This is the only indication I have ever given that I had a more than formal interest in this particular execution. I should not be believed if I said that I always acted as a mechanical, which is a non-human, arm of the State apparatus. I read the newspapers like any other man. I formed my own conclusions and no doubt made my own mistakes. The cases of some people seemed intensely interesting for criminological reasons. Others stood out for me because they were landmarks in my own career, even though the public never heard of them. I used the strap on the wrists of the first German spy I took the responsibility for hanging – and the mark is there to this day, where Otto Schmidt burst the strap from eyehole to eyehole. I used it on Josef Kramer, the original 'Beast of Belsen', on Neville Heath and on John Haigh. Deciding whether or not to use it has been the only sign of personal involvement in an execution which I have permitted myself to show.

But I left it behind for the hanging which, as I found out at the last moment, involved me most closely. I did not know the name of the rather sad-faced, thin man who used to come into The Struggler on Saturday nights. I know it now, but it is my privilege to withhold it. He was one of my regulars but he never called me Albert. He used to greet me with 'Hallo, Tosh' and I used to answer 'Hallo Tish, how are you?' It was a catch-phrase of the time. Tosh and Tish suited him. He was everybody's friend and no one knew a thing about him. He was lively and easy-going, with a loud tie and a cheap blue suit, and he had a good singing voice.

Almost as soon as he had got a beer in his hand he would start to sing. And people hushed to hear him. It was one of those voices they call 'pub tenors' that can cut clean through the smoke and the clatter, and reach into you and say something. Even if it is only 'Oh, Danny boy . . . '

> . . . the pipes, the pipes are calling
> From glen to glen, and down the mountain side.
> The summer's gone, and all the roses falling,
> It's you, it's you must go and I must bide.
> But come ye back when summer's in the meadow,
> Or when the valley's hushed and white with snow,
> It's I'll be here in sunshine or in shadow,
> Oh, Danny boy, oh Danny boy, I love you so.

He would sing that song, and his eyes used to fill with tears, and so did some among the customers who listened to him. He obviously also appreciated the chorus of 'What'll you have lad?' when he had finished the song. Sometimes, when I heard that *Londonderry Air* from where I was serving, I would come in and sing the second verse with him. He was certainly the only murderer I ever sang a duet with:

> But when ye come, and all the flowers are dying,
> If I am dead, as dead I well may be,

Ye'll come and find the place where I am lying,
And kneel and say an Ave there for me ...

He often brought a girl with him on those Saturday nights. A girl ... well, she was not young and she wore a wedding ring. We took it that she was his wife. He sang all his songs right at her, and sometimes she listened and wrinkled up her face at him. At other times she didn't take much notice. He was always watching her intently. She hardly ever said anything at all and had a remote, unreadable look about her. She sat there, a woman, being sung at, in a pub. A woman, not everybody's woman, no eyes constantly turning towards her, plain, but a woman: mysterious, withdrawn ... treacherous?

She wasn't his wife, and in the only true sense of the words he was madly jealous about her. He had written in his diary: 'My intentions are to win her affection completely, and when she cannot do without me I will play my final card ... I could have finished her on Saturday night, she must have been born under a lucky star ... Praying for one more chance to get Liza in a position to finish her off ... Headaches all day, think I'm insane, must proceed cautiously ... Always seem to be in trouble, mental strain, losing control of my brain, think my brain is turning, must be what I was afraid of ...'

And I shall hear, though soft you tread above me,
And all my grave will warmer, sweeter, be,
For you will bend and tell me that you love me,
And I shall sleep in peace until you come to me.

A pub tenor, belting out a pub song. How could any of us know that it wasn't the beer that was pushing the tears into his eyes?

He left my pub early one Saturday night. He called 'Good night, Tosh.' I called, 'Good night, Tish.' His girl went with him. She just smiled and gave a half-wave of her hand. Next morning they found her dead body in a bedroom in a respectable little hotel at Ashton-under-Lyne, five miles from The Struggler. She had been stripped naked and strangled. Across her forehead was written the word WHORE in indelible pencil. I read about it in the papers, but her name meant nothing to me. And I did not recognise the description of the man who had spent the night in the hotel with her, and whom the police now wanted to interview: 'Shortish, thin-faced, wearing navy blue pinstripe suit, looks like a musician.' This was in the days when long hair was more remarkable than it is today.

Three months later I accepted an engagement from the Under Sheriff of Lancashire to execute a man at Strangeways Gaol. The name of the prisoner meant nothing to me, I reported at the prison, and, as usual, discussed the condemned man with the Governor – his temperament, his behaviour, what attitude could be expected in the morning.

'You'll have no trouble with this one, Albert,' said the Governor, who had stopped calling me Pierrepoint years before. 'He's very quiet. But there's one thing you might want to watch. He keeps insisting that he's a friend of yours. He told me he has often sung in your pub.'

'What's his name again?' I asked, and he told me. 'Never heard of him,' I said.

I recognised him, of course, at the time I had officially to inspect him without his knowledge. The Governor left the cell door full open for me to observe him while they had a chat. That night one of the death-watch officers had a word with me: 'Albert, I've got a queer sort of request to make. He keeps insisting that he knows you. It seems important to him. He says you had a nickname for him. He keeps saying "I wonder if Albert will let on that he remembers me – it would be easier for me".'

'So what do you want me to do about it?' I asked.

'I just thought I'd tell you how it was,' he said. 'I leave it to you what to do.'

At twenty seconds to nine next morning I went into the death cell. He seemed under a great strain, but I did not see stark fear in his eyes, only a more childlike worry. He was anxious to be remembered, and to be accepted.

'Hallo, Tosh,' he said, not very confidently.

'Hallo, Tish,' I said. 'How are you?' I was not effusive, just gave the casual warmth of my nightly greeting from behind the bar.

The man relaxed. Then he breathed in so cheerfully, as if he were greeting a bright morning, that he brought his shoulders forward and his arms high in front of him, and if he had wanted to make trouble I should have needed two men on him. But I gently took his arms in their flow and guided them behind his back, and strapped them in an instant and said in his ear, 'Come on, Tish old chap.'

He went lightly to the scaffold. I would say that he ran. He was on the drop before I turned round, and he lifted the noose with the crown of his head and tried to get his head inside it, so anxious to please, but of course it was wrong. I took off the noose and I put on the cap and I did the right things, for the drop fell and the rope stayed still.

When the pianist in my pub struck up *Danny Boy* I did not stop him. It was not just one man's tune or one man's tears. But I thought, as I polished the glasses, if any man had a deterrent to murder poised before him, it was this troubadour whom I must call Tish, coming to terms with his obsessions in the singing room of Help The Poor Struggler. He was not only aware of the rope, he had the man who handled it beside him, singing a duet. ' . . . And all my grave will warmer, sweeter be . . . ' The deterrent did not work. He killed the thing he loved. And it came to me to receive his body. Not kneeling, or saying an Ave, for that is not after my fashion, but I extended gentle hands.

7

A Time of Passion

I was now to enter the most active and, in its public capacity, the stormiest period of my life. The name of Pierrepoint had been on the list of British executioners for half a century, and had been recognisable in the context of brief Home Office announcements of executions, but not more extensively. Yet suddenly it achieved a wider notoriety, for reasons which had nothing to do with me personally. The mood of the public towards executions and executioners had changed. The treachery trials in England and the long series of hangings of convicted war criminals in Germany occurred at a time when people had become habituated to violence by the war and accepted the emotional relief of vengeance. Each case was allotted a fair amount of newspaper space and people were quite familiar with the idea of judicial execution. There had also been a number of most dramatic murders, and colourful murderers – and there were more to come. The mood of the Press and of newspaper readers was also more tolerant, almost more greedy, for details of death and the dealers of death: it was, in my view, the beginning of today's so-called permissive society.

I myself kept a public house, which was no new occupation for an executioner. It did by sheer chance have a memorable name, 'Help The Poor Struggler', which the Press did not restrain itself from mentioning in some jokey, cynical context. People came on special journeys to the pub to see me, although I rigorously denied them any satisfaction from discussing my craft with any member of the public – I did this politely, discreetly, and without snide cracks: it was at this period that I became very angry at the completely false newspaper fabrication, often repeated, that I had a notice on the counter reading 'No hanging about this bar'.

It was also a time when people were getting more mobile

after the banning of pleasure traffic during the war, so that when I moved to my second pub I found it was a regular destination or calling-point for coach parties. And, though the mood of the casual customers was undoubtedly curious, I do not think it was ghoulish. They would ask to shake my hand not only because I had hanged Haigh, but also because I was a reasonably jovial character.

Alongside this blossoming personal interest among the general public, there was the political and intellectual movement for the abolition of capital punishment. I would not pretend that, even at the time of the final abolition in 1964, and for many years afterwards, a national referendum of the population of Great Britain would ever have cast a majority for the ending of the death penalty – but a number of laws have been passed by Parliament, and are law today, which emotionally the majority of electors do not approve, though they accept and obey them. The abolitionist movement was gaining strength in the post-war years, and was certainly gaining much publicity. That, in its turn, threw more publicity on me. My movements were reported, my ordinary life was detailed, my wife was quite mercilessly quizzed, in far greater depth than I ever anticipated.

It was, as I have said, a stormy period. The climax came when I was summoned to give evidence before the Royal Commission on Capital Punishment; when my evidence – which was far more revealing than any detail or comment that the Official Secrets Act consistently forbade me to disclose – was printed; when the Royal Commission's Report was presented; and when all this turmoil coincided with some of the most notorious murder trials and controversial executions ever to occur in one period of British social history. I refer to the cases, in chronological order, of Timothy Evans, Derek Bentley, John Christie, Louisa Merrifield and Ruth Ellis.

In 1832 there were two hundred and twenty offences for which the punishment was death. By 1837 the number of capital offences was reduced to fifteen, and in 1861 the death penalty was confined to the offences of murder, treason, piracy with violence, and arson in the Sovereign's vessels, arsenals and dockyards. An early opponent of unlimited capital punishment was Sir Samuel Romilly, who in 1870 unsuccessfully introduced a parliamentary bill to abolish the death sentence for stealing five shillings from a shop. A century later, the movement for full abolition gained force.

In 1930 a narrow majority of eight out of fifteen members of a House of Commons Select Committee recommended the abolition of capital punishment for peace-time crimes experimentally for five years. It was ignored. In 1938 a House of Commons motion suspending capital punishment for an experimental period of five years was carried, but ignored, and next year a similarly-phrased amendment to the Criminal Justice Bill was defeated. In 1948 an amendment to the Criminal Justice Bill advocating a five-year suspension of capital punishment was narrowly passed in the Commons but defeated in the Lords, and the Bill was passed without it. But in the interim period between the votes an abnormal number of reprieves was granted by the Home Secretary. As a result of this activity a Royal Commission was set up in 1949 to consider whether 'capital punishment for murder should be limited or modified'.

The Commission was not to report for four and a half years. Fifteen months after its inception I was asked to give evidence.

It may justifiably seem strange that an intellectual body appointed to make a very wide investigation and consideration of theoretical aspects of capital punishment should consult the Public Executioner. I thought so myself. This was surely the province of the Home and Scottish Offices, the Director of Public Prosecutions, The Lord Chief Justice and the Archbishop of Canterbury. These dignitaries were duly consulted. But at a late hour, after the terms of reference had been drafted, Mr. Attlee, then the Prime Minister, had requested that the Commission should also consider whether any change should be made in the method of execution. This involved an on-the-spot investigation in various parts of the world into the practical advantages and disadvantages of execution by means of the guillotine, the firing squad, electrocution and lethal gas. It was also thought necessary to interrogate me.

But it was put more mildly than that. A letter from the secretary informed me that 'the Commission would be glad to have the advantage of hearing evidence from you on certain aspects of their inquiry.

'The terms of reference of the Commission are as follows:

to consider and report whether liability under the criminal law in Great Britain to suffer capital punishment should be limited or modified, and if so, to what extent and by what means, for how long and under what conditions persons who would otherwise have been liable to capital punishment should be detained, and what changes in the existing law and the prison system would be required; and to inquire into and take account of the position in those countries whose experience and practice may throw light on these questions.

'The Commission has also agreed,' the letter went on, 'at the request of the Prime Minister, to consider the question of the method of execution.

'The Commission would be glad to have the benefit of any information you can give and any views you feel able to express about the existing method of hanging, in the light of your experience as executioner. Generally, the questions which the Commission have to consider are whether the present method is quick, certain and humane; whether any other method of execution would be preferable to hanging in any of these respects and should be adopted in its place; and whether, if hanging is retained, any changes or improvements should be made in the present procedure.'

The letter went on to say that, if I were willing, the Commission would send me in advance details of the questions on which they would like to hear evidence from me, and they made an appointment for my attendance in private session, though the Commission reserved its decision whether to publish the evidence later. It also stated that the Prison Commissioners had agreed to arrange for a dummy execution to be carried out in the presence of members of the Royal Commission, and 'the Chairman would be glad if you would also assist the Commission by attending at Pentonville Prison for this purpose' on the morning before I was to be questioned in the afternoon.

I replied saying that I was willing to give evidence and I asked for their summary of questions to be asked. In answer, I received a list of twenty-three questions, ending with an invitation to comment on the merits of other methods of execution including the gas-chamber. But the fourth question was one I did not welcome. It asked, simply, 'How many executions have you carried out as executioner?' I replied that I did not feel inclined to answer this question.

On the appointed morning I went to Wandsworth for the dummy execution. For some reason Pentonville was not convenient to the Commission. There was a company of at least a dozen in the audience. I went through all the movements as best I could, patiently expounding the routine, explaining how I adjusted the noose, and other details. I thought that I had managed to get over the essentials of the action, though I was not helped by the fact that the prison officer who had been selected to act as the prisoner took fright half-way through, and refused to be 'executed'.

The Commission had already had the advantage of receiving from the Home Office a memorandum detailing the routine of the last days in the life of a condemned man, and this was published, to the accompaniment of sensational exclamations from the Press, which had hitherto only been able to hint at or surmise the facts which were now so clearly stated. Since the Official Secrets Act had previously barred official revelation of these procedures, it is interesting to follow the authoritative text:

> Immediately a prisoner sentenced to death returns from court, he is placed in a cell for condemned prisoners and is watched night and day by two officers. Amenities such as cards, chess, dominoes, etc., are provided in the cell and the officers are encouraged to – and in fact invariably do – join the prisoner in these games.

> Newspapers and books are also provided. Food is supplied from the main prison kitchen, the prisoner being placed on hospital diet, with such additions as the medical officer considers advisable. A pint of beer or stout is supplied daily on request and ten cigarettes or half an ounce of pipe tobacco are allowed unless there are medical reasons to the contrary. The prisoner may smoke in his cell as well as exercise.

> It is the practice for the Governor, medical officer and chief officer to visit a prisoner under sentence of death twice daily, and the chaplain or minister of any other denomination has free access to him.

> He may be visited by such of his relations, friends and legal advisers as he desires to see and as are authorised to visit him by the Visiting Committee and the commissioners, and he is given special facilities to write and receive letters.

> The executioner and his assistant arrive at the prison by 4 p.m. on the day preceding the execution, and are not

permitted to leave the prison until the execution has been carried out.

They see the prisoner at exercise and test the execution apparatus with a bag of sand approximately of his weight. The bag is left hanging overnight to stretch the rope.

The statement dealt tactfully with official efforts to secure a confession before execution and to obtain other information which would enable the police to close outstanding files on other murders or assaults:

It is common practice for the Governor to visit a prisoner before he retires for the night to talk to him and give him an opportunity to say anything he may wish. Some like to take advantage of this opportunity, others do not, but no one is forced to say anything.

On the morning of the execution it is usual for the chaplain to spend the last hour with the prisoner and remain with him until the execution is over.

Some 20 minutes before the time fixed for the execution the High Sheriff, or more usually the Under Sheriff, arrives at the prison, and a few minutes before it is due, proceeds with the Governor and medical officer to the place of execution.

The executioner and his assistant wait outside the condemned cell, with the chief officer and officer detailed to conduct the prisoner to the execution chamber. On a signal given by the Sheriff they enter and the executioner pinions the prisoner's arms behind his back. He is escorted to the drop with one officer on either side. The Sheriff, the Governor and the medical officer enter the execution chamber directly by another door.

The prisoner is placed on the drop on a marked spot so that his feet are directly across the division of the trap doors. The executioner places a white cap over the prisoner's head and places the noose round his neck, while the assistant pinions his legs. When the executioner sees that all is ready he pulls the lever.

The medical officer at once proceeds to the pit and examines the prisoner to see that life is extinct. The shed is then locked and the body hangs for one hour. The inquest is held the same morning.

Burial of the body takes place in the prison graveyard during the dinner hour. The chaplain reads the burial service.

Burial within the prison precincts, where suitable space is strictly limited, gives rise to increasing difficulties. In some prisons bodies are already buried three deep. It is clear that in course of time some other arrangement will become inevitable, and notwithstanding the legal and religious difficulties attendant on cremation, the commissioners feel that it is not too soon to face these difficulties.

The duty thrown on prison staffs and others concerned is a distasteful one not only in carrying out the execution itself, but in the long-drawn preliminary stages. Indeed the actual execution may come as a relief from the mounting tension of the previous days.

Anything tending to increase this atmosphere of tension in the prison generally has been, as far as possible, eliminated. The hoisting of a flag and the tolling of a bell were discontinued many years ago, and today the prisoners are no longer locked in their cells during an execution. The time fixed is after the normal routine of the prison is under way, and all prisoners are out at work or about their normal business.

With these details in front of them, I thought, and the memory of the morning's dummy execution only a few hours distant, and a written reply from me to their advance skeleton questions, the Royal Commission would find that they could polish me off in no time at all. But it did not work out exactly as I had forecast. I attended the offices of the Commission, in Spring Gardens by Trafalgar Square, and got there early, which is my version of punctuality. I went upstairs and was told that previous witnesses were still giving evidence. Soon a door opened and they came out. They were Mr. H. N. Gedge, the Under Sheriff of London, and Mr. J. W. Wilson, the Under Sheriff of Lancashire. They acknowledged me when they saw me, but we did not exchange any words, and I was shortly called in to the commission. I went in to a long room with an elongated table that made it seem far longer, and there at the far end was someone whom I took to be the Chairman, Sir Ernest Gowers, who asked me in a friendly fashion to sit down.

I looked round incredulously. The only empty chair I could see was at the near end of the table, but jammed up alongside it there was a woman seated. They couldn't mean me to sit there!

There were two women members of this Royal Commission, Dame Florence Hancock, the chief woman officer of the Transport and General Workers' Union, and Elizabeth Bowen, the author. Neither had attended the dummy execution in the morning, and I had been given to understand that they would also be absent during my interrogation. This had been very pleasing to me. I detest speaking about my craft in front of women, and until this moment I had never done so. I had never discussed executions with my mother or my wife, and never yielded a word to casual women who had questioned me – a thing my own family would never do.

I looked at the woman beside my chair and gathered that she was a secretary. She was tidying what I suppose was a transcript of the previous evidence. I had no option but to sit down in the vacant chair, but I was very much put out.

The secretary poised her pencil and looked at the Chairman.

'We are very grateful to you for coming, Mr. Pierrepoint,' said Sir Ernest Gowers in an easy manner, and he went straight into the first question. *'How long have you been an executioner?'*

I thought: 'Eh, these are intelligent, highly educated people. And here I am in front of them with a very short education indeed. If Anne and I had ever had children, I'd spend all the money available on education. Because you don't know until you meet these people how dumb you can feel.' *'About twenty years,'* I said aloud. 'And you've got to be careful what you say,' I went on to myself. 'In case one statement crosses with another. It has to be perfect. Because it's all to be checked, after. It has to blend in.'

'How did you come to be appointed?' asked the Chairman. *'What put the idea into your head, and what did you do in order to secure the appointment?'*

'It's in the family, really,' I explained. *'I am the third in our family to hold the position – my father, my uncle and myself.'*

'It is a sort of hereditary job?' Sir Ernest observed pleasantly. I could hear through the years the voice of my father: 'This is my eldest son. And one day he will be the Official Executioner.' *'It seems like it,'* I said.

'How long before your appointment did you serve as an assistant executioner?'

'*About nine years.*'

'*What did you do in order to get the appointment? Did you make a written application?*'

'*I made a written application to the Prison Commissioners.*'

'*What is your other occupation?*'

'*Licensee.*'

'*In what town?*'

'*Manchester,*' I said. 'Hallo Tosh. How are you Tish?'

'*Did you receive any training before you first acted as an assistant executioner?*'

'*Yes. Everybody has to have a week's training in prison, and he goes through the same procedure which you saw this morning – only a dummy execution, naturally.*' 'Same procedure! Not so simple as that,' I was thinking, and the driving voice of my trainer came through to me: 'Haul him up and do it again. Get those traps up. Let's have some speed. Pinion and scarper. Cap noose pin lever drop. You've got to get it right.'

'*When you are an assistant executioner what are your actual duties?*'

I was beginning to feel more at ease, and I explained quite conversationally. '*It's really not much, but it's always handy to be there in case the executioner is sick or anything like that.*' Or in case he panics. '*The assistant executioner straps the legs of the prisoner on the drop itself. He doesn't play a big part really: it's just experience he is there for.*'

'*You say you were an assistant executioner for nine years, so I suppose you attended quite a number of executions as assistant executioner?*'

'*Probably about forty.*'

'*How many executions have you attended as executioner?*' asked the Chairman.

Suddenly I was not at ease at all. This was the question I had boggled against from the time of the preliminary paper. All my training, as well as my personal discretion, rebelled against casually disclosing this number. It was like trying to claim an entry in a popular Book of Records. I had the facts to bolster such a claim, but I was absolutely opposed to putting them forward. I can say now that I was executioner under four reigns. I have attended more executions in one day than any other man in this country has done in a year, more in twelve months than any other man has done in twelve years, and more in twelve

years than any other man in a lifetime, though my uncle was
on the list for forty years. This is the measure of my experience,
but I don't think the actual number is anything to boast about.
I must condense the details of my resistance against giving this
information, which I realised *was* going to be published in the
official record, because the argument between myself and the
Chairman went on for four months. I said I did not think it was
fair for me to have to answer this question. I told the Chairman
that the Press had offered me a large amount of money to disclose the figure, and I had refused on the principle that to give
the number was to claim a sort of accolade which I did not
want. Yet now the Press would publish for free – through the
pressure of the Royal Commission – what I had, out of
principle, refused to disclose even for payment. The Chairman
said that I should have to give the number. I gave it, but still
protested, and followed it up with letters after the interrogation.
The Chairman asked me in what form I should like the total to
be indicated in the printed evidence. I said I would be content
if the answer read 'Some hundreds'. He said he would accept
that. And it is my intention that the number of executions I
have performed shall still remain a secret that I shall take to my
grave.

'How many executions have you attended as executioner?'

Eventually I gave a figure. But I shall limit my indication of
it to what appeared in the official Report.

'Some hundreds.'

*'Then you are in a very good position to express an opinion
on this question: do you consider that the method of execution
by hanging as followed in this country is as humane and as
quick as any method of capital punishment could be?'*

Quick? I thought of the Austrian executioners who had hung
on to the legs of their strangling prisoner to finish the job, until
I brought them the British method. I thought, in contrast, of
the man I had hanged whom the doctor following me into the
pit could not trust himself to examine. 'Take the stethoscope,'
he had muttered. 'The heart. Is is palpitating? Irregular?' And
he gave me the headset and held the cup on the man's chest
and repeated, 'The heartbeats?' I listened to the sound of an
engine dying from lack of compression. 'They're going up and
down,' I said, 'and they're going fainter.' 'Oh, that's good,' he
said.

'Yes, I think it is quick, certain and humane. I think it is the fastest and quickest in the world bar nothing. It is quicker than shooting, and cleaner.'

The Chairman nodded. '*I suppose you must, in so many executions, have had things go wrong occasionally?*' he asked mildly.

'*Never.*'

Sir Ernest looked at me. I had given an honest blanket answer, not even then recalling the one exception in a full career, not realising that the Commission was interested in exceptions.

'*Have you had any awkward moments?*'

'*No, I have only seen one in all my career.*'

Sir Ernest Gowers was seventy years old, but very sharp, and I realised he had not written a handbook called *Plain Words* for nothing. He seized on the word 'seen' which I had used.

'*Were you the assistant executioner?*'

'*No, I was the chief.*'

It was the incident of the German spy. I realised that I had been a contestant, and no spectator. The crack of his skull against the wall as he dived to knock himself out; the six-man scrum on the floor with the priest looking on in anguish; the cry 'Come back, Albert!' as he burst his wrist-strap from behind; the final leap off the trap – the sequence could certainly be classed as an awkward moment.

'*What happened?*'

'*He was rough. It was unfortunate; he was not an Englishman, he was a spy and he kicked up rough.*'

'*He went for you?*'

'*Not only for me, he went for everybody.*'

'*That must be the case Mr. Gedge was telling us about?*'

I had no idea what Mr. Gedge, the Under Sheriff for London, had been talking about. He had given evidence just before me, and we had not spoken during the change-over. But he had certainly been present at that scene in Wandsworth.

'*It was the same case.*'

'*That is the only case, is it?*'

I was thinking of every possible 'exception' now. '*I have had probably three more, like a faint at the last minute, or something like that, but it has not been anything to speak about.*' Not really a faint. But there had been times when I sensed that the man might not last much longer, and the escorts had taken their warning from my book. One prisoner in particular, perhaps the most notorious criminal who came into my hands, seemed so uncertain that as I faced him waiting for his arrival on the drop I went to meet him, adjusted the cap and the noose while he was moving and had drawn the bolts before he was still. But professionalism in action was nothing to speak about in this context. I decided that the Commission would not wish to hear about the officer witness who fainted at the military execution.

'*Can you think of any improvements which you would like to suggest?*'

'*On the English method, no. I could not suggest anything to improve it. I think it is perfect and foolproof, that is, provided an experienced man is doing the job.*' 'And not only an experienced man, but a man with confidence,' I thought to myself. 'You are one man doing a job, and you've got twelve witnesses who all think they know it.' I remembered the prison doctor who had insisted that I should alter the drop to his own calculation, but who withdrew it at midnight when I said the responsibility was entirely his. There was another medical officer who said to the engineer: 'I can always tell if it's a perfect execution before I examine the body. You see that mark on the pit? If the head finishes by it, it's a perfect execution.' The only condition that would back his theory would be a relatively constant drop of about seven foot six. On the next occasion when he was present I decided to give a five-foot drop so that the head in the hood was still visible above the level of the scaffold when the fall stopped. I looked at the engineer. 'Perfect?' I asked.

The Chairman was reacting alertly to my answers. '*When you say "English", are you drawing a contrast with "Scottish"?*' he asked.

'*No, I would not say that. The Scottish is very good, but I think it is very, very old, antediluvian. It is about time it was altered in Scotland.*'

'*What is the difference?*'

I thought back to the time when I had first gone to Scotland with my uncle Tom and we had gazed at the fixed ring in the roof to which the end of the rope had to be attached. '*The apparatus is very old,*' I explained. '*Every prisoner has to have a different drop; you have got to get him somewhere near that* drop. *In England we can work it out to half an inch.*'

'*Is it because the attachment of the rope is an antiquated system and does not allow for adjustment?*'

'*It doesn't allow for any adjustment at all.*'

'*Do you have to tie the rope in a different place?*'

'*Yes, if you want to shorten the rope you have to put a knot in the rope.*'

'*And I suppose the knot tightens when the drop comes, and you have to allow for that too?*'

'*Yes.*' And you don't put the knot in overnight, but at the early morning adjustment. Yet you have to stretch the rope overnight with the sandbag, because it is when a rope has not been stretched that you get the whip on it when the drop comes.

'*So it is much less exact?*' prompted the Chairman.

'*It is not perfect. It is all right if you understand the job and you can work these things out, but a stranger can soon make a blunder of it.*'

'*It is a question of getting new apparatus?*'

'*They want it badly in Scotland, badly, but their ideas are very good without that. They are very old and I think in some places they have a mobile one that is moved from prison to prison.*' And makes it very difficult to get your prisoner up the hinged slope of the fit-up set. And it would help if they sometimes didn't set up the execution chamber in a cellar store with a literal pit underneath it. I decided that I was being enticed to say far too much about Scotland, but fortunately the Chairman seemed to think so too.

'*Would you tell us, so that we may have it on record, exactly what you do from the moment you arrive at a prison in order to carry out an execution, until the end of the operation?*'

'*We have to report at the prison before four o'clock in the afternoon the previous day.*' And the chief had better get his trains right for himself and not rely on what the assistant tells him, or he might still be at Crewe when Number Two is seeing the Governor with, 'Albert must be sick, I'll take over.' '*On arriving at the prison we are shown to our rooms. Shortly afterwards we are shown the execution chamber and we prepare. We have a dummy execution, a rehearsal, on that afternoon when we arrive. Then in the evening, say at five o'clock or six o'clock, we see the prisoner, probably at exercise or in his cell. Then we ask for his age, height and weight and in the evening we make*

*out his drop. Every person has a different drop. That is all for
the first day. Then in the morning at seven o'clock you go to the
execution chamber again and get all ready, make the final
arrangements for the job itself. Then we finish there about half
an hour before the execution is going to take place, and that is
all there is to it.'*

Well, that is all unless you think you need a special last-
minute caution or suggestion to the escort officers. Or you
haven't got to curb an engineer who always wanted to be an
actor. I remembered old Charlie, dead now, God rest him, who
always wanted to get in on the act at an execution. So he wrote
himself into the drama as The Man Who Pulls The Cotter Pin
From The Lever. 'I'll be bending on the floor while you adjust
the noose,' he told me enthusiastically, 'and then when you cross
to the lever I'll pull the cotter pin and you can stay upright –
it'll save you a movement and the whole thing will be quicker.'
I could not expel this scheme from his mind, although the very
principle of the safety catch is that the man who operates it also
pulls the trigger – if something went wrong I could go down the
drop as fast as the prisoner. So it was left to the actual occasion
of the execution to convince him that it did not work. I pulled
down the cap over the prisoner's head, adjusted the noose, flew
to my left, and heaved the grey lever away from me. Charlie
had managed to get the cotter pin out in time, but not to get out
of the way himself. The lever hit him in the middle of the skull
and sent him crashing into a corner with blood pouring from
his head. It was a perfect execution from every point of view
except Charlie's, who ruefully concluded that there might well
have been a second corpse. That was the end of the run for the
engineer in the supporting role of assistant executioner.

*'Do you see the prisoner without the prisoner knowing you
are seeing him?'* asked the Chairman.

*'Definitely. We see him through a spy-hole, or we look
through a window when he has his exercise.'* Definitely? Well,
there's always an exception even to that. I was working in my
pub one night when a chap came in, and said that by rights I
ought to have executed him by now. He had been convicted of
murder some years ago. He said he had been a chauffeur and he
had a boss who was always niggling at him. One day he was
changing the wheel of his big limousine when the boss came
nagging at him, so he hit him – but he had forgotten to drop the
wheel-brace when he lashed out, and the boss died. Sentence of

death was pronounced, and I went up to Glasgow to execute him. But a reprieve was announced after my arrival, so I had no work to do. The Scottish authorities, being a bit more generous than some of the English, gave me half my fee for my trouble as well as my travelling expenses, whereas I have known some sheriffs refuse to pay a cent after a reprieve. The point was that this prisoner said he had seen me in the prison, though I myself was not aware of it, and now that he had served his time he was glad to make my acquaintance. He had taken a job as a heavy transport driver, and whenever he came through Manchester he would drop in for a drink. I saw him frequently for a considerable time.

'*You say that you have to have his age, height and weight. I know why you want his weight, but why do you want his age and height?*'

'*We have to have his age.*' I glanced uneasily at the woman near me, taking it all down, and paused, then continued. '*If you get a person of say 24 years of age, he weighs nine stone; you might get a man of 65 years of age and he weighs nine stone, but the man of 65 has feeble muscles and the young man of 24 might have a strong, powerful muscular body; and we have to allow for that, so as to have it perfect and instantaneous.*' Explaining the difference in the drop between a 24-year-old and a 65-year-old with a woman sitting beside me was difficult and embarrassing. I just do not speak of this sort of thing before women. How far did they want me to go into detail? One of the men I had to execute soon after I was courting Anne was a dwarf. I didn't even tell her I was going on a job, let alone discuss the problems of the length of coil, the height of the noose, and the drop to be calculated for the abnormal muscular formation of a dwarf.

The questioning went on, very calmly. '*Do you allow for that by putting something on the drop?*'

'*More inches on the drop for a stronger man.*'

'*A longer drop?*'

'*A longer drop for a muscular man; that is why we see him on the previous day.*'

'*There is no formula for that? You have to trust your experience to do that? – you can't do that by mathematics?*'

'*No, just experience.*' And sometimes the experience of insisting on accuracy can make you look a right fool. I was in

Wandsworth once, looking through the spy-hole, and the prisoner would not get off his bed. The bed was on one side, and I couldn't see properly round the corner. I said to the prison officer 'I can't get a good view of him at all.' The officer said 'Why not put on my cap and tunic, and go in as if you were on the works staff inspecting the plumbing.' So I put his uniform on and he unlocked the door and I went in. I looked all around, looked at the prisoner, and went round the plumbing. 'All these pipes will have to go,' I said. I looked again at the prisoner and saw that he was looking at my feet. I had a blue suit on, which matched after a fashion with the uniform jacket, but I was wearing small pointed shoes which were nothing like a prison officer's boots. The prisoner just eased himself up in his bed, gazed at my shoes and then let his eyes travel all the way up to my face as if to say 'Some joke this is!'

'*I suppose it takes a good deal of experience to make sure of doing it right?*'

'I think so myself, yes.'

'*Have you ever known a case where, either by not getting that quite right or for some other reason, you have not given exactly the right drop and have either nearly decapitated him or strangled him instead of dislocating his neck?*'

'I have never seen any signs of it.'

'*Never!*'

I thought: 'This chap's doing some spadework. Everybody seems fascinated by decapitation ever since Berry pulled a man's head off seventy-five years ago. I suppose it could happen, if you didn't get it right. But I've never seen any blood.'

'*Never.*'

'*The knot, as you showed us this morning, must always be under the angle of the left jaw?*'

'Yes.'

'*That is very important, is it?*'

'Very important.'

'*Why is it very important?*'

'If you have the same knot on the right hand side it comes back behind the neck, it finishes behind the neck, and throws the neck forward, which would make a strangulation. If you put it on the left hand side it finishes up in front and throws the chin back and breaks the spinal cord.'

'*It depends on where he is standing on the drop*'

I thought: 'It didn't make any difference when the German spy jumped, even though the noose opened. He fell absolutely straight, and after Sir Bernard Spilsbury had conducted the post-mortem he said it had been a perfect execution. And my Uncle Tom has told me about Patrick Mahon, whom he went to execute while he sent me to collect his bets. Mahon jumped forward with pinioned feet as my uncle released the bolts, and his body pitched backward so that the base of his spine crashed against the platform edge, but death was instantaneous. They were the only mishaps in fifty years' experience, but they made no difference.'

I said, '*No, I don't think so. The knot is the secret of it, really. We have to put it on the left lower jaw and if we have it on that side, when he falls it finishes under the chin and throws the chin back; but if the knot is on the right hand side, it would finish up behind his neck and throw his neck forward, which would be strangulation. He might live on the rope a quarter of an hour then.*' And he might live just as long with an American 'hangman's knot' and their standard five-foot drop. Field Marshal Keitel was said to have lived for twenty-four minutes on the rope at Nuremberg. And Goering's American Army chaplain, Mr. Gerecke, told a newspaper correspondent that the Reichmarschall had committed suicide because he was convinced that his hanging would last a quarter of an hour. 'I have hanged several people myself,' he told the chaplain, 'and I know how it's done. The hangman will make the knot somewhat loose and I shall be slowly strangled.'

'*Would you agree with those who tell us that the great majority of condemned prisoners, when their time comes, go calmly and collectedly to the trap?*'

'Lord!' I thought. 'I've seen them almost running to the scaffold. And calmly? They've even had the reserve of courage to be courteous. "I've always wanted to meet you, Mr. Pierrepoint," said one, "but not, of course, under these circumstances." And he put his arm towards mine, but couldn't take it because of the pinion, so I put my arm through his and we strolled together on to the drop. But people differ. Some are as overcome as if they were dead already. I have had to use strength to lift a man's chin for the noose, because it was sunk so deep on his breast with abandonment.'

I replied: '*In my experience I would say ninety-nine out of every hundred go that way, and that's a big majority, isn't it?'*

'I think you told us this morning that you were against blind-folding a man before you take him on to the trap?'

'Yes.'

'Because it would make the proceedings longer?'

'It makes it a lot longer. I have tried it on three or four occasions abroad, and it has been a bad failure.'

'Where abroad?'

'In Germany, and also in Austria. I trained Austrians in the English method of execution.' And weren't the Austrians glad to give up what they called their barbarous necessity to hang on to the prisoner's legs!

'Did you execute condemned war criminals in Germany and Austria after the war?'

'Yes. After the war was finished they were all sentenced to death by shooting, but I believe after a few shootings it was stopped and they all had to be executed by hanging.' And the authorities told me what a mess had been made with those first few firing squads.

'Did that all go smoothly?'

'Perfect.'

'Would you give us your views about double executions?'

'I don't think there is any view. It is only like a single ex-ecution to me. I have done a large number and it is just like a single execution, only a few seconds longer.'

'Have you ever known a case where the man who went on to the scaffold first found the strain of waiting too much for him and started collapsing?'

'Never, no, because it is all worked out to seconds. They work out the time, and he is only there two seconds at the longest.'

'In such a case do you put the noose round one of the men and your assistant the other, or do you do both?'

'I put it round myself, to be sure it is correct.'

'What does the assistant do?'

'One assistant straps the legs, and the other assistant brings the second prisoner on to the scaffold.'

'Do you always pull the lever yourself?'

They always say 'pull', but I push. 'Yes, the executioner must do, that is the executioner's job.' It is a question of responsi-bility. The executioner takes full responsibility, and if anything goes wrong, he takes the blame.

'*Do you pinion both men, or does the assistant executioner pinion them?*'

'*I pinion them: the executioner does all the pinioning.*' And sometimes, for reasons of my own, I take my own special soft strap, as a substitute for the Home Office pinion.

'*Do you know of any assistant executioner who would be fitted to succeed you at the present time if unfortunately for any reason you were not able to go on with your work?*'

'*Every man on the list is supposed to be trained for an executioner, and should a case arise he is supposed to be a fit man to take charge.*'

'*Do you know whether any of those who are at present on the list have ever carried out an execution?*'

'*Only one, and he has done five or six.*' Steve Wade, a good, reliable man.

'*How are they appointed? Do they apply to the Prison Commissioners?*'

'*Yes.*'

'*Do the Commissioners advertise vacancies, or what?*'

'*I have never seen one advertised yet.*' What need, when they say there are five applications a week?

'*They have lists, do they?*'

'*They have lists, and when a vacancy comes they send for the people.*'

'*Anyone who wants to go on the list sends his name?*'

'*Yes.*' Women, too, I expect. One woman begged my father to get her appointed.

'*Is the distance between the condemned cell and the trap usually much the same as we saw this morning at Wandsworth?*'

Pentonville had originally been set up for the dummy execution, but Wandsworth was substituted. '*Yes, they are all pretty general now.*'

'*Do you know of any place where there is a much longer distance than that?*'

'*Yes, I know about two. They have all been rebuilt now; the Prison Commissioners are rebuilding them to the idea of the one you saw this morning. I think they are all being altered.*' There was one, in particular, where the execution chamber was placed at the far end of a wing, and married quarters of prison officers were fairly near. The occupants said they could hear the drop fall from inside their houses.

'*What would you say was the average time that elapses in a place like Wandsworth between your entering the cell and the drop?*'

'*I should say it would be between nine and twelve seconds.*'

'*What would you say would be the longest time that would elapse in any less convenient prison that you know of?*'

'*Twenty to twenty-five seconds.*' It has been normal for me to hear a nearby church clock still striking the hour in the dead silence after an execution.

'*At what stage in the proceedings do you get the length of the rope right? The evening before?*'

'*On the morning of the execution.*'

'*What is the prisoner doing then?*'

'*He is in his cell. He cannot hear anything at all.*'

'*Then you adjust the length of the rope in the way we saw and you take the loop up and tie the loop with twine?*'

'*That's right, all ready.*'

'*Would you say there was anything either particularly difficult or particularly unpleasant in the execution of a woman?*'

This was a simple question with controversial implications. I had lived through many a public outcry at the execution of a woman, and the subject was delicate even in the highest quarters. A Home Office memorandum to the Royal Commission had said plainly: 'There is a natural reluctance to carry out the sentence of death in the case of a woman and there have been occasions on which the Home Secretary of the day has expressly had regard to the prisoner's sex in deciding to recommend commutation.' But I had to speak as I found.

'*No, I think a woman is braver than a man, and I have seen more executions than anybody living.*' Certainly more than anyone in Britain, but I suppose there are still countries which use execution for political liquidation, and I don't really want to be listed in competition with them.

'*Have you ever known a case in which it was too much for a woman at the last?*'

'*I have never known it. I have never seen a man braver than a woman.*' But not the sort of glamorous bravery you used to see at the end of a spy film, with a disdainful Mata Hari slinking sexily to the execution post. Murderers are so often ordinary people, caught on the wrong foot. Ordinary men, without eloquence. Ordinary women, rarely beautiful. Square-faced, thin-mouthed, eyes blinking behind National Health spectacles which I have to take off at the last moment, hair scraped thin by curlers, lumpy ankles above homely shoes, in which they have to slop to the gallows because prison regulations demand that there are no shoe-laces. It is not easy to go to die like that, but the fortitude of a woman comes through.

'*Are there any other differences between the English and the Scottish systems, besides the difference in the apparatus you told us about?*'

'*They are identical except for the dual scaffold; that's all. That is all right for an experienced man, but if you get an inexperienced man it might be very dangerous.*'

'*Is the apparatus equally good in all English prisons?*'

'*Yes, perfect.*'

'*Is it not the custom in Scotland for the Provost to have to identify the prisoner?*'

'*Or a witness; not only the Provost.*'

'*Somebody has to?*'

'*Somebody has to.*'

'*Does that add to the length of the time the operation takes?*'

'*It just prolongs it probably by two seconds. He just asks him – "Are you so and so?", and he says "Yes"; that's all.*'

'*This is after you have gone into the cell, is it?*'

'*After we have gone into the cell; we bring him out of the cell and he is tested.*'

'*It just takes a couple of seconds?*'

'*A couple of seconds. It is hardly worth speaking about.*' I recollected that at one execution in Glasgow the Hanging Bailie, after confirming the identity of the prisoner, had asked if he had anything to say. 'Nothing to say,' said the man. I suppose it added seconds more to the interval before death.

'*Do you find your duties very trying?*' asked Sir Ernest Gowers. '*Or have you got accustomed to them?*'

'*I am accustomed to it by now.*'

'*You do not turn a hair?*'

The question was put drily. I answered '*No*' immediately. I do not think he was needling me, but I thought he had his spade out again. He was digging. I don't care who is the executioner, he can have done it for years, but I do not believe any man who has done it and says he doesn't get butterflies for just a few seconds before the action starts. You may have to wait three minutes outside the door of the condemned cell while the Sheriff's procession comes, and I do not believe it is possible not to be keyed up, and I would not trust anyone who wasn't. Even my uncle, looking absolutely stolid, with a strap over his arm and a sweet in his mouth . . . he was not unconcerned. When I saw the procession approaching, I got the butterflies. They were a cell's width away when I got the signal from the Sheriff, and at that moment the tension went, and I was in action.

I wondered if I should tell the Chairman of others who had turned more than a hair. At one execution the Under Sheriff came earlier in the morning than usual and sought me out personally. I was in the execution chamber and I met him outside. 'Have I got to go in there?' he asked. 'I didn't think I had to go in there.' 'The prisoner is your body,' I said, 'and by law you are supposed to witness the execution.' 'I don't like this, Mr. Pierrepoint,' he said in a low voice. 'Listen,' I said. 'You stand here in the corridor outside the chamber and let all the people go through. When they are all inside, just put your head round the corner and bring it back. In that way, you've officially witnessed it but you've never seen anything. As soon as you hear a thud, walk out.' 'Thank you very much, Mr. Pierrepoint,' he said, and he went off to the Governor's office. At the appointed time his procession approached, he gave me a shaky signal just as I had drilled him – and what happened after that I don't know, because the door of the condemned cell was being unlocked and I was going in. But he was very grateful to me afterwards.

I decided not to relate this incident to the Royal Commission.

'*Have you had any experience of judging,*' the Chairman asked, '*what the general opinion of ordinary people in England is about capital punishment? I imagine that people must talk to you about your duties?*'

'*Yes, but I refuse to speak about it. It is something I think should be secret, myself. It is sacred to me, really.*'

It is sacred to me, really. I suppose that is the statement of mine that has been quoted most often about me, and on occasion it has been used in such a way as if I were somebody simple. I didn't have to reflect what I should say in answer to that question. I always had that in mind, I hadn't to think about it at all. I always believed my craft was sacred. But for a long time in that interrogation I had been at the end of a table with the questions digging deeper and deeper about a subject which my official training had taught me was confidential, and my own inclinations said was absolutely private, sacred to me and the men and women I had had to deal with. I had no mind to divulge these things at all, and I had been under legal duress all my career not to say anything to the newspapers on this subject, but now I thought, 'What a fool! Why should it be sacred to me when they've let it all go here, and in a short time it will all be banged in the newspapers.'

The Chairman kept on to his theme: '*Then have you had no special opportunity of judging what people think on these things?*'

I looked at him and said as openly as I could: '*I have thought that, if I say anything either way, they will say –* "*It's his job*" *and think I am biased towards it, so I keep quiet. I am not in a position to judge, because if I agreed with it they would think, naturally, that it was because I wanted to carry on my job.*'

The Chairman thought for a moment, and then seemed to run out of steam. '*Did you say that you had an assistant at every execution that you have done?*' he asked.

'*Yes, at every execution there is always an executioner's assistant.*'

Sir Alexander Maxwell, one of the Commission, took up the questioning. '*You said that among this large number of executions at which you have been present, there were two or three at which some kind of minor episode occurred, such as a prisoner fainting at the last minute?*'

'*Yes.*' For some reason I thought of a previously forgotten man who had struggled and bitten my assistant's thumb.

'*What happens if a prisoner faints at the last minute?*'

'*They carry him on to the scaffold, but I have not seen it yet. I have never done that; they have just managed to get there.*'

'*But what happens if he gets on to the scaffold and then faints?*'

'*He has to go just the same; they push the lever and away he goes.*'

'*Just at that moment?*'

'*Yes.*'

'*Supposing he faints before you get him to the scaffold?*'

'*We would have to carry him there.*'

'*And put the rope round his neck?*'

'*Yes. You saw on the trap this morning that there are some planks. There is an officer on each plank holding him up. There is a rope for the officer to hold on to and he stands on the plank and holds him up.*' There is also a flat board the size of a stretcher in the corner, with straps that can fasten an unconscious man upright, but I have never used it, and am not going to mention it now.

Sir Alexander looked round for someone to toss the ball to, and Mr. Leon Radzinowicz, a criminologist from Cambridge, caught it. '*Did not today's execution take a little longer than usual?*' he asked.

Speed! I had not gone through the dummy execution to turn in a good time, but to demonstrate the details of what went on. And the man who was acting as the prisoner was panicking more than most I have met. '*That was not really an execution,*' I said in a conciliatory manner. '*The atmosphere was not there; and we had no assistant.*'

'*What do you mean by saying the atmosphere was not there?*'

'Well,' I thought, 'does it need so much imagination to see the difference? And the prisoner was so scared by the time he got to the drop that I had to tell him to walk off, and went through all the motions of the cap and the hood and the sweep to the lever in dumb show, without anyone to work on at all.' '*You gentlemen there made the atmosphere different,*' I said, '*We had no assistant executioner for another thing. You have not got the man there to perform on, you have to imagine it, and it all upsets your calculations a little bit. That this morning was very slow.*'

The gentleman from Cambridge yielded to Professor George Montgomery, Professor of Scots Law at Edinburgh.

'*As compared with the real thing?*' he elucidated.

'*Yes,*' I confirmed.

Dr. Eliot Slater, Physician in Psychological Medicine at a London hospital, asked: '*Do you wear anything special in the way of clothing, like gloves?*'

'*No,*' I said, '*just as we are.*' When I was a child I used to think that an executioner wore black gloves and a long black habit. Once, of course, he was masked to conceal his identity from a vengeance murderer. Now it is the prisoner who is hooded and the executioner is almost a public personality.

Sir William Jones asked: '*Would you tell us how you carry out a double execution? You have got the two condemned cells as we saw them this morning, and when you arrive you go into one of them. Would you just tell us from then on what happens?'*

'*I enter the first cell with my assistant and I strap the prisoner's arms there and then, and leave him there for a second while I slip into the second cell and strap the second one. Then I go into the first cell, take the first prisoner on to the scaffold and as soon as he is walking to the scaffold I give the signal to bring the second man out, and they almost meet on the scaffold.'*

'*You give your assistant the signal?'* he queried. A grotesque version of any alternative to signalling came to my mind. What were they imagining that I did? Lift my hand to my mouth and yell 'Right, Billy-boy, let's have yer!'? They seemed incapable of reconstructing the tenseness of the situation, the silence which one never wanted to break, the communication only by a lift of the finger or a slight nod of the head.

'*Yes,*' I said. '*We each take one, you see. I lead the way.'*

'*So it really means,*' said Sir William a little truculently, '*that you go into the cell, you tie up the man's hands, and you tie them up quicker than you did the officer this morning?'*

'*Yes,*' I said patiently.

'*But he was much more willing to be tied?'*

I remembered how the prison officer who was standing in as the prisoner had stiffened his arms as soon as I went to pinion him. I marvelled that the observers had not seen how scared he was at even play-acting the moment of execution, and how these intelligent people did not seem able to imagine the impact of the moment on a real condemned prisoner, who had had three weeks to reflect solely on this instant, and on most occasions seemed to have a tremendous urge to surrender at the last, in a way a drowning man finally ceases to struggle and slips under the sea. All I said was:

'*He was not as willing, believe me.'*

'*I should have thought he would have been more willing?'*

'*I should have thought so too, but he wasn't.'*

'*So that took longer than usual, because he was unwilling?'*

'*Yes.'*

The Chairman took up the questioning: '*Why does not the assistant pinion the second man while you pinion the first?'*

'*It is the thing we have always done. It's what we have all been brought up to do. It happened once where the assistant was helping in the second execution that he forgot to put the hood on the man.*' This never happened with me, and, as far as I can remember, it never happened with my uncle. It was hearsay, the sort of gossip about a famous blunder that becomes a sort of folk-tale in the prison service.

'*You mean,*' said the Chairman perceptively, '*you cannot trust the assistant.*'

I had not meant to convey this impression at all. But I did not feel inclined to deny it, except on behalf of my mate Steve Wade, who had never let me down. I remembered the one terrible occasion when, although I could not positively prove it, the circumstances left me with no other logical conclusion but that someone connected with an execution had toyed with the idea of sabotaging the execution, and the effect of that technical failure would have been the disgrace of the executioner and the promotion of the assistant in his place. A rope had been found to be defective after an execution. It had not actually broken, but it had partially disintegrated as if from the effect of acid. Another person who handled the rope complained of an acid burn on his fingers. An official enquiry had led to an inconclusive report. The possibility that anyone would let a prisoner go through the agony of dropping off the rope and being taken back later for a second execution horrified me. I said:

'*As things are, we have a lot of young assistants now, who really have not much experience.*' The fact was that at one time in the recent past there had been a period when there were only my uncle and myself on the list. Two assistants had died and another resigned, so that there was some urgency to recruit and train other suitable assistants.

Sir William Jones pressed on with the subject of double executions. I am not saying this with any hint at all of disapproval. The concentration of the Commission on double executions led me to give the matter long reflection afterwards, and I did slightly alter my technique as a result of it. He said:

'*If I understand you rightly, you pinion the first man and then you leave him standing there and rush to the second man through the two bathrooms and pinion the man in the further cell. You then walk back again to the first man and take him and put him on the drop, and then, having got him on the drop, you signal to your assistant, who is in the cell beyond the two bathrooms?*'

I corrected him: '*The second man is walking on to the scaf-*

fold before the first man walks on to the trap.'

'When do you give the signal to your assistant to bring the second man?'

'When I am leaving the first cell I give the signal to bring the second man out. There is only the width of the cell in between. When the first man walks from his cell on to the scaffold, the second man is in the first cell, and he has only to walk from there to the drop.'

'The furthest man has two cells plus the distance on to the scaffold to walk, the two cells – the two bathrooms are equal to one cell – and then they both, as you say, get there at practically the same time?'

'It is only a matter of three seconds longer than a single execution.'

'When the person to be executed is walking towards the trap, he sees in full view of him, level with his eyes, the rope, does he not?'

'Correct.'

'He also sees the trap?'

'He sees everything.' If he is the second man he also sees his companion already hooded and noosed. I discovered later that the Commission had, just before I gave evidence, keenly questioned the Under Sheriff for London, Mr. Gedge, on this point, and the view was expressed that the sight would be something of a shock. I have no doubt that the sight of a naked noose awaiting one, whether a companion is already hooded and noosed or not, can be a shock, but the desire to avoid all shock can sometimes be taken too far. There have been shocks enough in the commission of the crime of murder, including the shock of a mother having to view the body of her ravaged daughter.

'And still you feel that, in order to save those couple of seconds longer to take him there, it is better not to blindfold him in the cell?'

'Yes, definitely.'

'It is better that he should walk in and see before him the whole of his doom?'

'Yes, definitely. I have tried this on many occasions in Germany, and a man who is blindfolded is frightened of walking, and he is struggling, wondering where he is going. He is frightened of walking down the hole, and imagines all sorts of things.'

'How many assistants are there at a double execution?'

'*Two; sometimes three, for experience.*'

'*You said that women, when they are going to be hanged, are quite brave?*'

'*Very brave.*'

'*What is the attitude of the woman officers who have to attend on them?*'

'*The women do not see the execution. The men take over out of the cell just before the execution.*'

'*So that there is no woman present at the actual execution?*'

'*No. They stay in the cell and the women do not witness the execution.*'

In this, by a fault of memory, I was wrong. The woman Governor – either the Governor of Holloway, which is exclusively a woman's prison, or, for example, the assistant woman Governor in charge of the women's wings at Strangeways – is bound to witness the execution of a woman who has been in her charge, and I have never ceased to pay my tribute to the fortitude of these Governors at the painful occasions which they must witness. I also learned when I read the evidence later that Mr. J. W. Wilson, Under Sheriff for Lancashire, in evidence given just before my own interrogation, had said that at Strangeways, when a woman was executed, 'the head wardress and another woman warder walked with her'. I have no recollection of this, but it is true that I was always walking ahead of the prisoner and did not necessarily identify her escort. Yet no woman prison officer ever took a place on the cross planks over the drop on either side of the prisoner. Only men took up this last position, and I only ever instructed men on the special duties that this might entail. The important truth is that the three-weeks' attention to a condemned woman, and the final parting, were a strain on the emotions of woman officers which I myself would always shrink from imposing.

Sir William Jones continued: '*Are there any prisons where the condemned person has to cross a passage to get from the cell to the scaffold?*'

'*Yes, many prisons in Scotland.*'

'*A person has to cross a passage-way, and that passage-way is open to the prison itself?*'

'*It is open to the prison, but the Governor of the prison sees that the wing is definitely cleared before any execution takes place.*'

'*But, as you know, at prisons generally there are opposite wings?*'

'*Yes, but nobody can see anything. The Governor clears the prison on the morning of the execution.*'

'*Which of the prisons in Britain has the worst accommodation for the condemned person?*'

I thought this was a naughty question. It was no part of my duty to tell the Prison Commissioners how to run their own institutions. I said, '*I wouldn't commit myself; I don't think there is a worst prison; they are pretty general.*'

'*There are none any worse than the others?*'

'*I don't think so, no, I wouldn't commit myself on that.*'

'*When they have got to cross a passage, that is no worse? The condemned cell accommodation is as good in one as another?*'

'*I should imagine so.*'

'*That is a question of imagination?*'

I thought: 'But I am not a house agent employed to estimate the value of fixtures and fittings. I go into a condemned cell as speedily as possible to do one particular job. They were talking earlier on about the alcoves separating the two condemned cells, which they called bathrooms because they were too polite to say water-closets. I never even realised on the spot that they were water-closets. I just walked through two open doors without looking for a chain to pull.' I said:

'*We only see these things for seconds.*'

'*You see the cells, you see the accommodation?*'

'*Sometimes we hardly see them. We are not like prison officers who are there all day. We just walk through the cell and do not see anything.*'

'*You never go back to the cell again?*'

'*No.*'

'*What are the arrangements like at Liverpool?*'

'*Very good, the same as this morning.*'

'*What are they like at Cardiff?*'

'*They are all right. I don't know a place in England where they are bad. I think the longest time for any execution in Britain is at the very most twenty seconds.*'

'*The night before the execution you have a practice, do you not?*'

'*In the afternoon, yes.*'

'*Where is the condemned person taken while that is going on?*'

'He is either out at exercise or at the chapel; he is always out of the way, and he hears nothing happening.'

'Because, if he were next door, he would hear?'

'Definitely. That is why; we always say he mustn't hear anything.'

'Then when you do the work the following morning, he does not hear anything?'

'In the morning all the banging is finished; the doors are not dropped any more. It's only adjusting the rope, and we don't make any noise adjusting the rope.'

'There will be two or three people there talking?'

'No, not on that morning. Everybody is dead quiet because the man is next door; and also the door adjoining the execution chamber is sound-proof.' Not in the early days, in fact. And not sound-proofed enough to stop the sound of Gerry Hutchins singing. 'Sally's come back and brought the sunshine home.' Poor old Gerry.

Mr. Horace Macdonald, another member of the Commission, spoke from the other side of the table: 'Are you alone responsible for calculating the drop? Or do you have to confer with the Governor?'

'No, it is the job of the executioner to calculate the drop. He will advise you sometimes on the drop, but if you say, "No, I don't agree with it," he won't take responsibility for it.' Nor will the doctor, however enthusiastically he has done his sums.

'Do you mention to them what drop you are giving?'

'When it is finished with we have to make a record. We have to give a record to the Governor.'

'Do you have to vary the thickness of the rope at all?'

'No, it's all standard, as you saw this morning.'

'If you had a man of twenty-five stone, for example?'

'It would make no difference, they are all standard ropes.'

Mr. John Mann took up the questioning: 'We have been told that when you go to Soctland you have no assistants?'

'That's wrong. We always have an assistant; every time I have been there I've had an assistant.'

'We were told there were no assistants?'

'Definitely there are.'

'It would be essential?'

'I think it is very essential to have an assistant. You don't know what might happen to the executioner. He might be ill, you never know, and if that happened it might be a bit of a *predicament. I think an assistant is very essential in any case.'*

'We were told in Edinburgh, by one of the Ministers I think, that no assistant was ever engaged?'

I thought: 'And which Minister would that be?' I said: '*I was in Glasgow last Monday and I had an assistant with me. In January of this year I was in Perth and I had an assistant there with me again.'*

Sir William Jones asked: '*Do I understand that what really happens is that you go to a cell, see a man who is in prison clothes and assume that that is the man you have to hang, and you hang him without further question?'*

I thought: 'Have they hit on that old story about the drunken executioner who tried to hang the chaplain?' I said: '*No, we see the prisoner the day before, and you know what you are going in for.'* As it happens, the condemned man is not in prison clothes on the morning of the execution, but wearing his own suit. But it would be funny if he had been a parson in Civvy Street.

'If he is there the day before, you simply hang the man who is given to you?'

'Definitely yes, that is why the Under Sheriff is there.'

'What does the Under Sheriff do?'

'He knows the man because he has seen him sentenced to death.'

'That is what I thought, but I hear that is not so in London.'

No comment.

'At any rate, so far as you are concerned, you simply hang the man ... they say? ... there?'

'Yes, the Governor says that is the man.'

The Chairman stacked his papers and looked round the table. Dr. Slater said: '*One last question: is there a lot of twitching after the body has dropped?'*

I thought: 'Aren't they asking what they shouldn't know about? All these years I have believed that this matter was sacred to me. Is it really necessary for them to know this, or are they being quite unjustifiably nosy? Why have I obeyed this conviction all through my career to divulge nothing on these matters if now they are going to print it in every newspaper?

'I have stood up for the discretion of my craft against every show of idle curiosity, even against people who thought they were privileged. I once went back to the pit after the body of a

condemned man had hung for an hour, and found that someone had let in the coroner's jury, who were gazing morbidly at
the dead man and who settled themselves to watch me take him
down. "Gentlemen, get out!" I told them. "You have no business here, and I do nothing until you go away." Once I had to
teach my own assistant the respect necessary for the dead. He
came down into the pit after I had laid the man in his coffin,
lifted his shirt, and made a crude remark about his past per-
formances. I blistered him until he was white in the face, and I
saw that he never worked with me again.'

I thought the Royal Commission owed me, not only respect
for the dead, but respect for my craft. Nevertheless, the question had been put, and I answered it: '*There is not a movement
on the body with a good executioner. You cannot see a movement on the body.*'

Sir Ernest Gowers stood up. '*Thank you, Mr. Pierrepoint,*'
he said. '*We are very much obliged to you.*' I left the room, and
went down into the street, and mingled with the crowds in
Trafalgar Square. I thought: 'This interrogation has made you
a different man, if you decide that it shall. This morning you
belonged to a remote and skilled mystery. Now you are at one
with this crowd, and tomorrow, or as soon as the typist has
written up her shorthand, we shall all be reading together all
the details you have so far concealed even from your dearest
friend. Your discretion has gone for nothing. Albert Pierrepoint, if this is what you want, you can now go public.' And yet
I did not want it. And my decision was that, as long as I was
connected with this craft, I should continue as a man apart.

I read the evidence when it came out. I was interested in what
Mr. Gedge had told the Commission just before I went in,
because in many respects it exactly corroborated mine. His
timing for instance, was the same: 'When I give a signal, which
I do at exactly twenty seconds to nine, the executioner goes in
and I have found that the drop is exactly at nine o'clock.' His
account of the trouble at the execution of the German spy used
almost the same restrained words as mine, not revealing his
nationality: 'He was a foreigner, and I personally have noticed
that Englishmen take their punishment better than foreigners.'
He revealed that there had been one incident where a condemned man who had fainted had been strapped in a chair and
hanged while unconscious – but that had been before his time
as Under Sheriff. I was pleased with his references to me: 'We

appoint the executioner, the Prison Commissioners appoint the assistant executioner, and over a number of occasions I can get a very good idea of the type of man from the way he acts as assistant. Therefore you say – "That man looks as though he will be efficient, he has been properly trained, I will try him." That was the way I first tried Albert Pierrepoint . . . Pierrepoint was not the senior one when the County of London appointed him for the first time as executioner. Since then he has gone to the top of the list because he has done so many.'

Mr. Gedge's evidence had clearly been one reason for the Royal Commission's rather insistent questioning of me on the subject of double executions. Mr. Gedge thought that 'the nervous tension of the prison officials and all concerned at a double execution is out of all proportion to that at a single execution. Should there be any difficulty with either or both of the prisoners, it would be far harder to restrain them than in the case of a single prisoner. Further, from the point of view of the condemned men, a double execution is more likely to bring about the collapse on the scaffold of one or both prisoners . . . We have tried on various occasions to get both men on to the drop at exactly the same time, and it cannot be done. The result is that one man has to stay on the scaffold slightly longer than the other, and I have seen knees begin to wobble, with the result that if he had had a few more seconds you might have had a collapse at the scaffold. From that man's point of view I think it is wrong. He should not have to go through even those few extra seconds. From the other man's point of view, the man who comes from the further cell, he must of necessity see the first prisoner on the drop, with the noose round his neck and very likely the cap placed over his head, and there is no doubt that that may be a shock to a man. I have seen them absolutely start when they have seen it, and I do not think it is right from that man's point of view.

'If executions, as they ought to be, are humane, then it can easily be stopped by having single executions, and, in my opinion, there should not be double executions.' Mr. Gedge revealed that on one occasion he had ordered a 'double' execution to be staged with an interval of time between the deaths: 'In that case they were two Poles; one had shot a man and they were both convicted. It was rather felt by the Governor that the man who had not actually fired the shot would cause trouble. He spoke to me about it and I said immediately – "We will have single executions." The result was that we had one an hour after the other, and that can quite easily be arranged.'

I remembered that incident well, if only because in the interval between the executions a prisoner escaped from custody and got on to the roof, and started ripping slates off and slinging them down to the front of Wandsworth Prison. The Governor sent up after him a big prison officer who was a judo expert and had in fact been in on the fight in the condemned cell when the spy cut up rough. 'Nip upstairs and get him down,' said the Governor, and in a few minutes they led him down screaming and put him in solitary.

The Royal Commission eventually rejected spaced executions carried out in one prison on the same day with an interval in between. But both Mr. Gedge's evidence and the importance that the Commission obviously gave to the subject gave me reason to reflect seriously on the routine I had followed until then. At later double executions I had my most trustworthy assistant pinion the hands of the second man in the farther cell. I would pinion the first man, and, because I was more experienced and in any case had less distance to go, I would have fastened the strap and have my man moving towards the drop while the assistant was still walking. Consequently I would have finished with the cap and noose of the first man as the second came to the drop. I did not delegate any other detail, but adjusted the hood and the rope on both, as was my final responsibility. I think the change saved a few seconds.

I was also interested in the evidence of Mr. J. W. Wilson, Under Sheriff for Lancashire: 'I have not seen the sentence carried out by any executioner other than Pierrepoint, who in my opinion is most capable and can always be relied upon to perform his duties in a completely satisfactory manner from the point of view of the Sheriff.' I suppose it would have seemed odd to include a reference to the point of view of the prisoner, yet, when all is considered, that is the standard which governs the insistence that an execution should be humane.

As I had expected, the subject of decapitation was trailed before the Sheriffs. Just as Mr. Gedge could only cite the experience of a previous sheriff regarding the fainting man strapped to a chair, Mr. Wilson had to rely on hearsay for his only evidence on that point: 'My senior partner, who was for some twenty-seven years Under Sheriff of Lancashire, was told by the prison doctor of a man who had received at some time a

very severe knife wound in the side of the neck. There was a
good deal of discussion between the medical officers in the
prison as to whether that man was fit to hang in case his head
came off.' 'Was he hanged?' came the inevitable question, and
Mr. Wilson replied: 'In fact he was hanged and his head did
not come off.'

When members of the Prison Commission were called before
the Royal Commission, they gave details which again interested
me. Dr. Methven confirmed that five applications a week were
made for the post of executioner. Captain Williams said that
stopwatch timing of recent executions had been, from the
moment the executioner entered the cell until the drop, seventeen and nineteen seconds respectively for two single executions
and twenty-two seconds for a double execution. Dr. Methven
categorically denied a suggestion that 'American-style' executions involving slow death could occur in Great Britain. 'Are
there not two ways of hanging?' he was asked. 'Because I did
see that in some of the executions that took place in [the
American-occupied zone of] Germany of the war criminals,
doctors who examined them seventeen minutes after they had
gone found life still in them. Could that happen in this
country?'

'Not in our experience,' replied Dr. Methven.

At the end of the transcript of my own evidence there was
printed an appendix consisting of a memorandum submitted by
Mr. W. Bentley Purchase, the Coroner for the Northern District of London, regarding post-mortem examinations which he
had ordered on thirty-eight prisoners successively executed for
murder between 1931 and 1950 at Pentonville Prison. This
complete and unselected series showed no suggestion of any
death by suffocation and there were no internal signs of
asphyxia. Commenting on the remarkable consistency of the
fracture dislocations of the spinal column – almost always at
the two-three cervical vertebrae – registered after 1943 (that is,
when I began to take over as virtually sole executioner) the
Coroner said that the pathologist Sir Bernard Spilsbury had
told him that he, Sir Bernard, had suggested that the standard
drops should be varied by some three inches to achieve this
uniform effect, and that once this was done the satisfactory
results which the Coroner was reporting had begun. But I
myself must state that Sir Bernard Spilsbury did not alter *my*
table of drops, which was dated 1913 and which I did not use

anyway except as a rough guide. At no time did I ever receive
instructions from Sir Bernard, either verbally or in writing –
and I should have needed written authority to make such a
change. If every execution between 1943 and 1950 was perfect,
I must modestly claim that it was because of my experience and
not Sir Bernard's three inches.

I took a new public house, the Rose and Crown at Hoole,
near Preston, in June 1952, and the Royal Commission went
into hibernation to consider what their Report should be. In the
meantime I was not only exceptionally busy but unwillingly in
the public eye. In January 1953 I had to hang Derek Bentley,
the nineteen-year-old youth of retarded intelligence who had
already been taken into custody by the police after a factory
break-in when his companion in crime fired a revolver and
killed a policeman. Because the killer was aged only sixteen
he was not sentenced to death. Bentley was sentenced, and
the execution was carried out after widespread national protest.

In July 1953 I had to execute John Christie, the self-
confessed necrophiliac murderer of seven women, including the
wife of Timothy Evans, the woman whose body had been found
in Rillington Place three years previously along with that of her
daughter Geraldine. Timothy Evans himself had been convicted of the murder of his child, and the principal witness
against him had been Christie, whose crimes had not then been
discovered. Evans was sentenced to death and I hanged him –
his post-mortem condition was an item in Mr. Bentley Purchase's memorandum on fracture dislocation. It now fell to me
to hang Christie.

In August 1953 I had to execute Mrs. Louisa Merrifield,
only the sixth woman to be hanged in Great Britain since the
death of Mrs. Edith Thompson thirty years before. Such a
succession of controversial executions was extremely rare. The
coachpark of the Rose and Crown was crowded every night of
the summer.

In September 1953 the Royal Commission on Capital
Punishment, appointed in May 1949, presented its Report,
which said nothing of any deep consequence. It made a few
technical recommendations about the law of constructive malice
and the law of diminished responsibility through mental abnor-
mality. It could suggest no alternative to hanging as a speedy
and merciful method of execution, 'defended on the score of

humanity by witness after witness'. It underlined the 'greater
degree of skill required by the hangman' compared with the
executioner using electrocution or lethal gas, and suggested
that 'Mr. A. Pierrepoint, the most experienced executioner in
this country' should delegate some of his experience. 'We
recommend that Sheriffs should vary their selection of executioner so as to ensure that there are always at least two experienced executioners on the list. At present, knowing which
executioner is the most experienced and competent, they tend
to select that person if he is available. The result is that most of
the executions are performed by the same executioner and the
other persons on the list have carried out few executions if any.'
This recommendation was not, in fact, adopted until after my
retirement.

'There'll come a day when they'll all get reprieved,' my
Uncle Tom had said a generation earlier, but the Royal Commission Report did nothing to hasten that day beyond keeping
the subject topical and increasing the heat of the argument for
and against abolition. Uncle Tom was never to know the outcome of this controversy. For he was eighty-four years old, and
dying. I went to see him, making the journey I had done so
many scores of times in the past. He was half sitting up in bed.
I had very recently completed an execution. He used to follow
them all. 'How did it go?' he asked. 'Everything went off
champion,' I replied, 'everybody were very pleased with it.'
'Good,' he said, and he smiled, with the light from the window
filling his blue eyes. 'Of course, it's not really my doing,' I told
him chaffingly. 'I had a good tutor, a very good tutor.'

He looked puzzled for a moment, because he was very old,
and then he saw that I was giving him my thanks and affection
for all he had meant to me through so many years. He smiled.
He lay against the high pillows, and the smile became broader
until it seemed to embrace the whole of his face, except that his
eyes were not puckered, but wide open and blue. It was the way
people smile when they are happy and listening, listening for
more, not wanting to miss anything. I suddenly recognised the
unclouded blue eyes and the deep smile of simple happiness
with which he had looked up at me, so long ago, as I sang the
Irish songs on our first crossing to Dublin, with the priests on
the Guinness in the saloon, and myself feeling that first freedom
that our strange career had brought me – and, I now understood, had brought to him, too.

>Oh no, 'twas the truth in her eyes ever shining
>That made me love Mary, the Rose of Tralee.

There was a spasm in my throat which stopped me from shaping the words, and I could only hum the tune to him. 'I had a good tutor,' I said again, and his smile shone on until it faded from weakness, like the sun going in. And I went away. And he died.

8

The End of the Road

On the 23rd of February 1956 I wrote out my resignation, requesting the Prison Commissioners to remove my name from the list of persons qualified as executioners. On the 26th of February the Home Office confirmed this fact to *The Times* newspaper. On the 29th of February the Prison Commissioners wrote to me asking me to reconsider my decision and to communicate with them again 'as a matter of urgency' as to whether I still held to my decision to be removed from the list. I confirmed that this was my wish, and I have never been inside a prison since except for social purposes – and I refer to both leisure-time entertainment for the prisoners and a frequent drink with the prison officers.

The authorities have asked me to keep the reasons for my resignation confidential, and I respect their wish. I only offer the details which I have already set out above in order to give the lie to two rumours which became current. The first was that I had been dismissed by decision of the Prison Commissioners, and the second was that I had resigned because of shock I had sustained through the recent execution of a woman, Ruth Ellis. One story cancelled the other, but it was quite unnecessary to pay any attention to either, because they were both absolutely false.

The outcry against the execution of Ruth Ellis in July 1955, after conviction for the murder of a lover who had discarded her, was the last great sentimental protest against capital punishment in Great Britain. Shortly afterwards, the imposition of the death sentence was restricted to a narrow range of crimes – murder by shooting or explosives, murder done in furtherance of theft, murder of a police officer or prison officer on duty, or effected in order to escape from legal custody. Later, even these offences ceased to be classed as 'capital murder', and there has been no judicial hanging since 1964.

Two assistant executioners were promoted to succeed me, as the Royal Commission had recommended. The series of thirty-four executions which they carried out in seven years ended, by chance, with two single executions which took place at the same time in different cities, so that no one can say that he individually performed the last execution in Great Britain. This historic date was the 13th of August 1964, when executions were carried out at 8 a.m. at Liverpool and Manchester.

I was glad that the changing of the law paid no formal attention to the hysterical agitation for respite of the sentence against one reputedly glamorous woman. For, a few months previously, I had had to hang another woman in Holloway on the same scaffold which I later prepared for Ruth Ellis, and there had been no great national outcry at all. The other prisoner had not been a blonde night-club hostess, but a grey-haired and bewildered grandmother who spoke no English, only the language of the tears that were on her cheek when I came to her – she was the Cypriot woman, Mrs. Christofi. And at the same time that I held in my files the written appointment for the execution of Ruth Ellis, I had another date in my diary. I was to go to Strangeways Gaol, Manchester, a week earlier and hang a woman of forty who had been sentenced to death for assaulting her quarrelsome eighty-seven-year-old neighbour, inflicting injuries from which she died. There had been a history of trouble between the two women, and the incident occurred on a day when the younger woman went to help her neighbour and was kicked and cursed by the old woman. The prisoner told the police: 'It has been going on for years . . . She would not be friends with me . . . I don't know what made me do it. I lost my head, picked up the spade and hit her . . . I seemed to be in a frenzy and could not stop.'

Two women therefore lay under sentence of death at the same time. For one a powerful series of national petitions was launched – someone even sent me a cheque for ninety pounds and said it was my fee if I did not carry out the execution: I have the cheque still. For the other, nobody except her devoted husband lifted a finger. As it happened, the woman in Strangeways was reprieved two days before the execution.

When I left Holloway after the execution of Ruth Ellis, the prison was almost besieged by a storming mob. I needed police protection to get me through. I knew that I would have walked out of Strangeways a week earlier into an empty street. At

Euston Station a crowd of newspapermen were awaiting me. I shielded my face from the cameras as I ran for my train. One young reporter jogged alongside me asking 'How did it feel to hang a woman, Mr. Pierrepoint?' I did not answer. But I could have asked: 'Why weren't you waiting to ask me that question last year, sonny? Wasn't Mrs. Christofi a woman, too?'

All public life is a field for controversy and misrepresentation. Some statements are made – sometimes in good faith, sometimes in malice – which are completely untrue. A denial never gets the publicity of the first false publication. But since this is a book of record, and there can never be another, written as it is from the documents of a unique family with a service of over half a century, I should like to correct some untrue statements which have particularly hurt me.

A few of them have appeared among the imaginative 'colour stories' about particular executions, written by people who were not present, as part of propaganda versions of various controversial cases. Others, more maliciously, have been invented to indicate that I had a flippant or cynical attitude to my craft, which no one who has known me could substantiate.

I never did make any jokes in my public houses, or in my social life about being an executioner. I never displayed a notice reading 'No hanging around this bar'. I never opened a restaurant named The Last Drop – I have never owned a restaurant in my life. I have never introduced myself as 'the executioner' to any stranger, although I have successfully stopped others, including an assistant, from trying to cash in on this unsought notoriety. To this day, when I take my wife on holiday we usually sign the register with an assumed name.

At the execution of Derek Bentley I did not shake hands with the prisoner on the afternoon before his death. I did not make any notes about him. The Governor of Wandsworth Prison did not have to urge me to get on with my job. Derek Bentley did not cry on the way to the scaffold. I cannot be provoked into giving the witnessed details which would disprove these tales, but I state unequivocally that they are false.

After the execution of John Haigh, Captain Dennis Neale of Rock, near Bodmin, Cornwall, did not send me a telegram: 'Am getting married to Mrs. John Haigh Saturday morning. Won't you congratulate? Remember Germany. Danny Neale.' A reply-paid telegram with this message was sent by an impostor, and Captain Neale sought legal action in consequence.

At the execution of Ruth Ellis no untoward incident happened which in any way appalled me or anyone else, and the execution had absolutely no connection with my resignation seven months later. Nor did I leave the list, as one newspaper said, by being arbitrarily taken off it, to shut my mouth, because I was about to reveal the last words of Ruth Ellis. She never spoke.

The only families who have been 'hereditary' executioners in Great Britain in this century have been the Billingtons, for a few years in the first decade of the 1900s, and the Pierrepoints, from 1901 to 1956. Other executioners have claimed that their sons were on the list, but this is untrue.

During my twenty-five years as executioner, I believed with all my heart that I was carrying out a public duty. I conducted each execution with great care and a clear conscience. I never allowed myself to get involved with the death penalty controversy.

I now sincerely hope that no man is ever called upon to carry out another execution in my country. I have come to the conclusion that executions solve nothing, and are only an antiquated relic of a primitive desire for revenge which takes the easy way and hands over the responsibility for revenge to other people.

I have seen prison officers faint on the scaffold, strong men weep, and woman prison officers sobbing helplessly. I have known prison doctors who could not examine the body after execution because the beat of their own heart was obliterating anything they could distinguish.

I have felt overpowering sorrow for the victims of crime, for little children murdered, for the families of all concerned, for the special worry which policemen's wives always suffer and for the tragic occasions when it is justified. Yet I have had many friends in the police and in the prison service who also feel very strongly against capital punishment.

It is said to be a deterrent. I cannot agree. There have been murders since the beginning of time, and we shall go on looking for deterrents until the end of time. If death were a deterrent, I might be expected to know. It is I who have faced them last, young lads and girls, working men, grandmothers. I have been amazed to see the courage with which they take that walk into the unknown. It did not deter them then, and it had not deterred them when they committed what they were convicted for. All the men and women whom I have faced at that final moment convince me that in what I have done I have not prevented a single murder.

And if death does not work to deter one person, it should not be held to deter any. As long as reprieves for the death sentence existed, the reason for a reprieve was always fundamentally political: an execution here would incite too much sympathy for the victim and must be restricted; an execution there will show that the Home Secretary means business. The public were allowed to blow like the wind for one popular reprieve of a favourite from Hampstead, and stay dead calm about an unattractive strangling in Ashton-under-Lyne precisely because the same basic inconsistency was being operated for the policy reprieves. The trouble with the death sentence has always been that nobody wanted it for everybody, but everybody differed about who should get off.

I have written as an executioner of experience, who has worked in nine countries, looking back on my life with all the honesty I can. I believed in what I was doing. I tried to join some dignity with death. I was anxious to maintain some status in my craft. I retired with what gravity I could: it was no part of my ambition to become a showman.

I conceived an early ambition, implanted by my father. My belief is still, as I look back at the obstacles I met, and the dangers I have surmounted, that I was sent on this earth to do this work and that the same power told me when I should leave it. I had an ambition, I have it no longer. All the desire is quite gone.